A Quiet Family Murder

A Novel

by Joseph A. Tringali

Calkins Harbor Publishing

CALKINS HARBOR
PUBLISHING

DEDICATION

Dedicated to my colleagues and dear friends
of the Bench and Bar.
If you recognize yourself in these pages, it's probably a
coincidence.*

(*But, remember, in creating characters, authors write what
they know best.
And you are certainly some of the best characters I have
ever known!)

PROLOGUE

This novel is based on a real murder that took place in Florida. The defendant in the case was convicted, appealed the conviction, and the conviction was affirmed. The defendant died in prison in 2013.

The legal principle underlying the appeal is discussed in the appellate court's opinion, reported in volume 626 of the Southern Reporter, Second Series, at page 968. The author of this novel was the Assistant Attorney General who represented the State in that appeal. Some of the places and characters in this novel appear in other novels by the same author. For that reason, the legal procedures, problems, sentences and strategies employed in this book are based on Florida law as it existed in 1985-86, some five years prior to the date of the actual murder.

Although much of the dialogue that takes place following the arrest and in the courtroom is taken from actual trial transcripts, the victims and witnesses are completely fictional. The public officials, attorneys, characters, and settings are fictional as well. Any resemblance to any lawyer or judge, living or dead, who practiced in the State of Florida (or, for that matter, in the

State of New York), within the last 40 years is coincidental: keeping in mind, of course, that when authors create characters, they often draw on their personal experiences. You be the judge.

CHAPTER 1

"There's a Sergeant Watkins here to see you."

"Who?" My middle-aged, recently-returned-to-the-work-force receptionist still didn't understand her job here at the Attorney General's Office. We don't take walk-ins. She was supposed to protect me from this sort of thing.

"Sergeant Watkins from the Sheriff's Office," she repeated. "He says he wants to see the person in charge of the office."

"Mary Ellen, we do criminal appeals in this office. We don't actually deal with human beings."

"Well he says he wants to talk with the Assistant Attorney General in charge of the office."

Whoever this guy was, he sure as hell wasn't going away. I figured I better go out front and see what it was all about. Damn, I hate interruptions; it was one of the things that drove me up the wall when I was in private practice.

"Sergeant Watkins? I'm Dave Bradley," I said, extending my hand.

The guy appeared to be at least fifty, paunchy around the middle, with slate gray eyes and hair to match. He looked tired, like a man who had been at it too long and seen too much, and he eyed me suspiciously.

"Are you the person in charge?" His face told me he thought we were hustling him.

"Don't let the knit shirt and docksiders fool you. We don't get many clients around here; we only dress up for court days. What can I do for you?"

"Well, I've got this case . . ." He broke off and looked around at Mary Ellen and the other secretaries. "Do you have an office or something?" he asked with an expression that said he didn't think I did.

"Sure, I'm sorry. Come on in." He followed me back to my office, and I moved some transcripts off a chair so that he would have a place to sit. "We don't deal much with real people around here. Most of our work is reading transcripts and doing legal research."

"Maybe I came to the wrong place. I thought you people did the really big cases."

"Office of Statewide Prosecution does. This is Criminal Appeals."

"Oh."

It was surprising how little information most people had about our office. Even Watkins, who looked like he had been around for a long time, had no idea what I was talking about.

"So where do I find Statewide Prosecution?"

"In Tallahassee."

"You mean you people don't have branch offices?"

I could see he was beginning to get aggravated, but the simple fact was they didn't have branch offices, at least not here in Bonita. In fact, the only reason our division was here was because the District Court of Appeal happened to be located here. And now it looked like I was going to have to explain that small detail to a detective sergeant who clearly did not want to hear it.

"Look," he finally blurted out, "I've got a murder case here and nobody wants to hear about it. Now if the State Attorney doesn't want to hear about it, and the Attorney General doesn't want to hear about it, what am I supposed to do, prosecute it myself?" His face began to flush with anger. He was obviously a man who had been getting the run around.

"Calm down, Sarge. I didn't say I didn't want to hear about it. I'm just as good as anyone else at giving advice."

"I don't need advice; I need an indictment!" he exploded.

"All right, calm down before I have to give you one of my heart pills. What's on your mind?"

"I've got a kid from Sabal Palms locked up who's got evidence of a murder. He sold a woman a gun who used it to kill her husband."

"So what's wrong with the State Attorney's Office, are they on vacation?"

"I told you, the State Attorney doesn't want to hear about it."

"Yeah, you said that. Mind telling me why?"

"The Sabal Palms coppers cleared the case as a suicide." He didn't say anything else, but his eyes spoke volumes.

"And now if you make a murder case out of it they're going to look pretty stupid."

"Something like that."

"So what? Since when has Deke Stoner worried about whether he makes some Podunk department look stupid?" I knew Deke. His motto was 'Say anything you want, just spell my name right.' He wasn't the kind to worry about somebody else looking stupid as long as he came out looking good.

"Since State Attorney Deke Stoner lives in Sabal Palms . . . at least that's one guess."

"Oh, come on Sarge. This is real life. What are they going to do, give out parking tickets the next time he has a party?"

"All I know is, I've got evidence of a murder, and nobody wants to look at it. And it looks like you can't be bothered either, right?"

"Hey, come on. I'm sworn to uphold the law just like you are." This guy's attitude was getting *me* pissed, and *he* was the one asking for help."

"Sure you are. So are the people in the State Attorney's Office. They went all out on this one. I couldn't even get them to talk to my witness before they took a shit."

"All right, calm down. You're going to bust a gut. What happened to his guy? What's his name, anyway?"

"Stempo. Joe Stempo. I might add, 'the late' Joe Stempo. The Sabal Palms coppers got called to his house by his wife. When they got there they found him lying in bed in his pajamas. He had a bullet hole in the left side of his head and the gun was in his left hand. The wife and daughter were both hysterical. The daughter's live-in boyfriend, Melwin Fanchie, said that he fell asleep watching TV in the living room. He was awakened by a noise and heard Mrs. Stempo screaming in the bedroom. He went in and found Joe lying in bed with a gun in his hand and a bullet in his brain. Mrs. Stempo was hysterical, so Fanchie called the police."

"What happened to the body?"

"Cremated."

"Cremated? You're kidding me! Any autopsy?"

"The usual. Death was caused by a single gunshot wound to the brain."

"Anybody scrub the hands for powder?"

"I guess the boys down in Sabal Palms didn't think it was necessary."

"How could they have made such a bush-league mistake?"

"I don't know. But I do know there's a lot of things in this case that don't add up."

"Like what?"

"Like the gun. None of the family admitted to ever having seen it before. Turns out it was stolen from some doctor's house during a burglary. Why does a nobody like Stempo use a stolen gun when he couldn've walked into any pawnshop in the state and bought one? I'd want to know about that, but they didn't follow up on that detail, either. And then . . . I don't know, maybe you haven't seen as much of this shit as I have . . ."

"Don't let the boyish good looks fool you, Sarge. I was an Assistant State Attorney here for six years, and then I put in seven more in Palm Beach before I had a heart attack and came back here two years ago. I've seen a lot of crime; I just don't see it up close and personal anymore."

He got up and started pacing around my office. "So in all those years, did you ever hear of somebody killing himself with his wife next to him in bed?"

"Maybe he wanted to give her something to remember him by."

"Nah, bullshit. People just don't do it that way. And besides, I've got this kid . . . all right, so he's a burglar . . . who says he sold the gun to Stempo's old lady. He even knows where it came from. And get this . . . she paid for it by cashing a check. I've got a copy of it."

"And the State Attorney's Office won't look at this stuff?"

"All they say is, 'The case is closed.'"

"Was this Stempo guy some kind of player? Why is everybody so afraid of the case?"

"He was just a nobody, Dave . . . I can call you that,

can't I?" I nodded my head in reply. "That's the hell of it. He was just a nobody, and the coppers screwed up. And now somebody has decided it's too much trouble to go back and make it right because . . . I don't know why . . . I guess maybe because he *was* just a nobody. So they close the file and Justice gets it in the ass again."

"You really know how to get to a guy, don't you?"

He was standing behind the guest chair across from my desk and looked at me as if he could read my mind. "Anybody that's been prosecuting this shit for what? . . . fifteen years? . . . must have some sense of justice. You do or you wouldn't be here."

"Maybe I just need the money."

"So how come you're not on the other side? They've got nice quiet offices over there, too."

"I like the title here better. Did you ever hear of anybody letting public defenders go when they get stopped for speeding? Anyway, can I talk to your witness?"

Watkins sat down again. The sales pitch was over and we were down to discussing details. "Sure, but he wants immunity."

"Immunity? I can't give him immunity. At least I don't think I can. Can I?"

"Hey, you're the one with the fancy title." It was the first time I had seen Watkins smile.

"When can I talk to this guy?"

"I've got you hooked, haven't I?"

"Not yet, you haven't. But there's nothing on TV and my wife is teaching a night school course at Bonita College. The problem is transportation; we only have one car."

"I'll have the kid in my office at seven o'clock; his name is Shawn Planer by the way. Give me your address. I'll send a car over for you." Watkins stood up and extended his hand over my desk.

"Sarge, I do criminal appeals. I'm not making any promises. Anything like this has to go through Tally."

"I understand. I'll see you at seven."

He was gone before I could even begin to try to sort out the politics in something like this. Ordinarily, the General didn't like stepping on the toes of any of the state attorneys, but Deke Stoner had given him a hell of a primary fight three years ago in 1982, and the rumor was that he was gearing up to do the same thing next year. I suspected the General wouldn't mind making an exception in his case. Besides merely aggravating the shit out of Stoner, if this case turned out to be big enough it might end his statewide political aspirations. The General never passed up a chance to eliminate possible competition. And then, of course, there was my old friend Tom Julian. I didn't think he'd pass up a chance to settle a long-standing score with Deke Stoner. Joe Stempo might have been a nobody, but in my business careers are built and destroyed by the prosecution of nobodys. Given the right spin, Stempo's killer could become the Lee Harvey Oswald of Southwest Florida. I wondered what Barbara would have to say about me going back into the courtroom, and that evening I casually raised the subject has we had dinner on the balcony of our small condo.

"A guy came in from the Sheriff's Office today."

"For what, to look at a transcript?"

"He says he has a murder case that one of the local departments screwed up. He wants the Attorney General to take a look at it."

She put down her wine glass and looked at me carefully. "Did you tell him that you're in Appeals?" she asked in her clipped English accent.

"I did."

"And?" she demanded softly. She had just come from

her studio and looked exactly like an elegant interior designer should look: blonde hair pulled back in a bun, print dress with a natty scarf tied around her neck, an elegant but not ostentatious bracelet on her wrist. It was a look ingrained into her by her British heritage, or maybe by her years in Palm Beach before we moved across the state to Florida's west coast where we were supposed to adopt a slower, and healthier, lifestyle.

"And nothing," I replied. "He just wants me to take a look at the case. If there's anything to it, I'll pass it on to Statewide Prosecution."

"David, remember your heart." Barb's blue eyes flashed icily.

"My heart is fine."

"I'd like you to keep it that way."

"I'm not going to try the case; I'm just going to assess it."

"Then why do you have that look in your eyes?"

"What look?"

"That old-fire-horse-when-the-bell-rings look. David you promised me. No more stress, remember?"

"I'm not going to be under any stress if I'm only looking it over for somebody else."

"No courtroom. Promise?"

"I promise. Anyway, I'll be gone for a couple of hours while you're at school tonight."

"A couple of hours? You should be resting!"

"Barbara, I'm all rested out. I'll be fine. They're even sending a car for me. What more could you want?"

"I don't want you doing any more trial work." She reached across the table and took my hand. "I don't want to be your widow, David."

"You're not going to be anybody's widow. Now let's do the dishes so we can get out of here."

The sheriff's car pulled into the driveway right on time, and I wondered what the neighbors would think if they saw me getting in. Whenever I talked about my job – which wasn't often – I went out of my way to tell people that it was no big deal.

"Mr. Bradley?"

"You got me."

"Sergeant Watkins wants us out at the S.O. as soon as we can get there. Better fasten your seat belt."

Thankfully, he didn't hit the lights and siren until we were out on the highway. I'm sure that being whisked away in a screaming police car would have turned me back into a middle-class celebrity. Better that Barb didn't know about this part of the evening, either.

Actually, my job isn't all that glamorous. I spend most of my time reading transcripts and looking over other people's mistakes. I guess it was interesting at first but let me tell you, after a while all drug deals look alike, and trying to figure out the difference between "probable cause" and "reasonable suspicion" can make you crazy. Even the murder cases begin to blend into an indistinct shade of gray. I don't know where writers get their plot ideas, but believe me; real life is a lot more mundane.

Except tonight. This jerk – whoever he was – wanted to talk. And he wanted immunity. I wasn't even sure if I had the power to grant it, but I did know one thing: I wasn't going to do it without a lot more information. The problem was that it sounded like he wasn't willing to part with information without some kind of commitment from me. The question was going to be which one of us would blink first. This was starting to sound a lot like the world I left two years ago.

I pondered the situation while we shot down Interstate 75, no doubt scaring the hell out of a lot of people who thought we were chasing them. I hadn't come up with any answers by the time we arrived at the Sheriff's Office. My driver kept the motor running.

"Aren't you coming in?"

"No, thanks. I've got to get back on patrol. I leave all that heavy-duty stuff to the experts like you. That's why you get paid the big bucks."

"Yeah, right." I closed the car door and headed toward the building. 'Big bucks.' That guy would probably laugh himself sick if he knew. Let's just say nobody ever got rich working for the State of Florida. My cousin who is an orthopedic surgeon sometimes gets called in after hours, too. But he's making five times more money than I am. And he doesn't have to talk to assholes. And when he walks into a hospital he's met by a good-looking nurse instead of a steel door and an unintelligible intercom like the one that greeted me.

"David Bradley to see Sergeant Watkins." The impersonal metallic voice that responded said either, "second floor" or "push the door," I couldn't tell which. A buzzer made a sound like the door was being unlocked from somewhere, so I took a chance and pushed.

"State Attorney's Office, right?" the young officer on the other side asked.

"Close enough."

"Come on; I'll take you up to Sergeant Watkins."

We went up a flight of steel stairs – maybe the voice had said "second floor" after all – and found Watkins waiting for me.

"Thanks, Al. I'll take it from here," Sarge said to my escort who left quickly. When we were alone Watkins nodded toward the door and said, "I've got our boy in there. The kid's been a real pain in the ass. We've got him made in three house burglaries and he's a suspect in five or ten more. Just listen to him, okay?" He opened the door to the interrogation room.

A scrawny kid was sitting in a hard, wooden chair and nervously flicking ashes into an over-full ashtray on the otherwise bare table. His fingers were stained nicotine yellow, and his face was covered with the worst case of acne I had ever seen. The kid's dirty blond hair looked like he might have washed it once, sometime in the distant past. I had to remind myself that my neighbors thought that this was a glamorous job.

Watkins spoke first. "Shawn, this is Mr. Bradley from the Attorney General's Office. He wants to hear what you have to say."

"I want immunity first," the kid replied.

I sat down heavily across from him. This was going to take some explaining, and I wasn't sure if either of us was up to it. "Shawn, I'm not from the State Attorney's Office. I'm an Assistant Attorney General. We operate out of Tallahassee, understand?" He flicked a couple more ashes over the dead butts in the ashtray and nodded dumbly. "Let me tell you about immunity. If you talk to me about a crime that's under investigation, you'll have transactional immunity for anything you did as a part of that crime. Understand?" His eyes went blank. I didn't mean to use the word "transactional" – it just slipped out.

"All's I know is, I want a piece of paper sayin' I got immunity. That's all's I know," he replied.

I motioned Sergeant Watkins outside. "There's no such thing as a 'piece of paper,'" I whispered after he closed the door.

"I know that. So just give him anything."

"I can't do that. I'm not sure the A.G. even wants to get involved in this. This is State Attorney business."

"I told you, they won't touch it with a forty-foot pole."

"I think I can see why." My sense of self-preservation kept telling me to run like a deer, but my old trial lawyer instincts wouldn't let me. "All right, let me see if I can explain it to him again," I offered.

"And Counselor . . ." Watkins grabbed my arm. ". . . this time leave out the word 'transactional.'"

I sat down across from the kid again. He had lit another cigarette. If he kept this up we would soon need radar in the room and Barb would go nuts when she smelled all the second-hand smoke on me when I got home. "Look, Shawn, let me try to explain the law. 'Immunity' is something you get by talking about your involvement . . ." The kid's eyes started to glaze over, and I tried again. "Shawn, Sergeant Watkins tells me you want to talk about a murder, right?" The filthy blond head nodded. "All right. Now if you talk to me about that, you'll have immunity for any crime you committed as part of that trans . . ." Watkins looked at me and raised his eyebrows. "You'll have immunity from anything you did as part of that murder, understand?"

"Hey, man, I didn't kill nobody."

"I didn't say you did. I'm sure you didn't. But maybe you helped move the body afterwards. That could be a crime. You'll have immunity from prosecution for that."

"I didn't move him. I didn't even see him after they done it."

"I don't mean to say you did. But whatever you did . . . if it was a crime as part of the trans . . . murder, you'll be immune from prosecution if you tell us about it. Understand?"

"What about these charges here?"

I looked at Watkins and nodded him outside again. "What the hell is he talking about 'these charges here'?"

"I told you the kid was a burglar," he shot back.

"You didn't tell me that he had pending cases!"

"Dave, they all have pending cases. That's why they're here."

"I can't immunize him on those. I can't even nolle prosse them, I don't think. Christ, I don't even know if I should be talking to him. Does he have a lawyer?"

"What difference does it make?" Watkins asked, deftly avoiding my question.

"It makes a lot of difference." I was shouting and trying to keep my voice down at the same time.

"Let me handle this," Watkins said as he reopened the door. His lack of a direct reply made me suspect the answer was probably something I didn't want to hear. This time around he took the lead and I listened.

"Shawn, Mr. Bradley's office is in Tallahassee. He doesn't have anything to do with the State Attorney here in this county."

"He's sort of the big leagues, right?" Shawn asked, looking like he wanted someone to say "yes."

"That's right," Watkins assured him. "He's the real big leagues. His boss is in charge of all of the state attorneys all over the state. Now, he can't say anything about the burglaries you're charged with because he hasn't taken over the case yet. But once he does he'll help you out, okay? But the only way he's going to come into the case is if you tell him about the murder, get it?"

Watkins was really laying it on thick. Some of what he said was true, but a lot of it was bullshit. I had the feeling to run like a deer again. Still, he did leave me with a way out. I could always say that our office chose not to be involved. Shawn could go off somewhere and do his time on the local charges and the murder – if it was a murder – could wind up on "Unsolved Mysteries." I decided to stay. Shawn's eyes darted back and forth between Watkins and me as he flicked more ashes with his skinny, stained fingers.

"I might as well tell ya' the whole thing. No one else wants to listen, so I guess I can't be any worse off. I mean . . . I can't believe you guys don't want to know about a murder."

"I want to know, Shawn," I replied. "I'm listening."

"See, there's this girl at school, Anita."

"School?"

"Sabal Lakes. That's my high school."

Christ, they were starting earlier all the time. He flicked more ashes into the over-full ashtray and continued, "Anyways, like she comes up to me one day an' goes, 'Like I hear you got a gun for sale.'"

"How did she know that?"

"A lot of the kids know that I get stuff an' sell it. It's like a business I got on the side."

I looked at Watkins. The kid was a professional burglar – in high school, no less. And he was selling a gun to another student. In my day the big problem was wondering if you could get arrested for trying to check into a motel after the prom.

"Anyways, I go, 'Yeah, I got a gun. You want it?' An' she goes, 'Like, how much?' An' I go, 'That depends, what do you want it for?' An' she goes . . ."

"Shawn, let's stop the dialogue, okay? Did you sell her the gun?"

"Yeah, she goes, 'My mother needs it. Can I see it?' An' I go, 'Okay, I'll bring it over to your house.' An' she goes, 'No, you can't do that. Me an' my boyfriend'll pick ya' up at your place. Just have the gun with ya'.' So like the next day, her an' her boyfriend an' her old lady pick me up after school, and Melwin . . . that's like her boyfriend . . . checks out the gun while we're in the car an' he goes, 'That's all you'll need.' An' then like her old lady goes, 'How much do you want for it?' An' I go, twenty-five.' I should of asked more, but these people were kind of weird, like they were really buying this gun to do somethin', not just to have it, and like I wanted to get out of there."

"So you sold them the gun for twenty-five dollars," I interjected.

"Yeah. So, anyways, like they don't have the money. I mean, like, I couldn't believe it, ya' know? So Anita goes, 'Well, will ya' take a check?' An' I go, 'Like, you're buyin' a gun, man.' An' she goes, 'Well, maybe we can cash a check someplace.' So Mel drives us to one a' them check cashin' places, and Anita an' her mother like go inside. An' then they come out an' get in the car an' like hand me two tens an' a five an' drive me back home."

"Shawn, so far you've told me that you most likely stole a gun. You probably carried it in a concealed manner. And you sold it illegally. When do we get to the murder?"

"I'm gettin' to that. Anyways, about a week later I'm talkin' to Anita at school, an' I go, 'Like how did you like the thing you bought?' An' she goes, 'Fine.' An' I go, 'Like what's it for?' An' she goes, 'We're gonna kill my old man.' An' then she laughs, like she's makin' a joke, only it don't sound like she's jokin'. An' like I laugh too, 'cause maybe if she does . . . ya' know . . . like really do it, like I could be next, ya' know?"

"So, anyways, a couple of weeks later, I hear her father committed suicide by shooting himself in the head with a gun. An' I figure it's my gun . . . the one they bought from me. An' like the next time I see Mel pickin' her up from school, I go, 'Hey, too bad about Joe.' An' he goes, 'Yeah, tooooo baaaad.' An' I go, 'Did you do it?' An' he grabs me an' slams me up against the car, an' goes, 'What do *you* know about it?' An' like I go, 'Nuthin'. I don't know nuthin' about it 'cept you got the thing from me.' An' he goes, 'Like you better just forget about that, man, 'cause you could be next. I hear the gators out in the swamp are gettin' hungry.' An' I go, 'Hey, man, take it easy. I forgot everything, man. Like I don't even know what you're talkin' about.'"

"Is that it?" It was almost a relief. Even if everything he said was true, nobody could prosecute anybody on this kind of drivel. I could tell Watkins he didn't have enough evidence and go back to my no-stress job.

"No, that ain't it. A few days after that, me an' Anita were doin' a little dope out behind one a' the portable classrooms. An' she starts tellin' me how there's gonna be a lot more money an' free time around her house now that her old man is dead. An' I go, 'You guys did it to him, didn't ya'?' An' she goes, 'Bet your ass.' An' I go, 'Like why?' An' she goes, 'Cause he was a miserable son-of-a-bitch an' he deserved to die.' An' then she goes, 'Are you gonna blow us in?' An' I go, "Hey, like I'm in this too, remember? Like I supplied the thing. Besides, what do I care if you blew away your old man?' An' she goes, 'That's good. 'Cause if you talk, Mel an' his friends'll do you next. You heard about Terrell didn't ya'?' An' I go, 'Yeah, I heard.' An' she goes, 'Well, Mel says the gators are always hungry.'"

I wish I could say the story shocked me. It didn't. I guess I had been a prosecutor too long. I know people are nuts. There isn't anything you can imagine that somebody hasn't already done to somebody else. "So why are you talking to me now?" I asked Shawn.

"Hey, man, like these dudes got me on a bunch of shit, and they're talkin' hard time. I don't mind the stockade; I've even done time in the county jail. But like I ain't interested in doin' State time. I figured I could help myself out a little bit."

I looked at Watkins and motioned him outside again. "I don't know, Sarge. I don't see the Attorney General getting involved in this."

"It's a murder for Christ's sake!" he protested.

"No, it's a death under suspicious circumstances. And it's a couple of kids shooting off their mouths."

"Yeah, well there's something else. I got a copy of the check the old lady cashed. It supports the kid's story all the way."

"So she bought a gun and her husband used it to do himself in. So what?" I protested.

"Why do you look like you don't believe that?" the good Sergeant replied.

I reopened the door and sat down for the last time with the burglar who Watkins wanted to make into my star witness. "Shawn, let me ask you one more thing," I said wearily. "This could be very, very important. Where did that gun come from?"

"Hey, man, like I got it, all right?"

"Where did you get it, Shawn?" There was a long pause while he stared at the tabletop and played with the butts in the ashtray.

"I don't know. I guess I robbed it."

"I knew that. Where?"

"Some doctor's house down in Palm Lakes. What difference does it make?"

"Palm Lakes, that's where you live?"

He shook his head. "Nah, I was just down there, ya' know, like scopin' the place out."

I looked at Watkins. "That's down in Cypress County, isn't it?"

Sarge nodded.

"It makes a lot of difference, Shawn. A whole lot of difference." I glanced at Watkins again before continuing.

"I can't say anything right now, Shawn. I can't say anything either to you or Sergeant Watkins. I'm going to go up to Tallahassee personally, and I'll find out what the Attorney General wants to do. In the meantime, relax and keep your mouth shut. Don't say anything to anybody. Especially don't say anything about this talk we had here tonight, understand? If anybody over at the jail asks you where you were, you tell them the S.O. is trying to clear all their burglaries by pinning them on you. You act real pissed off, get it? Sergeant Watkins tells me the State Attorney already passed on this case. I think it's in your best interest to keep things quiet. Don't let anybody know that anyone else might be interested."

"Okay, man. But, like, it's a real bitch, ain't it? I mean, like those dudes got away with murder."

"They didn't get away with it yet, Shawn. Sometimes things just take a little longer to square up.

CHAPTER 2

B arb and I drove up to Tallahassee a few days later. She insisted it was no problem for her to take off from the design studio, although I suspected she was afraid of letting me drive that far alone – afraid that I might keel over or something. Besides, her daughter was a pre-med student at Florida State University, and any excuse to visit Tori was a good excuse.

I had spent much of the previous time huddled in my office with Watkins, going over what he had. Frankly, it wasn't much. We knew Shawn sold the gun, and we knew who he sold it to. About the most damning thing we had was Anita's admission to Shawn while she was "doing dope" with him. Would that be admissible as an admission against interest? It might be in Anita's trial, if we ever got that far, but it would be pure hearsay as to the other two defendants unless we could indict them all on a conspiracy theory. In that case, would the admission of one be admissible against all? I hadn't been an "appellate lawyer" long enough to be sure; I would have to do some research on that. Then there was the problem of Shawn himself. I couldn't see anyone getting indicted much less convicted on the word of a teenaged professional burglar. Conviction required proof beyond a reasonable doubt. Hell, he was my witness and even I had trouble believing him. I guess I was too quiet for too long, and Barbara suspected something was up.

"Well, it will be nice for you to see the people in Tallahassee and let them know the Bonita office is still there."

"I guess."

"Any money in the budget for raises this year?"

"They'll say 'no' right up until July first and then somebody will find some laying around in an unused account, just like they always do."

"I wish we had one of those 'unused accounts'." She was silent for a minute and then added, "You were thinking about that case, weren't you?"

"Just speculating," I answered noncommittally.

She reached across the seat and touched my arm. "David, I'm not trying to hold you back."

I looked over at her. Damn, she was beautiful. Her blonde hair was parted on the left and pulled back into a ponytail; with her crystal blue eyes and youthful face and figure, it was a look that never failed to knock my socks off. Barbara didn't look like a woman with a daughter in college. I had been lucky to find her six years ago over in Palm Beach following my divorce and subsequent escape from Bonita. She was an interior designer for one of the more exclusive studios, and she thought my job as a trial prosecutor was exciting. It was a whirlwind romance and we had some heady years in the Palm Beach social scene before I was, you might say, "required" to take a low-stress job. Barbara never complained. Rebound marriages are usually a disaster, especially those from Palm Beach, but Barb stuck by me through a very bad time. If she wasn't one in a million, she was at least one in several hundred thousand. All right, I admit it: I'm still in love with my wife. When that becomes a crime, indict me; I'll plead guilty. I ran my hand gently through her hair and across the back of her neck. "You're not holding me back, my love. And if you ever do, I'll be happily held."

"It's just that you don't know what it was like, that day I got the call at the studio from Judge Nelson's court clerk. She said they had taken you out on a stretcher and you be being rushed to Good Samaritan Hospital. I don't ever want to go through that again."

"It was no picnic for me," I groused. Barb's blue eyes started to get misty. "Hey, come on," I said, caressing her cheek, "I don't want to go through that again, either. And we're not going to go through it again. We're going to drive up to Tally; I'll talk to the General and you'll spend the day with Tori. And then we'll take a long, slow ride back home. I hear there are a lot of deserted beaches up in the Panhandle. I hope you remembered to pack your thong bikini."

"God, David, is that all you think about?"

It was difficult not to think of her in a bikini – or less. We had some great times together in the sack, and the best part about it was they weren't always in the sack. Beneath that cool ice maiden exterior, Barbara was a hot little minx and she often had trouble keeping her clothes on when the beach was deserted. Whenever I reminded her she could never get away with that back in her native Southampton, she would laugh at me and say we Americans were the real Victorians.

We got to Tally late in the afternoon. I had an appointment with my friend Tom Julian, the General's third in command, for early the next morning, so we checked into a motel and headed straight for the F.S.U.

campus where Tori was waiting for us.

Tori was the image of her mother: smart, vivacious and inquisitive; nothing escaped her notice. I suspected there would be a lot of broken hearts in Tallahassee during the next few years.

"Hello, Mother. Hi, Dave," she said with a hug that squeezed her full breasts into my chest.

"Watch it, Dear. I'm only a stepfather, and I'm not made of asbestos."

"Mother! Is he always like that?" she squealed. Tori was smart but she was not an actress. I would have given her an "F" for "showing indignation."

"Yes, he's always like that, Dear. That's why I married him." Leave it to Barbara to come up with the perfect answer.

Greetings over, we headed out for dinner – after Tori asked if it would be all right if we took her roommate and another friend. Of course it was all right. I used to be a student once, remember? Besides, what man would complain about being surrounded by four beautiful women? After dinner we took in a movie – on me, of course. Hey, "Dad" is a big shot in the State government, isn't he? It was after midnight before Barb and I got back to the motel.

She was in my arms as soon as the door closed. "I thought it was really sweet the way you treated Tori's friends," she said with her lips brushing mine.

"Is this my official 'thank you'?" I asked, returning her kiss.

"You know motels always make me horny," she sighed as I began to unzip her dress.

"Yeah, I remember that," I said while she unbuttoned my shirt and started to kiss her way down my chest.

"Remember the first time I did this?" she asked softly.

We didn't get to sleep for a long time, and even though morning was going to come a lot earlier than I wanted, there's nothing like good old aerobic exercise to keep the heart muscle in shape.

It was difficult to leave Barb's nude body between those warm sheets the next morning. Well, as the poet said, I had promises to keep. We'd have time for more of this later.

Tom Julian was in a staff meeting when I got to his office. I took a rain check on the coffee his secretary offered me and browsed though some old issues of The Florida Bar Journal: "The Challenge of Peremptory Challenges." Good Lord! Did anybody actually read this stuff?

"Dave!" Good to see you!" Tom almost shouted as he blew into the waiting room with his hand outstretched. "Come on in and take a load off. How's the mainspring?"

"Good, Tom; real good."

"That's great. Is your heart okay, too? Damn, some guys will do anything for a mistrial."

Same old Tom. His hair had receded a little more, but his wit was as sharp as ever. We had been Assistant State Attorneys years ago back in Bonita. He was a workaholic then, too. Tom's other fault – if you could call it a fault – was loyalty. He was loyal to the death; which meant that if you ever crossed him you could count on never, ever, being forgiven. Ever. That loyalty cost Tom dearly back in the old days when one of the guys in our office – a fellow by the name of Deke Stoner, by the way – resigned and ran against the man who had given all of us our first jobs. I agreed that it was a shitty thing to do, but I was already divorced and in Palm Beach and into a new life. Tom, on the other hand, was right on the scene and took it personally. He told Stoner straight out exactly what he thought of him. After the election Tom was out of a job.

Fortunately, he was able to hook up with the Attorney General even though it meant selling his house at a bad time and moving his family several hundred miles upstate. Once his life settled down though, Tom moved up the ranks quickly. He's the consummate government lawyer and works well in a structured environment. We kept up our friendship over the years, and it was lucky for me we did. Tom really came through for me when I needed a place to land after the big one hit.

"Seriously, Dave, you haven't had any more problems, have you?" I could see the concern on his face.

"Tom, I'm great. Never felt better."

"So what brings you to the capital?"

"Besides seeing you?"

"There's still no money for raises." The story was so old that it had become an inside joke and we both smiled.

"No, this is different, Tom. This is about a case. I thought that you and the General might be especially interested." I summed up what I knew as quickly as I could. Tom was one of those people who couldn't sit still — a real "Type A" personality. By the time I finished my story he was pacing the floor, slamming his fist into his palm.

"Payback time! I love it!"

"Take it easy, Tom. This might turn out to be a big zero."

The General's going to want to hear this right away. He's got a score to settle with The Deacon," Tom said, using the nickname he hung on Deke Stoner years ago. He looked at me, smiled and added, "And I've got one to settle, too."

"Tom, take it easy," I warned again. "Let's think this thing through." I began to worry that I might have set off an avalanche.

"Of course we'll think it through. We'll think it through and then we'll squash that bastard like a palmetto bug." He picked up the intercom. "Gloria, I need to talk to the General right away." There was a short pause before he spoke again. Apparently Tom didn't need to wait long to speak with the most powerful lawyer in the state. "General, David Bradley, our bureau chief from Bonita his here with me. He has some information that you need to hear . . . No, sir, I think you're going to want to hear this in person . . . Yes, sir, whenever you say. We'll be right over." Tom hung up the receiver. "Come on, we're going to take a walk."

I hurried out the door after him. The General's office was two blocks away – uphill, no less – in the Capitol building, and I already knew I was going to have trouble keeping up with Tom's brisk strides. "Tom, at some point we're going to have to slow down and take a careful look . . ."

"Do we have enough to get us in?"

"Not much, except the gun was stolen in one judicial circuit and bought and used in another."

"That's thin, but it'll have to do."

He looked at me and slowed his pace a little. "So how does Babs feel about you getting back into trial work? You do want this case, don't you?"

"You know she hates it when you call her that."

He smiled an impish grin and his eyes sparkled behind his wire-rimmed glasses. "I know. That's why I do it. What does she think?" he repeated.

"She'll probably have a fit."

That stopped him in his tracks and we stood there on the sidewalk halfway between his office and the Capitol. "Really?" Tom was suddenly serious again – serious and concerned. It was nice to know Barbara's feelings really meant something to him even if it did enjoy tormenting her with that "Babs" business. "If it's going to cause a problem,

Dave, I can keep you out of it. But tell me now."

"I need to get back into it, Tom. Just a little bit; just a taste. Barb is going to have to accept that."

Tom began walking again. "Are you going to tell her, or am I?

"I'll tell her."

He looked at me and picked up the pace again. "Well, you can always sleep on that couch in your office." The impish grin was back. "Just remember, 'Abstinence makes the heart grow fonder.'"

The Capitol building is a huge modern tower that dwarfs the "Old Capitol" building that is attached and kept for ceremonial and historic purposes. All the real work of government takes place in the new building. We breezed though security where most of the guards greeted Tom by name, and quickly made our way to the Office of the Attorney General – two doors away from the Governor's Office. The receptionist greeted Tom with a wave and in a minute we were in a small area. It led to three offices: one for the General himself; another for Gloria, his personal secretary; and a third, vacant office for a press secretary. "He's expecting you," Gloria said, and she ushered us into the inner sanctum where the Attorney General waited behind a giant walnut desk. His tailored jacket was carefully strewn over the back of a side chair, and his shirtsleeves were rolled up in a pretty good imitation of a working lawyer. The General glanced up from the legal pad he was studying and laid it down on an otherwise barren desk. Whatever he did here, drafting pleadings obviously was not one of his duties. He stood up and extended a manicured hand toward me.

"Come in, gentlemen. Dave, it's nice to see you again. How are things down on the west coast?"

"Fine, General. Criminal Appeals is keeping the bad guys

in jail." I was amazed at the effect he had on me. I've been around the block as they say, and I've known my share of politicians. Intellectually, I knew this guy's only interest in Southwest Florida was the number of votes it could deliver in the next election. Nevertheless, I found myself falling under his spell. His manner was a smooth as the top of his head.

"David has some information about a case that might interest this office, General." Tom, as usual, couldn't wait to get down to business.

"Let's hear it, Dave," the General said.

I told the story for the second time that day. This time Tom didn't leave his seat in the overstuffed leather chair. I got the impression that no one was supposed to stand up here until the boss stood up. There was a long pause when I ended my story.

"Dave, it's no secret that Deke Stoner has not been a friend of this office." The General had a way of talking that made it sound like he always was on camera. "I have no intention of using the power and prestige of the Attorney General's Office to punish him for that." I waited for the "but" which came two beats later, right on cue. "But, if he has failed in his duty to the people of this State to prosecute a murder case in his own jurisdiction, I believe it is our obligation to step in. Of course we could go directly to the Governor and ask him to appoint a special prosecutor, but he might appoint another state attorney who is no more competent than Stoner has been. I would prefer that a matter this serious remain in our hands. I believe the people of this State would best be served by keeping this in-house under the aegis of the Statewide Prosecutor."

I saw the case slipping away from me. In about five seconds I would be thanked for bringing "the matter" to his attention and sent packing. And the political big shots would divvy up the spoils. Tom Julian came to my rescue.

"General, if I may . . . Dave here is an excellent trial lawyer, and . . ."

"I'm sure he is, Tom. I have no doubt that Dave is one of our more capable assistants. But Helene Hizer is the Statewide Prosecutor, and I doubt she would be pleased if I took this case way from her."

Tom wasn't about to give up the fight. "General, jurisdiction here is very thin. It's possible that we could spend a lot of time and money on an investigation and get blown out of the water on a pretrial motion. You might be doing Helene a big favor by keeping her out of it."

"What are you suggesting, Tom?"

"Dave is an Assistant Attorney General. During the last campaign you often talked about cross-training assistants so the State could get the full value of its employees. Dave has loads of trial experience; it would be no problem to give him an extra assignment . . . sort of a pilot project. If the case falls flat, we can confine the damage to Bonita . . ."

"And if he gets a conviction?"

"You and Helene fly in, hold a press conference and announce the beginning of another successful program under your administration."

"We sweep up the glory. Does that offend you, David?"

"General, I've been around too long to be offended. I just want to get back into the courtroom and pick up a check every two weeks."

"We're agreed, then." The General stood up, and we followed his lead. "Make it happen, Tom. Dave," he extended his hand and I took it again. "Give 'em hell."

Tom and I were back out on the sidewalk before I knew what hit me. When I finally spoke up it was to ask, "Whose side were you on in there, anyway?"

"What the hell do you care? You got what you wanted, didn't you?"

"Sometimes you scare me, Tom."

"My boy, in politics, gall is all."

We were silent until we got back to the building that housed Tom's office. As we were about to enter, Tom turned to me and said, "Dave, we'll want the F.D.L.E. to do the investigation in this case."

The Florida Department of Law Enforcement is our state's version of the F.B.I. It meant the Attorney General was calling in the big guns. It also meant that Sergeant Watkins of the Calusa County Sheriff's Office was out on his ass.

"I can't do that to Watkins, Tom."

He looked at me coldly. We had been friends for a long time, but both of us knew he was now my boss. If he wanted to pull rank he could do it and there was nothing I could do about it. He had just gone out on a limb for me. I owed him more loyalty than I was showing.

"The Deacon's been the State Attorney down there for what: five, six years?" The smile was gone and his voice was as frigid as a winter night could get here in Tallahassee.

"He just started his second term," I agreed.

"He's got his fingers into everything down there, David. He's in shit up to his eyeballs, but we haven't been able to prove it. Have you ever heard of the Jolly Boys?"

"Are they some kind of rock group?" Another frosty look from Tom warned me I should cut out the smartass answers. He appeared deadly serious, as in "very deadly" serious.

"They were a gang of small-time thugs. Shitheads. But they're moving up in the world. They're in line to become the enforcers for a major drug operation that's moving into the west coast."

"You can't be serious Tom." The words "drug operation" and "enforcers" sent a shiver up my spine. Surely this couldn't be happening in a quiet little backwater like Bonita.

"Drug money, Bubba. There's lots of it out there and it comes from some very high players. I suspected it fueled The Deacon's campaign against us three years ago, and the word is his war chest is building."

"I don't believe it! A little place like Bonita?"

"It's everywhere, David. Anywhere they bring in boats or fly in planes. And as far as The Deacon goes, it would be pretty nice to have the Attorney General of the State in your pocket, wouldn't it?"

"Can you prove any of this?"

It was the wrong thing to say to someone like Tom, and I instantly regretted it. His eyes froze me from behind his glasses. "If I could prove it, The Deacon would be honing his legal skills as a prison law clerk somewhere," he said coolly. Tom opened the door and began walking into the lobby. I had to hurry to keep up.

"Anyway, Tom, even if Sto . . ." Tom shot me a look and I knew instantly what he meant: never mention names in public, even in your own lobby. "Even if that guy has his fingers in things, I don't think . . ." The elevator doors opened. Thankfully it was empty and I could continue my thoughts in privacy. "Tom, even if Stoner is as dirty as you say, his fingers can't possibly reach as far as Bear Harper and the Sheriff's Office."

"I hope you're right, Bubba. I like Bear." He looked at me earnestly. "I hope he's clean. I truly do."

"Even if he isn't, Tom, this shit doesn't go down as far as Watkins. He's just one of those old timers who wants to see justice prevail."

The elevator doors opened. We were on Tom's floor

now, and obviously he didn't mind continuing the conversation. Tom had personally vetted everyone on this floor. There were no leaks in his office. "I'd be a lot more comfortable if we pulled an end run and eliminated all of the locals," he replied without turning his head.

I had to grab him physically and hold him back to get him to look at me. He stopped; it was going to be my last chance to save a little something for the man who brought me the case. "Tom, you just went to bat for me, and whatever you say goes. But I honestly, truly feel that it would be wrong to pull the rug out from under Watkins. Besides . . ." I played my trump card much like he had done with the General . . . "he's got a rapport with this kid Shawn. I don't know if the kid will cooperate without Watkins around."

We had reached the door of Tom's office. He was silent for a minute. "Okay. But whatever Watkins does has to be on his own time. No files in the local S.O. Agreed?"

"Anything you say."

"And we'll use the F.D.L.E. for the balance of the investigation. Watkins can work with them as a liaison . . . on his own time."

It was the best deal I was going to get, and we both knew it. "Okay, Tom."

Tom extended his hand and I took it. "Like The Man said, 'give 'em hell,' Bubba." The old smile came back and I felt a lot better.

"Thanks, Tom. Thanks for everything."

I got back on the elevator and rode down alone. Tom's speech to the General kept ringing in my ears. He had been up here a long time, and it sound like he had learned the first rule of politics – always cover your own ass. I wondered how far our friendship would go in covering mine if I blew this case. I suspected it would not go very far. That's great. It was just what I needed. Instead of a garden-variety murder case, I was now carrying the political baggage of some of the most powerful lawyers in the state, as well as God-knows-what in other, unknown agendas. I began to regret my decision of sticking up for Watkins. If something did go wrong, if Deke Stoner somehow managed to muck things up, my stubbornness would be ample reason for Tom to cover his ass by pulling the plug on mine. I figured no matter what happened I'd better keep this information from Barbara.

Which brought up another problem. How was I going to tell her? I had promised her that I would stay away from this case, even though I knew I was lying when I made that promise. Now I had to tell her. I wouldn't blame her if she packed up and walked out on me right here in Tallahassee. Except I wouldn't let that happen. I couldn't live without her. If it came to that, I would call Tom back and beg off. I'd have to. I couldn't lose her, just to prove a point to myself. I couldn't lose her for anything.

I made it back to the motel by 10:00 a.m. It's surprising how much you can get done when your day starts at 7:30. Barbara was in the bathroom and came out wearing a monogrammed terrycloth robe I had given her.

"How did it go?" she asked as she ran a towel through her hair.

"Fine. Fine. No problems." I still hadn't come up with a way of breaking the news.

"Did you see Tom Julian?"

"Yeah." I advanced on her and ended up with my arms around her waist. The only thing she had on under that robe was perfume. A very interesting evening started out like this last night.

"Does he still call me 'Babs'?"

"Afraid so," I said as I began kissing her neck.

"Hey, you're not being fair," she protested as she tried to pull away. I'm supposed to spend the day with Tori."

"What does being fair have to do with that?" I asked as I began working my way toward her ear. That always drove her crazy.

"We were supposed to go shopping," she gasped as I nibbled her earlobe.

"I'll come with you."

She laughed throatily. "You just want to 'come'."

I continued my attack on her ear while my hands roamed over her back and down to the two luscious globes below.

"Did you have breakfast?" Leave it to Barbara to ask something practical at a time like this.

"No," I whispered as I continued my exploration of her body. Her skin felt creamy soft under the robe.

"Aren't you hungry?" She was squirming in my arms now, not sure if she wanted me to stop of continue what I was doing.

"Only for you," I breathed in her ear.

She signed heavily. I had gotten to her. "Maybe that can be arranged," she said with a soft moan. She broke away from me for a moment and took a step backwards. "I've got a little surprise for you," she said as she looked directly into my eyes and slowly opened the robe. My jaw dropped. She had completely shaved off her pubic hair. Her body looked like an alabaster statue. Every crease was visible and I drank in the sight. She really knew how to turn me on.

"You really drive me crazy, you know that?" I couldn't conceal the smile that spread over my face. I must have looked like a kid who knew he was about to be let loose in a candy store.

"Show me how crazy, Sailor," she breathed.

I couldn't have stopped myself if I wanted to. I fell to my knees and began kissing the smooth softness where her legs met. She grabbed my hair with both hands and forced me deeper. After a few minutes her legs began to buckle and not long after than I had her sprawled on the bed where every delicious fold was open to me. I kept it up until she was screaming for me, and when I finally moved up over her she held on so tightly that I lifted her off the bed. We had some wild times in the past, but this was among the best. My "point of no return" came and went, but it didn't matter. I couldn't get enough of her. She didn't act like she had enough either, and I kept pounding into her like a man possessed. Barb matched me stroke for stroke. We were both drenched with sweat when we finally exploded. I was my second; I have no idea what her count was. I collapsed on top of her. It was a few minutes before I could roll off her.

I was lying next to her; breathing heavily and hoping my heart would stay inside my chest. Funny, she never worried about another attack at times like this. Barb kissed my neck. She finally spoke. "Did you get the case?" she asked softly.

"Yep," I answered staring at the ceiling. "How did you know?"

"You haven't made love to me like that in a long time." I turned and looked at her. She stroked the side of my face and continued. "I don't want to lose you, David."

I turned away again and looked at the ceiling. I couldn't bear to see the hurt in her eyes. "You're not going to lose me, Barbara. I just want to know that I can still do it, that's all."

Barb kissed my cheek lightly and said, "You can still do it, Lover. Believe me, you can still do it."

CHAPTER 3

"What the hell kind of double-cross is this?" Watkins shouted from the other side of my desk.

"Keep your voice down! It's not a double-cross."

"Then what the hell is it, if it isn't a double-cross?"

"We'll take the case, but the people in Tallahassee want the F.D.L.E. to do the rest of the investigation."

"But I brought it to you, goddamn it."

I looked at him carefully. "Sarge, you walked in here off the street and said that you wanted a murder case prosecuted because you wanted to see justice done. We're going to prosecute your murder case . . . at least we're going to try. We'll do our best to see that justice is done."

"But you guys are cutting me out."

I didn't need any more ego trips and I cut him off quickly. "I didn't know that 'justice' required you to be in on the case," I said without raising my voice. Watkins must have realized how silly that sounded, and he looked down at the floor, properly chastised.

"Look, Sarge," I continued, "I work for other people just like you do. They're going to let me try the case, but the rest isn't up to me. If you want to work with me, it'll have to be on your own time. Any files will have to stay right here, not at the Sheriff's Office."

His eyes came up off the floor and met mine straight on. "Your boss is afraid of Deke Stoner, isn't he?"

"You're asking me for a conclusion," I said, hiding behind the rules of evidence. "I can't possibly know what another person thinks."

"Shit, you're all afraid of him."

"Sarge, I leave the politics to the politicians. I just want to try a simple little murder case. I'm already in trouble with my wife; am I going to be in trouble with you, too?"

Watkins shook his head and smiled another one of those rare smiles. "All right, Dave. I guess it's not your fault. Deal me in. But I still say I've been double-crossed."

I picked up the intercom and asked Mary Ellen to send in our new teammate from the conference room where I had stashed him. Watkins and I waited in silence until my door opened. When it did, I introduced Watkins to Agent Jim Harcourt from the Florida Department of Law Enforcement.

Jim extended his hand and I could see that Watkins took it only reluctantly. "Sergeant I want to compliment you on a fine piece of police work."

"Come on, knock off the soft soap," Watkins mumbled.

"No, I mean it," Harcourt continued earnestly. "Most officers just want to clear cases and close files. It takes a real cop to dig deeper. You're to be congratulated."

"Well," Watkins let go of Harcourt's hand, "you know, I was just trying to do my job."

"Yeah, well if we had more local police officers doing their jobs like you, we wouldn't need the F.D.L.E."

"Or the Attorney General," I interjected. The bullshit was getting pretty deep in here, and I wanted to get down to business before we all drowned in it. Harcourt and Watkins took their seats across from me. It was time to talk turkey.

"Gentlemen," I began, "as I see it, our first problem is a lack of admissible evidence."

"I got you Shawn," Watkins replied defensively.

"And Shawn knows what Anita said to him, which, as an admission against her own interest, may be devastating against Anita. But what did Melwin say to him?"

Watkins fished a small notebook out of his pocket and thumbed through the worn pages. "Like you better just forget about that, man, 'cause you could be next. I hear the gators out in the swamp are gettin' hungry," he said in a flat monotone.

I exchanged a glace with Jim Harcourt. I could tell that this time he really *was* impressed. "What's wrong with that?" Watkins demanded.

"Kind of vague, isn't it?" I replied. "And who's this 'we' that everyone's always talking about? Is it Anita and her mother, Anita and Melwin, the mother and Melwin? What the hell is the mother's name, anyway?"

"Grace." Watkins appeared to be an inexhaustible font of details.

"The 'we' is all three of them," Harcourt interjected.

"Prove it, Jim," I replied. "Beyond a reasonable doubt. And besides," I continued, "there's the very real problem of Shawn. Who's going to believe him?"

The credibility problem cast a very large shadow over our conversation. Harcourt hadn't met Shawn yet, but I had filled him in. Jim was an experienced cop who had seen his share of cases go down the toilet when the prosecution tried to convict a criminal on the word of another.

"And then there's the little matter of *corpus delicti*," I continued.

"I told you about the body; it was cremated," Watkins protested.

"I don't mean the 'corpse' body; I mean the *corpus delicti* . . . the 'body of the crime.'

Under Florida law you can't prove a defendant's guilt by his confession alone. We need to have some independent proof that a crime was committed."

"We had a body with a bullet in its head." Watkins was still stuck on the corpus/corpse connection.

"The medical examiner said the bullet wound was self-inflicted, remember? We need independent evidence that a crime . . . any crime . . . was committed, before we can bring in the defendants' statements." Watkins was writing in his notebook and I surprised myself with my explanation of the technicalities. The past two years had been a lot like earning a master's degree in criminal law.

"How big a problem is Shawn's credibility?" Harcourt asked, going back to our first problem.

"Real big." I figured I might as well lay it on the line.

"Can we get him to use a wire?" Leave it to an F.D.L.E. agent to start thinking high-tech.

"I don't know" I responded honestly. "Sarge?"

"You mean wire him for sound and have him try to get Anita and her boyfriend to say something else?"

"It could solve the credibility problem," Harcourt replied.

"How do we get him out of jail to do it, without tipping off the State Attorney that we're trying to steal an indictment from right under his nose?" I asked. There was no reason to be coy. Watkins had already figured out we were all pawns in some kind of bigger political game. I might as well lay everything in the table.

"Somebody bails the kid out," Harcourt repeated matter-of-factly.

"Jim, I can't do that. I can't put up the bail. I think it's illegal and I'm sure it's unethical."

"Who's talking about you?" he replied.

"I can't let you do it, either. In this case you're acting as my agent. Besides, where would either of us get the money? We'd need a bondsman, and that means signatures. It can't be done."

"Who's talking about either of us?"

"Well what the hell are you talking about?"

"Suppose I have a friend who wants to help some poor, misunderstood child who's rotting away in the Calusa County Jail waiting for his trial to come up. And suppose this same friend decides . . . out of the goodness of his or her heart . . . once I bring the matter to his or her attention . . . to post bail for the kid. Are you telling me that's illegal?"

"I don't know; it might be. Who's your friend?"

"If I tell you, does that make my friend your 'agent'?"

"It might."

"Then I'm not telling you."

"You know, Dave, springing Shawn would really cement us in tight with him," Watkins said. It didn't take a psychologist to see he liked the idea.

"I don't care how badly we want this case, I'm not going to cross the line," I protested. "I'm not happy about talking to the kid without a lawyer present. If we start taking any more shortcuts, it will always be 'just a little more.' It's a slippery slope that can end with me getting disbarred."

"You're not doing anything, for chrissake!" Watkins exploded. "His friend is putting up the money!"

"Who's his friend?"

Harcourt's smile reminded me of one of the dolphins at Sea World. "My friend is an anonymous do-gooder who wishes to remain anonymous." The smile vanished and he got serious for a moment. "But I give you my word, David, I really do have a friend. There's no secret state fund for bailing out informants." Harcourt looked at me earnestly, although I still didn't believe him. On the other hand, the story was plausible. Maybe it was better not to ask too many questions at this point.

"All right, say we get him out," I replied. "Then what?" Even if we get somebody to talk on a wire, we're still in no better shape in terms of *corpus delicti*.

"I'm not so sure about that," Watkins interjected. "The Sabal Palms police report says there was another kid in the house when it happened. And the word on the street is that some people have been talking."

I looked at him quizzically. "You never told me about this before."

"There was no reason to. I wasn't going to put in any more time into chasing down a bunch of kids if nobody was going to listen to me. Besides . . ." he smiled his own 'Flipper' grin . . . "I wasn't about to shoot my whole wad until I knew you guys were serious."

I had to admit he made sense. "Anyway, according to the coppers' report, the girl didn't have much to say," he continued. "But you said we need evidence 'tending to show that a crime was committed'." Watkins was reading from his notebook. He never failed to amaze me. It was an almost verbatim statement of my *corpus delicti* explanation. I nodded in response. "All right, any crime?" he asked. "Possession of a firearm?"

"That's not a crime in Florida; you know that."

"It is if it's stolen; or if you carry it in a concealed manner. How about aggravated assault?"

"Do you have evidence that somebody in the house was put in fear of deadly force?"

"How the hell do I know? Watkins protested. "I haven't

talked to the kid. I just want to know: is that enough?"

"Just barely, but it's enough."

"Okay, here's what I say," Watkins continued. "I say I go talk to this girl and these other little sons-of-bitches, whoever they are. I can do that because I'm a local cop. Local cops are always asking questions. If Stempo's family gets wind of it, so much the better. Maybe they'll get nervous and make a stupid mistake. Meanwhile, Jim can talk to his friend and work on getting Shawn out of jail."

"Suppose Deke Stoner gets word of you asking questions about the Stempo case?"

"How's he going to find out?" Harcourt protested. "And so what if he does? Sarge is investigating house burglaries where guns may have been stolen. He's a local; he has every right to do that."

"This gun was stolen in another county; in fact, it was a different judicial circuit," I reminded them. "Neither Sarge nor Deke Stoner have jurisdiction down there."

"I'm investigating burglaries here in Calusa County. Are you going to take Shawn's word for where he stole the gun from? He's so coked out most of the time he doesn't know where the hell he is. And I'm not arresting; I'm only investigating. So let me do my job, okay?"

"And while you guys are out having fun, what am I supposed to do?"

"Go back to your books, Counselor," Watkins chided. "Find out everything you can about those *corpus delicti's*. And when you're finished with them, do a little research on admissions. Agent Harcourt and I are about to bring in a case; we don't want the Attorney General screwing it up."

It was late in the week before we got together in my office again. This time Shawn was with us. Harcourt's friend, whoever he or she was, had come through. Shawn looked thinner and paler than when I had seen him last.

Apparently the county jail didn't agree with his health. The acne was still there, even more pronounced against his pale skin, and his hair still looked like it had never seen soap. As I looked at him in the well-lit, air-conditioned office, I began to wonder if I could actually get away with using him as a witness. It would take a lot of window dressing. Maybe Barbara would have some ideas.

"So, Shawn, how does it feel to be out?" I began.

"Like, okay, I guess."

"You know Agent Harcourt from the Florida Department of Law Enforcement? It was a friend of his who put up the bail."

"Yeah, thanks," he said, nodding at Jim.

"Are you going back to school? I asked, wondering how we were going to break the news about wiring him.

"I don't know. Like I guess I got to, right? I mean, like I don't have a choice, do I?"

"You could always drop out," Watkins suggested. What the hell did he say that for? We wanted the kid back where he could be in daily contact with Anita and Melwin. Why the hell did Watkins want to put ideas in his head?

"Sure, like and have my old lady kill me, right?" Shawn protested. Why did I suddenly feel like Watkins knew that answer all along?

Harcourt went to work. "Shawn, we helped you out. We got you out of that smelly old jail. Even if you do have to go back to Sabal Lakes, it can't be as bad as that, right?"

"Yeah, like, I guess."

"Well now we want you to do something for us," Jim continued.

Shawn looked up and his eyes darted back and forth among the three of us. "Yeah, like what?" he asked suspiciously.

"We need you to talk to Anita and Melwin. Get any

information you can about this murder," Harcourt responded.

"Like, I don't know if they'll say anything else, man."

"I understand. We're not asking you to do the impossible. Just try, okay?"

Shawn looked at the floor and nodded.

"And Shawn," Harcourt added, "I'm going to want you to wear a bug while you're doing it."

Shawn looked up and his eyes widened. "No way, man! No fuckin' way! I heard back in the slammer that Mel's a Jolly Boy. He sees anything like that, I'm gator meat! I'm dead! I ain't wearin' no bug!"

"It's perfectly safe . . ." Harcourt began.

"I said I ain't wearin' no fuckin' bug, man!"

"Shawn, that friend of mine who put up the money for your bail only did it because I said you were cooperating with us. Now, if you're not going to cooperate, I'm afraid my friend may decide to do something else with that money."

"I don't care, man! Take me back to jail. It's better'n what happened to Terrell."

"Who? What are you taking about?" Watkins asked.

"This kid at school named Terrell. At least he used to be at school. Anyways, he screwed over one a' the Jolly Boys on a drug deal or somethin'. Ripped 'em off, I guess. An' like the word is one night they grabbed him in front of his house an' wrapped him in duct tape. His own fuckin' house, man! An' they like drove him out to the swamp somewhere and thew 'im into a lake full a' gators." Shawn's hands began to shake violently and he ran them threw his greasy hair. "An' they say the Jolly Boys stayed around an' watched Terrell get eaten alive."

I looked at Watkins. "Could this be true?"

He shrugged. "Who knows? A missing person case

involving some punk? Happens all the time." He handed Shawn a cigarette and lit it for him. I didn't bother to point out that this was a smoke-free building. "Shawn, look, I understand you're upset, but let's talk about it. Maybe we can work something out."

"We ain't working nothin' out, man, 'cause like I ain't wearin' no fuckin' bug! Not for no fuckin' Jolly Boy! I can't even believe I'm talkin' to you dudes about this, man. If the Jolly Boys find out, I'll be gator meat out in some swamp." He looked up at us and added, "Those guys play rough man," as he flipped ashes into the palm of his hand.

"Shawn, that's ridiculous. I've wired up hundreds of people, and we've never . . ." Harcourt began before Sergeant Watkins interrupted him.

"Shawn, suppose we fit you up with a bug that can't be detected; can't be seen. That would be okay, wouldn't it? Something there was no way for anybody to see?"

"I don't know, man," the kid whined.

"Sure you do, Shawn. You said yourself you didn't want these people getting away with murder. Now if we need a little more evidence, you could help us with that, couldn't you?"

"I don't know, man. Like I never expected it to go this far."

"None of us thought it would go this far, Shawn. But we're into it now. We can't walk away from it, not if we're real men. We're into it this far and we've got to go through with it."

Watkins gave a hell of a sales pitch. I wasn't sure why any of us "had to" go through with anything, but I was hoping Shawn wouldn't notice the flaw in that argument. He didn't.

"I guess," he finally mumbled.

"That's what I like to hear, buddy!" Watkins slapped him

on the back so hard he almost knocked him out of the chair.

"There just can't be, like, you know, any wires showin' or anything man. 'Cause if Melwin sees anything at all, I'm like gator bait."

"There's not going to be anything showing, Shawn," Jim Harcourt assured him. "We're not even going to do anything right away. We just wanted you to know about it, so you wouldn't think we were pulling any surprises if the time comes."

"Like I'm surprised, man. Okay?"

"How are you getting home, Shawn?" Watkins seemed to really care about the kid.

"Same way I got here. My bike."

"You have a motorcycle?" I asked.

"Bicycle, man." Shawn looked at me like I was an idiot.

"Okay, here's five bucks," Watkins said, handing him a bill. "Stop at Burger King on your way, okay? I'd go with you but I've got to talk to these guys about something else. Besides, I don't think it's a good idea for you to be seen with me, understand?"

Shawn nodded.

"All right, scram," Watkins said abruptly.

Shawn looked at us. No one said anything. I was about to extend my hand, but it didn't look like he was used to that, and I didn't want to embarrass him. I lifted my hand in sort of a half wave. "We'll be in touch, Shawn."

"Yeah," said the kid. And then he was gone.

It was a long time before Watkins spoke. "It looks like the gang problem the Sheriff is always talking about is really here."

"It has a foothold all right," Jim Harcourt added. "And it's going to get worse."

"How much do you know about this Jolly Boy thing,

Jim?" I asked.

"Not enough. At least not yet. But whether you call them "Tenth Street Gang" or "Marauders," the gang problem is fueled by drug money that's also reaching into some very high places." I looked at Jim and thought about Tom Julian's suspicions, but it appeared Sergeant Watkins's thoughts were elsewhere.

"Makes you wonder, doesn't it?"

"Wonder about what?"

"Kids like that. People like that. Where's he going: What's he doing with himself? Don't you ever wonder how some kids wind up in law school and others wind up like him?"

"You're starting to sound philosophical, Sarge," Harcourt reminded him.

No. No, I mean it. I've been running around putting little assholes like him in jail for what, twenty-five years? And nothing changes. Christ, if Shawn has kids and I live long enough I'll be putting *them* in jail. Where the hell does it all end?"

"It doesn't end, Sarge," I reminded him. "We're just here holding our fingers in the dike and hoping for the best."

It was a fitting way to end the meeting. Here we were, investigating a murder. It looked very much like a woman and her daughter – maybe with a little help from the daughter's boyfriend – killed Daddy in his sleep and then made it look like a suicide. That might be okay on the Movie of the Week, but this was real life for chrissake! These were regular people just like us. For all I knew, Anita Stempo might be the checkout girl at the supermarket; her father might have been one of the guys who passed the basket in church. It made you wonder what went on in people's houses after the doors were closed. Even a nice quiet little condominium like the one Barbara and I lived in might hold secrets of violence and brutality that would never make it past a network censor. It wasn't a pleasant thought.

My mood had not improved by the time I got home. Barb was waiting with hors d' oeuvres and wine out on the patio. It took a couple of glasses before I was ready to talk.

"It's not going well, is it?" she finally asked.

"No, it's going just fine. Well . . . it's going as well as can be expected at this point."

"You've been awfully quiet for a couple of days."

I didn't reply for a long time, and Barb was smart enough to not ask more questions. The silence got to be deafening after a while. "You know, Watkins had a point today. We were talking to this kid Shawn. He's a burglar, Barbara, a real, professional burglar, and he's only in high school."

"And?"

"Watkins just asked how a kid gets that way. Look at Tori; she's in college, on her way to medical school. This kid is a few years behind her and is on his way to Nowheresville."

"I believe the place is called 'Palookaville', Darling. And the answer is 'genetics.' Tori's father may have been a rat, but he was a very intelligent rat." She smiled at me coyly and added, "You see, I have a 'thing' for smart men."

"Sure, genetics is part of it. I'm not saying Shawn was ever going to be a brain surgeon, but I'm sure he could do a hell of a lot better than being a burglar.

"David, it sounds to me like both you and Sergeant Watkins have become philosophical. Perhaps that's why criminal prosecution is best left to younger men . . . they tend to see the world in much more severe colors: black and white, for example."

"Is that an 'age' comment?" I asked defensively.

"Just an observation," she added with a peck on my lips. She stood up and headed for the kitchen and I followed her, glass in hand.

"Well, let me tell you, the problem with a lot of those younger prosecutors is that they have no sense of perspective." Barb poked around the refrigerator instead of politely listening to my speech. "They haven't been around long enough," I continued, warming to the topic, "they don't know when to cut someone a break."

She took a platter out of the 'frige. "I think it's time to grill these salmon steaks, Darling. The wine is getting to you. I'll make the salad."

"You're not listening to me, are you?"

"Yes, of course I am. You're old enough to know when people deserve a break. Do you think the Stempo's deserve one?" she asked, handing me the platter.

"No, of course not. I mean, you can't just blow your husband's brains out . . ."

"Why not? I had a husband once, and I thought about blowing his brains out any number of times."

"Present company excepted, I hope," I said with a smile.

"Do you want fat-free Ranch or olive oil and vinegar on your salad?" she replied.

We had dinner on the patio, just the two of us. It was the way we usually did things around here. Living with Barbara was like that. We were both old enough to know what was important, and we knew that time alone together was the only thing that mattered. Every once in a while I wonder if we would have related to each other differently if we had met when we were still young enough to have been thinking about a family. But then I reminded myself that we have Tori, and that's enough. I don't think I could handle any more demands on Barb's attention right now. At the moment she was talking about a new client whom her employer was trying to capture: a young lady over on Bonita Key who was spending a ton of money trying to create an upscale restaurant. It was an interior designer's dream, as it is in any profession when the client says the magic words, "Price is no object!"

The sun was setting out over the Gulf of Mexico when the telephone rang. Barb picked it up and handed it to me. It was Tom Julian calling from Tallahassee.

"Aren't you at the office pretty late, even for you?" I asked as I took the receiver.

"Nah, I'm calling you from home. "I've been here for at least half an hour. I'm already on my second Bourbon and Branch."

"What's on your mind, Tom?"

"Nothing. Just calling to see how you're doing."

I didn't believe that answer. Tom never called anybody for no reason. He especially didn't call people at home — from his home — for no reason. Something was definitely on his mind, but I would have to wait for him to tell me when he was good and ready.

"How's the case going?"

"Fine, Tom." What did he want? There had to be a reason for the call. Why not just come out with it?

"Any new evidence?"

"No, not yet. But it's still early in the investigation."

"I thought maybe your buddy Sergeant Watkins had a chance to talk to some other kids. There was one in the house when the shooting took place, wasn't there?"

I smelled a rat, and I could feel my blood pressure rising. "How did you know about that?"

"I'm your boss, David. It's my job to know . . ."

"It's Harcourt, isn't it?"

". . . and it's the General's job to know what I know," he continued, ignoring my question.

"I don't like being spied on, Tom."

"David! 'Spying' is such an ugly word!"

"That's what you guys are doing, isn't it?"

"You know, David, the Attorney General of our State is a lot more perceptive than most people give him credit for. You'd be surprised how carefully he thinks things through before he makes a decision."

"Harcourt's down here keeping an eye on me, so that if things start to go bad somebody from Tally can come down and pull the fat out of the fire, right?"

"David . . . you're jumping to conclusions," Tom warned.

All of a sudden it hit me. Tom didn't have to make this call. He certainly didn't have to mention Watkins and the additional witness. He was tipping me off, without tipping me off, of course. It's called "plausible deniability." I hesitated for a minute. I'd better cool off and listen to the meaning behind the words.

"I appreciate your concern, Tom," I said quietly.

"We've been friends for a long time, Darlin'."

"I know."

"Well, I'd just be careful about who I call an 'asshole,' if I were you. And for chrissake don't make any 'bald' jokes."

"I'll be careful, Tom."

"You do that. Hey, and Bubba? I didn't tell you anything. Any conclusions that you drew, you drew them for yourself, you hear?"

"I've always been real good at drawing conclusions, Tom."

"I know; that's why I hired you. You were always a little naïve about politics, though."

"Yeah, I guess I needed to be reminded about that."

"Take care of yourself, Bubba. There's bears in them woods, and they're just waiting for a Little Red Riding

Hood like you. But you're still the best goddamn Assistant Attorney General we've got. Besides me, of course."

"Take care of *yourself*, Tom."

"I always do. That's why I've survived up here for so long."

I hung up with a vague sick feeling. I had begun to like Jim Harcourt; now I would have to treat him a little more carefully. He would still do his job for me, of course. But now whenever I said anything in his presence, I would have to pretend I was saying it in front of the Attorney General himself. Like Tom said, "No bald jokes." And while we were on the subject of spies, how about Watkins? He might be a hell of a cop, but was he making daily reports to the Sheriff? Nothing on the record, of course. But did they have some secret agenda that included the dethronement of State Attorney Deke Stoner? Nothing serious enough to take directly to the Attorney General, of course. Politics doesn't work that way. Doing things directly can sometimes forge an alliance that one side or the other might later regret. The better way is to find somebody – some pawn – who is your enemy's enemy, and find a reason to help the pawn. If the pawn succeeds, your enemy perishes and you're owned a favor. On the other hand, if the pawn does not succeed, you simply withdraw your support and look for a new pawn. I wondered who was playing me. The General? The Sheriff? Both? Barbara's massaging hands on my neck pushed a lot of dark thoughts out of my mind.

"You look like someone who has just lost his best friend," she said softly.

"On the contrary, I just found out how good a friend Tom Julian really is."

"Problems with the General?"

"Nothing I can't handle," I replied. "As long as I can keep track of the players.

CHAPTER 4

Mollie Sussman's mother wore a silky yellow blouse and a matching tight skirt, and the heel of her right foot bounced up and down on my carpet. She blew a cloud of cigarette smoke across my desk as she spoke. "I don't know what you think my daughter has done, Mr. Bradley," she began.

"We don't think she's done anything, Ms. Sussman," I replied. "If we did, I would be the first one to tell you." I was trying to put out a small brush fire before it burned down our entire case. Mollie was the kid who was at the Stempo house the night of the shooting, and when Watkins tried to talk to her, Mollie told Mama who promptly went though the roof. Discretion being the better part of valor, the good Sergeant then hustled Mama over to my office for a heavy application of soft soap. Now she was sitting on the other side of my desk, demanding to know why the big, bad State of Florida was harassing her little girl. Watkins sat next to her and kept his mouth shut. I was the soft soap expert on this team.

"I don't like lawyers, Mr. Bradley. I had a lawyer for my divorce, and he turned out to be a bigger skunk than my husband's lawyer, who was also a skunk. Both of them were only out for themselves, you know? When they got through with the two of us, we couldn't even go out for coffee together because we couldn't afford it. I mean, not that I'd want to get together with the jerk again . . . my husband that is . . . but we could have done things a hell of a lot easier and cheaper ourselves."

I nodded my head, and wondered whether the divorce had been particularly difficult or if indeed some of my brethren of the legal profession had performed a cashectomy on two unsuspecting victims. There was no way to tell but, as usual, the lawyers got the blame. "You may very well have been better off representing yourselves," I agreed. "Of course, that depends on whether you could have talked to each other without drawing blood at the time." I thought I was being cute; but she did not smile.

"Anyway, I can't afford to go out and get a lawyer for Mollie now, and I'm sure her father won't do it. The skunk barely gets his child support in on time." It sounded like they couldn't talk to each other even now.

"There's no reason to, Ms. Sussman. Mollie's not charged with anything. Of course, if you'd be more comfortable with a lawyer present, you're entitled to have one."

"Maybe I should get the Public Defender."

"The Public Defender's Office represents people who are charged with crimes. They don't represent witnesses."

"So you mean, if I want a lawyer for Mollie, I'll have to go out and hire one, right?"

"I'm afraid so."

"Well, that's not going to happen. No way. Not unless she's charged with something real serious."

"She's not being charged with anything, Ms. Sussman.

We just want to talk to her as a witness. We think she might know some details about Mr. Stempo's death."

"So she's not in any trouble."

"Not at all."

"Will you give me your word on that?"

"Absolutely. You have my word."

"Can I stay here while you guys talk to her?"

I looked at Watkins who clenched his lips and shook his head. "I think Mollie would be more comfortable if you waited outside," I suggested.

The woman stood up. "I'm putting a lot of faith in you, Bradley. Don't let me down," she said as she marched out of my office. Sergeant Watkins escorted her to the waiting room and returned with Mollie. She was dressed pretty much like her mother, but looked twice as nervous. Her hand was cold and clammy when I shook it and asked her to sit down.

"Mollie, we're doing a little follow-up work on the death of Joe Stempo. You were there the night he . . . the night it happened, weren't you?"

"Yeah," she said quietly. She slunk deep into the chair and looked a lot younger than her sixteen years. I couldn't help but wonder if Mollie ever hung around the mall with her friends, and if she acted as shy and insecure as she appeared now.

"Mollie, you're a friend of Anita Stempo aren't you?" Watkins asked from the chair beside her.

"Yeah." This interview might take a while if Mollie confined herself to one-word answers.

"Well, we just want to clear up a couple of things about her father's death, that's all," Watkins persisted.

"Is Anita in trouble?"

"Why do you say that?" Watkins asked.

"I don't know. I mean, like, because her father was shot,

you know, I mean, like shot himself and everything. Anyways, I told the Sabal Palms cops everything I know."

"I know that. But see, there's a couple of things that don't make sense, Mollie, and we've got to clear them up." The girl did not respond, and Watkins continued, "See, when a guy commits suicide he usually thinks about it, at least for a minute or two. He doesn't just wake up in the middle of the night and pow!" – Mollie flinched visibly at the word – "blow his brains out. And if he thought about it in advance, well, he probably wouldn't go to sleep right before he did it, right?"

"Maybe he woke up in the middle of the night, and he was . . . like, you know, depressed or something," she protested.

Watkins inched his chair forward and hunched closer to her. He looked like a jungle cat stalking its prey. "There's lots of time," I could almost hear him thinking. "No need to hurry; just keep her talking. She's already said too much."

"Yeah, but, see, Mollie," he continued, "where did he get the gun? Nobody in the family ever saw it before, right?" Mollie looked at the floor and did not answer. It appeared that Watkins had hit a nerve.

"Nobody saw it before, right, Mollie?" Watkins repeated. Still no response. He did not press the issue for the moment, and instead continued talking as if he were only thinking out loud. "See, the problem we're having is if the gun was just laying around, well, I guess it might be possible he just picked it up and pow!" – she flinched again – "did it on the spur of the moment. But, see, the gun wasn't lying around. He had to get up and get it from someplace. Now if he did that, he wouldn't go back to bed with his wife laying there, would he?"

The girl slunk deeper into her chair and her hands

trembled slightly. She did not respond.

"Mollie? Would he?" Watkins persisted.

Still no response.

"You know what I think, Mollie?" Watkins said leaning very close and whispering in an almost conspiratorial tone, "I think Joe Stempo didn't kill himself. I think somebody else did it and tried to make it look like a suicide. He didn't kill himself, did he Mollie?"

A tear started to run down the girl's cheek, and she brushed it away with the back of her hand.

"He didn't do it, Mollie," Watkins continued, whispering so softly I could barely hear him. "And you know who did it, don't you Mollie? Come on, tell me, and it'll be off your shoulders. It'll all be over, and no one will ever have to know that you told. Who did it, Mollie?"

"I don't know," she sobbed into her hands.

"Yes, you do Mollie. You just don't want to tell. You don't want to tell because you're protecting your friend Anita. She put it all on your shoulders, didn't she? And she's making you carry the guilt for her. She killed her father, didn't she? And she's making you carry the load for her. It hurts, doesn't it, Mollie? It hurts keeping it all inside like that. Come on, let it out and it will all be over."

"It wasn't Anita," she sobbed. "It wasn't Anita. It was somebody else, one of the other two. I don't know who. Oh, God, please believe me, I really don't know."

Watkins pulled a fresh handkerchief out of his pocket — why did I get the feeling that he had stashed it there on purpose? — and he handed it to the young girl and gently stroked her hair. "That's all right, Mollie," he said, his voice was as low and warm as a compassionate grandfather. "You just have a good cry. They've put you though a lot, those people. Carrying all that guilt around for them. You go ahead and cry for a minute. We're going to help you.

We're going to straighten everything out for you. And you won't ever have to think about it again."

I had a pounding headache as I watched the sixteen-year-old girl across from me sob into Watkins' handkerchief. I had read a lot of transcripts in my years of practice and had even participated in a number of interrogations. But this was different. Mollie wasn't a suspect; she was some innocent young kid who had been caught up in a web of evil. I was certain she was shielding someone else and I knew – and I think Mollie knew – that Watkins wouldn't let up until she told him every detail of what horrific night. I wondered how much more brutal the grandfatherly, paunchy Sergeant Watkins could get with an actual suspect.

"Come on, Mollie. Tell us which one of them did it so we can get this over with. And then we can all get on with our lives. Right, Mollie?

"It wasn't Anita," she repeated though her sobs. "She tried to do it once, she told me. But she couldn't go through with it. She didn't do it. It wasn't her."

My feelings wavered between pity and disgust. A young girl was telling us that her friend had tried to murder her father by putting a gun to his head while he slept in his own bed. It seemed the only reason Joe Stempo lived long enough to have someone else kill him was because his own daughter couldn't find it in her heart to pull the trigger when she tried to do it herself.

"How did it happen, Mollie? Watkins was relentless. If he had any feelings – shock, sympathy, anything – they must have been sublimated in the thrill of the pursuit. "You can tell us," he was saying. "You can tell me, and I'll straighten it all out for you. It'll all be over, once and for all."

"I was in her bedroom with her when I heard the shot

just like I told the Sabal Palms cops." She looked up a me, pleading with her eyes. "We were in there, the three of us, Anita, Melwin and me, watching videos, just like I told them. But, see, what I didn't tell them was, a couple of minutes before it happened, Mel said something to her, real quiet. And then he took the gun out of a drawer and said he would be right back." Mollie was breathing heavily, gasping for air, and sounding like she might become hysterical at any moment. "And then Anita started crying, and a couple of seconds later, I heard a noise, I guess it was a shot, and Anita started crying harder. And I put my arms around her, and she kept crying. And then I heard Anita's mother crying, too. And Mel came back in and he said that Joe had shot himself and that he was going to call the police."

"You're sure about that, Mollie? Anita started crying right before you heard the shot; before Melwin came back in?" I asked.

The girl nodded.

"How about the gun, Mollie? Did Melwin have the gun with him when he came back into the bedroom?" Watkins was speaking again.

She shook her head "no."

"I'm going to get you a Coke, Mollie, I said as I picked up the intercom. I think we all need one." I asked Mary Ellen if she could get some soft drinks out of the vending machine in the break room and bring them in.

"Why didn't you tell the Sabal Palms police about the gun, Mollie?" I asked while we waited.

"I guess at the time I didn't want to get involved and I . . . I don't know. Do you have to tell my mother?"

"We'll only tell her what you want us to tell her," Watkins replied. I looked at him quizzically while he continued; "We're going to help you out all we can.

Nobody but us has to know anything for now. Okay?"

Mollie nodded and Mary Ellen came in before I could ask Watkins what the hell he was talking about. "Do you want me to bring her mother in here?" Mary Ellen asked, looking at Watkins and me as though we were a couple of child molesters.

"Mollie?" I asked. "Can we bring your mother in now?" The girl and Watkins both nodded and Mary Ellen left with an expression that looked like pure disgust. It was a minute or two before Ms. Sussman reappeared, and her daughter had composed herself. Watkins stood up and offered Mollie's mother his chair.

"Your daughter is a fine young lady, Ms. Sussman," he said, taking the woman's hand. "Talking to her has really helped us out."

"You mean she didn't tell the police everything?"

The girl looked at Watkins. "Oh, no. Nothing like that," he replied. "It's just that sometimes you get a much better handle on things when you hear it firsthand. Talking to Mollie gave me the chance to put a couple of small details into focus."

"Then she's not going to have to testify or anything like that?" the woman asked.

"Well, I . . ." I began before Watkins cut me off. "I doubt that very, very much, he said. "Now that Mollie has put me on the right track, I'm sure we can get the rest of this straightened out with no trouble at all."

Mollie finished her soft drink. "Can we go?" her mother asked.

"Of course," I replied. "We'll be in touch if there's anything else." Watkins shook the woman's hand and patted the girl on the shoulder. I escorted the two of them to the lobby and then returned to confront him in my office.

"What the hell do you mean, 'she won't have to testify'? How the hell am I going to prove this case without her?"

"Dave, take it easy. Melwin did it. Put him in a room alone with Jim Harcourt and me and we'll have a complete confession in thirty minutes, maybe less. There's not going to be any trial; the son-of-a-bitch will plead guilty."

"To first-degree murder?" I demanded.

"First-degree, second-degree, who cares? This case is wrapped up. Melwin did it, and I'm going to nail his ass."

"How do you know the old lady didn't pull the trigger?"

"In her own bed for chrissake? Give me a break, Dave."

"It's possible."

"Yeah, it's also 'possible' that Mollie did it. But Melwin is the odds-on favorite in this horse race. I'll see you; I've got work to do."

Jim Harcourt was in my office the next day. "Of course you know Watkins is full of shit."

I had insisted on full disclosure between Watkins and the F.D.L.E. The last thing I needed was two separate investigations going on with two different suspects as targets. Watkins had squealed like a stuck pig when I told him, but I wouldn't back down. He assured me the Tallahassee boys would do nothing but try to torpedo him at every opportunity. Now it looked like they were about to prove him right.

"Come on, Jim," I protested. "The guy was up front enough to update you on Mollie Sussman. Why can't you give him a little credit?"

"I do give him credit. I give him a lot of credit. He's obviously a much better cop than the Sabal Palms officers."

"So what's the problem?"

"The problem is that he's drawing the wrong conclusion from the information she gave him. Melwin didn't do it; the wife did it."

"Jim, be reasonable. The kid said she saw Melwin take a gun out of a drawer and leave the room with it. A couple of minutes later there's a gunshot, and Melwin comes back in and announces Joe killed himself."

"I know, I know," Harcourt replied. "But in the final analysis we're going to find out he handed the gun to the old lady and she pulled the trigger."

"How the hell can you say that?"

"Did you ever kill anybody, David?" he asked in response to my question.

I looked at him as if he were insane. "Kill anyone? No, of course not."

"I didn't think so; I doubt if Watkins has either. I have. I killed a guy once during a drug raid in Tampa. It wasn't an instantaneous, bang-bang kind of thing, either. He was advancing on me with a very large machete. I told him to drop it or I'd shoot. I guess he didn't believe me. Anyway, he didn't drop it. He took another step toward me and I shot him." He paused for a moment and then repeated, "I shot him, David, right through the heart."

Harcourt looked away for a moment as he said it. I could tell that regardless of the circumstances and how long ago the incident happened, the memory of it still affected him. "The point is," he continued, "I had enough time to think about it, and the longer I thought about it, the harder it was for me to pull the trigger. Now you tell me what the motivation was for Anita's boyfriend to put a gun to the temple of a man who was asleep in his own bed and pull the trigger."

"I don't know. Mollie said that Anita tried to do it herself. Maybe he was just trying to be 'macho man' . . . show her he could do something she couldn't do."

"I can think of a whole lot of things he could do that she

couldn't do," he said with a snicker. "It's not enough of a reason."

"Maybe Anita had been sexually abused by her father. She might have told Melwin about it. Jealousy is a pretty strong emotion," I suggested.

"Still not enough," he repeated. "A lot of hatred went into that gunshot, Dave."

"All right, so who's *your* suspect?"

"The wife, of course. She's the only one who knew Joe well enough to hate him that much."

"And what's her motive?"

"Who knows? It could be jealousy, like you said. It could be revenge. It could be greed; she might want to collect on his insurance. My guess is that it was nothing more exotic than plain old hatred. She hated his guts."

"Can you prove that?"

"To the best of my knowledge, Counselor," he said, getting to his feet, "in this State we don't need to prove motive."

"We don't need to, but it helps," I replied.

"Give me a couple of days. I'll prove it," he said as he closed the door behind him.

After he left I put in a call to Tom Julian in Tallahassee.

"Tom, I need some legal advice," I began after I got past his secretary.

"Well they always come home to Papa when the goin' gets tough," he chuckled.

"Come on, Tom. I'm serious."

"You must be if you'll admit you need legal advice from me."

I reminded him of the details of Shawn's story and filled him in on Mollie Sussman's statement.

"Did you get her down on paper yet?" he asked.

"Not yet, Tom. Her mother was talking about getting a

lawyer. I don't want any additional publicity right now."

"I can understand that, but don't wait too long. It sounds like the gal is an important witness. You're going to want to get her story nailed down as soon as you can."

"I agree, Tom; and I will. That's not my problem right now."

"Lay it on me, Bubba."

"Watkins wants to pick up Melwin Fanchie and sweat the truth out of him. I've seen Watkins work. There's no doubt in my mind that he can do it."

"Can't do that, my friend. You pick up that guy on a murder-one charge and State Attorney 'The Deacon' Stoner will impanel a local grand jury the next day. Remember, the point of this exercise is to keep our office in control of the case."

"And to do that we need to get a sealed indictment out of the Statewide Grand Jury, right?" I asked.

"Which means you tell Watkins that nobody gets arrested until after those indictments come down," Tom confirmed.

"As I see it, Tom, the problem is if we wait for the indictments, the suspects might go out and get lawyers. Then you can pretty much kiss off the possibility of confessions."

"And that's another reason to keep it secret," he reminded me. "Once you get your indictments, Watkins and Harcourt can pick up the defendants on arrest warrants before anybody can make a move. I repeat, David, secrecy and speed are essential. When can you get your witnesses together?"

"I'd like to hold off for a while and see what else we can develop."

"Man, you've got enough for an indictment. All you need is probable cause!"

"Yeah, but to get a conviction I need proof beyond a reasonable doubt. You haven't met Shawn. I don't know if he can stand up under cross-examination. Hell, I'm not sure if he can stand up to direct examination. And besides, I checked the case law on admissions of conspirators."

"And?"

"They're only admissible against co-conspirators if the statements are made in furtherance of the conspiracy. Most of the things Anita said to Shawn were said long after everything was over. So even if I can get a jury to believe Shawn . . . which will be a miracle . . . most of what Anita told him can only be used against her."

"How about the new girl?"

"Mollie's great, but what does she tell us? Either Melwin did it or the old lady did it. That'll be a hell of a trial: me trying to prove murder-one and the two of them point fingers at each other. Talk about reasonable doubt!"

"Well you sure as hell have evidence of a conspiracy."

"I thought the point of this was to get a murder conviction."

"No the point of this is to make The Deacon look very foolish and bury him politically."

"I'm a lawyer, Tom, not a politician. I need admissible evidence. I don't want just an indictment; I want a conviction."

"Well don't wait too long, Bubba. The General's been asking me about this case. I'd hate to have to tell him that Stoner grabbed it away from you while you were dawdlin' around. Now what's the legal advice you need from me?"

"I guess the only thing I really need to know is how fast you can impanel a Statewide Grand Jury."

"Helene's got one going on in Orlando right now. You can always tag on to hers. We'll pay to get everybody up there. You make sure you keep me posted, understand?"

"Why? Did Harcourt forget how to write reports?"

"Now, David, I'm going to ignore that last remark."

"I'm sorry, Tom."

"No offense taken, my friend. You just make sure you stay in touch with me. Don't worry about anyone else."

We signed off as friends, which was probably more than I deserved. I had to learn to watch my goddamn mouth, even with Tom. Without his help back in the General's office, Statewide Prosecutor Helene Hizer would be running this thing right now, and I'd be stuck in the library affixing my 20/20 hindsight on some other prosecutor's mistakes. God, I had to admit I liked the excitement of this part of it, being on the front line, bringing it together — even the part about outmaneuvering Deke Stoner. I knew things were going to heat up quickly from here on out, so I definitely had to learn to keep my size 10D's out of my mouth.

Two days later, Watkins, Harcourt and I met in my office where, through the blaze of another headache, I reiterated the fact that there would be no pre-indictment arrests.

"Well you better get a move on, Dave," Watkins warned. "I'm not going to get much further until I can get Melwin where I can squeeze him."

I looked at Harcourt. "I've got bad news and bad news," he began. "It seems that our office *did* do a gunpowder swab test for the Sabal Palms Police Department. Only it was on Mrs. Stempo. And the results were negative."

"I told you Melwin pulled the trigger."

My head was pounding. I hadn't felt headaches like this for a long time. I put my fingertips to my temples and pressed hard. "What's the rest of it?" I asked with my eyes closed.

"There's no motive," Harcourt continued. "Maybe the

old lady hated him, but if she did kill him, it wasn't for any reason we could find. The guy pretty much kept to himself: not exactly 'Husband of the Year' material, but not all that bad, either. The neighbors say he was pretty much of a 'couch potato.'

"The neighbors? Christ! You didn't star flashing your I.D. on them did you?" I demanded.

"Relax, Dave. Take a couple of aspirin. I was just some stumblebum from the insurance company asking a few questions. You'd be surprised by how much people need to talk, especially when the guy next door blew his brains out in his own bedroom."

"Insurance," I muttered. "Did you check on insurance?"

"Of course I checked on insurance."

"And?"

"And nothing; at least not enough to make a difference. No million-dollar policy or anything. No, I'm afraid if the wife did it, she did it out of pure hatred."

"That's why I'm telling you it was Melwin," Watkins insisted.

"Guys, come on," I pleaded. "We don't need to get into that again. All we need is one good witness," I looked at Watkins before he could interrupt and added, "one *credible* witness who can survive a trial, who either saw something or heard something . . . some admission . . . and who's willing to go through a trial."

"You realize you're not asking for much," Harcourt said sarcastically.

Mary Ellen buzzed the intercom. "There's a Sylvia Mendez on the line for you."

"I'm in a meeting, and I don't know any Sylvia Mendez."

"She knows you're in a meeting. She's from the Bonita Journal, and she says it's very important."

I picked up the receiver. Whatever the rest of Mary

Ellen's message was, the whole office didn't need to hear it. "The Bonita Journal? Christ! What do they want?"

"She said you'd know. Something about the Stempo case."

I felt my stomach tie itself into a knot and a lump form in my throat. The game might be up. If this investigation hit the papers we could kiss it goodbye. There'd be no way to stop Deke Stoner from sending out a couple of investigators to make arrests, then get his own Grand Jury to come up with indictments. We were close now, so close. All we needed was a couple more witnesses. Hell, I'd settle for one – one good, strong witness with no criminal record. If we indicted now, with what we had, we would polarize things too soon. The defendants would exercise their right to counsel and clam up. If nobody else came forward, we'd be stuck going to trial with a half-assed case. Even now, with what he had, what did we know? We needed more – just a little more – to solidify our case. I picked up the receiver expecting the worst.

"Hello, this is David Bradley. Can I help you?"

"Mr. Bradley, this is Sylvia Mendez from the Journal. I have a report that you're running an investigation into the Stempo killing." This broad didn't fool around. She got right to the point. I could feel my blood pressure rising.

"Ms. Mendez, this is Criminal Appeals. We don't get involved in ongoing investigations."

'Yes, I know. That's why I was surprised when your name came up."

"My name came up? From whom?"

"I'm afraid I can't reveal my source, Mr. Bradley, but I can assure you it's a very good one."

Shit! Was she bluffing? I looked at the two men across from me. Either one of them could qualify as a "very good source'; not to mention the Sheriff – or the General himself for that matter. How much did this Mendez woman really know? Was she just baiting me to get me to confirm something she was only guessing at?

"Ms. Mendez, at any given time the Attorney General's Office might be involved in any number of cases."

"This is about the Stempo case, Mr. Bradley. I'm only interested in Joe Stempo."

"I'm afraid I can't say anything about any particular case at this time."

"Then you want me to run the story saying there's an investigation but you can't comment on it?"

"Can we talk off the record?" She hesitated. If she said "yes," at least I couldn't be quoted. But then I had to give her something. Just by asking the question I was letting her know there was more here. She had the ball.

"All right, it's off the record."

"I don't want you to run any story right now, Ms. Mendez. If you do, it could create real problems for us."

"What do I get if I hold off?"

There was no choice. I was going to have to risk it. Either I gave her what I had so far and begged her for time or she might blow the whole thing out from under me in tomorrow morning's paper.

"Why don't you come down here this afternoon, and I'll go through our entire file with you?"

"You've got a deal, Mr. Bradley; temporarily at least. I'll be there at two o'clock."

I hung up the receiver and looked at my companions. "Gentlemen," I announced, "we have a leak."

CHAPTER 5

"Leak? What do you mean, 'leak'?" Watkins exploded, his eyes darting from me to Harcourt.

"Leak," I repeated. "As in, 'Someone leaked information to the press.'"

Harcourt stared at him coldly. If looks really could kill, Sergeant Watkins would be visiting the late Joe Stempo at the moment – wherever he was.

"Hey! You don't think it was me!" Watkins shouted.

"You're the local," Harcourt said evenly.

"So what the hell's that supposed to mean?"

"It means you want your case prosecuted and you don't give a damn who does it. Whether it's us or Stoner's office, it's all the same to you." Jim summed up my thoughts pretty well.

"Except that's not the way I play ball, goddamn it!" Watkins turned to me. "Dave, I gave you my word!"

"And I gave you mine, Sarge."

"Well whoever talked to the press, it wasn't me! How do we know it wasn't the Tallahassee boys over here?" he said, jerking a thumb in the direction of Harcourt.

"Because we don't talk to the local press."

"So you say."

"So I know," Harcourt retorted.

"All right, all right," I pleaded, looking for the aspirin bottle that was supposed to be in my top drawer. "We're not going to get anywhere accusing each other. I'm going to work under the assumption that whoever tipped off the Journal . . . that person is not in this room. So who else could have done it? The Sheriff?"

"I haven't made one single official report since you took over the case. I swear to God, Dave," Watkins interjected. He was protesting a little too much, I thought.

I didn't believe him, at least not completely. I know all about that Hollywood crap where some cop goes off alone and solves the "BIG CASE" after being ordered off it — or maybe even fired. Let me tell you, it doesn't happen in real life. Today's word is "lawsuit." Nobody, *nobody* goes out on the street today without insurance or executive immunity or both. All you need to do is look at some felon crossways and the next thing you know you're the defendant in a civil rights suit. And if the county attorney finds out there's no official investigation going on you're left twisting in the wind. Watkins would have to be a fool to continue working on the Stempo case unless somebody at the Sheriff's Office knew something about it and gave him at least tacit approval. And whatever Sergeant Watkins was, he was nobody's fool.

"You've never *talked* to the Sheriff about this?" I demanded.

Watkins eyes darted from me to Harcourt and back. "Well of course I talked to him . . . privately . . . in his office." He looked back and forth between us again. "Well what the hell was I supposed to say I was doing with my time? Checking out adult bookstores?"

"So the Sheriff knows what's going on," I confirmed.

"The Sheriff knows what's going on. And . . . yes . . . I am keeping him apprised . . . unofficially . . . of the situation."

"Well, there's our answer," I said.

"No. No way," Harcourt interjected. "No way is Sheriff Bear Harper anybody's leak."

"What's this, Jim? Now F.D.L.E. is sticking up for a local?"

"Bear Harper is more than a local, David. He's a legend. His word is rock- solid-gold everywhere in Florida." Jim shook his head for emphasis and added, "No, whoever our leak is, it's not The Bear."

"All right, so it looks like we're not going to find out who the leak is . . . in fact, we may never find out," I said quietly. "We'll just have to accept that there is a leak somewhere in one of our offices, and from here on out we'll have to play it that way."

"What do you suggest?" Harcourt asked.

"I suggest we're running out of time. I'll talk to Ms. Mendez this afternoon, but if she's anything like the other reporters I've dealt with, she's going to be pressuring me to break the story. If I don't give her enough information to keep her quiet for now, she might go over to the State Attorney's Office and start asking questions . . . and that will really blow us out of the water." I looked from one to the other, dividing my attention between them. "I'm telling you guys we need at least one more solid witness, and I'd say we've got about forty-eight hours to come up with one. I'll stall Mendez for as long as I can, but you guys are going to have to come up with somebody."

They nodded and headed for the door, and I went to the break room for a glass of water to wash down the aspirin. A couple of the other Assistants were headed out for lunch at a pizza place in the mall across the street, but I declined their offer to join them. I planned to spend my lunch hour in my office with the lights off, thinking about Barbara and our trip to those beaches in the Panhandle. Even if I still had a headache when Ms. Mendez from the Journal arrived, at least I would be able to smile at her.

She arrived sooner than I expected. Not that her arrival was all that bad. The tall, leggy redhead with green eyes certainly added to my office décor. If I had not been so much in love with my wife or so politically correct, I might have said that Ms. Mendez was "all right." The problem was that she was a reporter, and attractive or not, that made her the enemy. And this meeting was D-Day. She must have read the surprise on my face.

"Don't tell me, I don't look Hispanic, right," she said, extending her hand.

"I didn't say that," I replied as I took it.

"You didn't say that, but you were thinking it."

"As far as I know there's still no law against thinking," I said, smiling at the so-far friendly banter. "Please sit down."

"My mother was Irish; my parents are from The City, Mr. Bradley." She said with a now-detectable Bronx accent. We moved to Miami when I was twelve. I guess I never lost the New York attitude. Mind if I smoke?"

She opened her purse and took out a pack of cigarettes, a lighter and a small portable ashtray. Ms. Mendez came prepared, and she was obviously going to smoke whether I minded it or not. She blew a cloud across my desk.

"So tell me about Joe Stempo. His wife killed him, didn't she? Insurance money?"

"As a matter of fact, there wasn't much insurance," I replied. "We've looked into that. Some, but not enough to murder anybody for."

"Depends," she retorted. "'not much' to you could be a

whole lot to somebody with nothing."

"I don't think greed was a motivating factor."

"Then you *are* running an investigation, and she's a suspect."

Ms. Mendez was good. She was very good. I was happy that she majored in journalism. A person with her instincts could be a killer in the courtroom.

"Have you ever thought of going to law school, Ms. Mendez?"

"Flattery will get you nowhere, Mr. Bradley," she said as she exhaled another cloud.

"Call me 'Dave'."

"Flattery will get you nowhere, Dave. And most people call me 'Sylvia'."

I held my fingertips to my temples again. "Headache?" she asked. "From me?"

"Yes, and it began long before you called. This has not been one of my better days."

"I'm sorry," she said as she put out the cigarette. She looked like she really meant it. She had lived in Florida for what – ten, twelve years? That is, if you consider Miami to be 'Florida'." Some people – native Floridians in particular – have grave doubts about that. Still, the Bronx aggressiveness seemed to have been softened by the Southern climate. I suspected Ms. Mendez might not be as hard-boiled as she would like to tell herself she was. I was ready to trust my instincts and level with her. Besides, there wasn't any other choice.

"Look," I began, "I'll lay the whole thing out for you. But you've got to promise me you'll hold off on publishing anything until after the arrests are made."

"How long will that be?"

"Two weeks."

"Two weeks?" she demanded. "You're joking. We could

all be dead and buried in two weeks!"

"Well, I think it was Oliver Wendell Holmes who said, 'There's no harm in the asking.'" It was a clear-cut cue for her to come back with a counter-offer and she took it.

"How much time to you really need?"

"We've got the facts pretty well figured out. It wasn't a suicide. We just need time to get one or two more witnesses."

"How much time?"

"Two weeks."

"Make it one."

"Sylvia, I don't know if we can get it all wrapped up in a week. We've got to get indictments out of the Statewide Grand Jury, and they're meeting in Orlando."

"So you never heard of airplanes? And why is the Attorney General doing this instead of the local State Attorney?"

"We have reason to believe the murder weapon come from another judicial circuit."

She looked at me like I had just told her the moon was made of green cheese and an animal of the family Bovidae regularly jumped over it.

"Right. And I suppose it has nothing to do with the fact that Deke Stoner ran against the Attorney General in the last primary? Or that he's gearing up to do the same thing next year?"

"Sylvia, it's no secret that the Attorney General and Deke Stoner are not the best of friends, but the General is not the kind of person who would use his office to punish Stoner because of that." Honesty be damned: win, lose or draw, I wasn't about to sacrifice my job over the Stempo case.

"Gosh, that was nice," she replied, putting her chin in her hand and batting her big green eyes. "Do you have that written down someplace? I didn't catch what you said after the words, 'use his office'."

". . . to punish Stoner because of that," I repeated.

"'Punish,' I like that. It has 'Press Release' written all over it, don't you think?"

I pressed my fingertips to my forehead again. "What do you want from me, Sylvia? I'm a pretty low man on the totem pole in this case."

"I want an 'exclusive', and I want to be able to publish in a week. Otherwise I guess I'll just have to go to ask Deke Stoner if his office is making any progress in the Stempo investigation."

She stood up and extended her hand. I took it. "All right, a week," I agreed. "But you give me your word that you'll publish absolutely nothing before then?"

"You have my word," she replied.

She left a heavy trace of perfume behind as she headed for the door. Maybe it was the cigarette smoke or maybe it was the tension, but I hadn't noticed it before. As I said, if I wasn't so in love with my wife —

Well, enough of that. It's funny but reporters never bag movie lawyers. The lawyers are always one step ahead. That's something that doesn't happen in real life, where we spend much of our time scratching and grabbing for answers. I've been interviewed on camera and in print any number of times and it's always a fencing match with the client as the prize. Any lawyer who tells you he enjoys it is either crazy or lying or both.

I didn't want to call Tom Julian and ask his opinion about this latest turn of events. You don't inspire confidence in your boss by running to him every time somebody pokes you in the nose. And even though Tom was a friend, he was still my boss. If I was ever going to advance in the Attorney General's office, his would be one of the recommendations I would need. I didn't want to discuss this with Harcourt or Watkins; even if neither of them was the leak, he could be the person who was inadvertently giving information to the leak. There was only one person I could trust, completely and absolutely.

I telephoned Barbara and told her not to pick me up. I planned to get a ride from one of the people in my office and go home early. She must have guessed something was wrong, because she was waiting for me out on the patio, wearing the hot pink thong bikini I had bought for her. I changed into something less formal than my casual office attire and I joined her.

Barb was laying face down on the lounge. I collapsed into a chair and poured myself a glass of wine from the chilled bottle in the ice bucket on the table. I sipped quietly and contemplated the sight of Barbara on that lounge. The view was magnificent.

"Are you all right?" she asked, looking at me over her shoulder.

"Now I am."

"You're a pervert. But of course you know that, don't you?"

"Guilty as charged, Your Honor."

She turned over and sat up. "You look terrible, David. I'm worried about you."

"I'll be all right," I said, rubbing my forehead.

She got up and moved behind me where she started massaging my neck and shoulders.

"Headache?

"No, thanks; I already have one."

"It's nothing to joke about, David. It's probably your blood pressure."

"Please, Barbara, not now."

"How was your day," she asked softly. Her hands felt

incredibly good as they rubbed the back of my neck and worked their way down my shoulders. And that English accent of hers never failed to get to me.

"Terrible. Awful. Horrendous."

"That bad?"

"No, it was worse than that. I just can't think of any more adjectives right now."

"Want to tell me about it?"

"There's not much to tell. We've got the same two . . . make that one-and-a-half . . . witnesses we had two days ago, with no apparent prospects of finding others. And now someone has leaked information to the Bonita Journal. If they print the story, Deke Stoner will grab the case out from under us, Jim Harcourt will go back to Tallahassee, and I, personally, will be the laughingstock of the Calusa County legal community for years to come. That's all."

She moved around and sat in my lap. "David, it's not that bad."

"It isn't? Tell me why it isn't."

"Most of our friends . . . even the lawyers . . . don't know that much about criminal law, and I doubt that any of them can understand the arcane political connections that you seem to think are so important."

I kissed her softly. "You're trying to tell me to look at the big picture, aren't you?"

"I'm telling you that you've narrowed your focus quite a bit since this horrid murder business started." She kissed me back.

"Of course, you know if I blow this case, I'll never get promoted. I'll be relegated to the Bonita office and criminal appeals forever."

She began nibbling my neck. "Well, you'll just have to find something else to occupy your energy. Maybe you could write a book or something."

"Let's discuss the 'or something'. I think my energy is making a distinct comeback." I kissed her again, harder this time. And longer, a lot longer. Among her other talents Barbara is an excellent kisser. Sometimes it seemed could spend hours with her on my lap, just kissing her without going any further, but reality always crept in and our glands took over. This was one of those times.

I really didn't mean for it to happen, but my hand found the two strings that held the top of her bikini halter-top in place. I untied the bottom one first. I repeat, I really didn't mean to do it; it just happened. Barb didn't object – she couldn't because her lips were still locked on mine – and I started upward to the other string.

"You're a naughty, naughty boy," she said when I got it untied. Well, at least we were even. We were both bare chested now. Our kisses became more passionate and I began to wonder what the possibility was of carrying things through to a much-needed conclusion right there on the patio. I held her left breast in my hand and gently massaged it.

"Be gentle. Please be gentle," she whispered.

"I'm being gentle," I protested with her lips still against mine. I lowered my mouth away from hers and began to lick the nipple that had already hardened to my touch.

"David, we shouldn't be doing this here. The neighbors might see us."

I moved my lips back to her mouth to drown out her protest; then I began to work my hand under the bottom half of the thong as the tip of tongue pushed past my lips. Freud would have said that Barbara's Ego was protesting, but if moisture is any indication her Id definitely had other ideas.

"Not out here. They'll see us," she gasped as my fingers found their target.

"How are they going to see, by climbing over the patio wall? Besides, they're not home and if they *are* home they should be doing the same thing we're doing."

"David! Your hand is in a very private area!" she squealed.

"That thong doesn't put very much in my way, does it? That's why I bought it for you."

I suppose in retrospect this might sound like some big seduction scene. It wasn't. We were just playing around after a long, miserable day at work. Not that I wasn't out to seduce her. I was. I very definitely was. But I wanted to play with her first, just for the fun of playing with her. Heck, we weren't going anywhere. We had all night. Of course things would eventually happen. I could tell she wanted it as much as I did. But right now it was time to play, and play we did.

"You know your hand isn't supposed to be there," she whispered wetly.

"Your tongue isn't supposed to be in my ear, either," I replied.

"But a tongue in the ear isn't equivalent to what you're going," she said, squirming in my lap.

I wondered who had invented the point system, but I wasn't about to stop playing the game. Her protests kept getting weaker; eventually she didn't even object when I slipped off the bottom half of the thong. Now she was nude in my lap, and there was no question that we could soon be making love.

"We really should go inside," she said as a warm breeze sprang up and washed over our bodies.

"We will in a minute," I replied. My problem at the moment was getting my own bathing suit off without destroying the mood. I needn't have worried; Barb's libido took over.

"Wouldn't you like to get more comfortable?" she whispered as she reached for my waistband.

"Now that you mention it, things are getting a little cramped in there," I replied as she stood up and pulled my suit off. I was ready; so was she. This time when she sat in my lap we were very closely connected. Once again, there was no hurry. We could stay here like this for a long time, enjoying each other's company as well as each other's bodies.

Barb was the first one to move. I don't mean to imply that I have better self-control. I don't. It's just that I was too damn tired. Besides, she was on top of me. She barely moved at all at first, just enough to keep us both excited and aware of what was happening.

"So how was the rest of your day?" she asked as her body moved gently in my lap.

"Not bad," I replied. My mind wasn't on the day anymore. It was concentrated somewhere below where my belt would have been if I had been wearing a belt.

"I've heard that when you're very, very tired, the best kind of pick-me-up is exercise."

"Yes, I've heard that," I replied.

"It increases your intake of oxygen, you know."

"So I've heard. I've noticed you're breathing a little heavier yourself." She was slowly picking up the tempo.

"Yes, I suppose I am," she said with a little gasp.

"Do you still want to go inside?" I asked.

She bit her lower lip and shook her head "no." The tempo had definitely increased and it kept rising. Her breath began to come in short gasps.

"Do you want to say right here?" It was a stupid question and I can't imagine why I asked it. Barb nodded her head and suddenly grabbed me and held on tight. Her entire body went rigid for a moment before she collapsed in my arms, breathing hard.

"Will you please not ask me silly questions while I'm having an orgasm?" she panted.

"I'm sorry."

"Now be quiet and concentrate. This one's for you." She began moving again, slowly at first and then faster. This time it seemed that her sole purpose was my pleasure. It didn't take long for me to join her release.

"Now, isn't that better?" she asked.

I nodded dumbly.

"Headache gone?"

I nodded again.

"I think we should go inside and take a shower."

I nodded a third time. We stood up and walked inside, hand in hand and completely relaxed and comfortable with our nudity. The long hot shower was the perfect aperitif to our lovemaking.

The telephone ran just as I stepped out, and I went to pick up the extension in the bedroom.

"Dave, it's Watkins," the voice said. "I've got your witness."

"When? Who?" It was difficult to ask an intelligent question after what I had just been through.

"I'd rather not get into details over the phone. Mind if I come over?" Barb was toweling off in the bathroom and I was stark naked and dripping water on the bedside table.

"Uh . . . well . . . I . . . we're a little busy right now."

There was a long silence on the other end of the line, then, "Jesus Christ, aren't you a little old to be fooling around in the middle of the day?"

It had to be a lucky guess. He couldn't possibly know what we had been doing. I was going to deny it, but then I figured, 'what the hell.' "No, as a matter of fact, I'm not too old," I replied. "Come over if you have to, but first give us a chance to put the chandelier back up."

"I'll see you in a couple of hours."

"Sarge, have you had dinner?" As I asked the question I realized I didn't even know if he was married. Come to think of it, I didn't know the man's first name.

"No," he said with a distinct hesitation in his voice. "No, I haven't. Why?"

"Well, I just thought you could have dinner here with my wife and me. If you'd like to, that is." Barbara looked at me quizzically. Neither one of us ever brought work home. This was quite a departure for me and we both knew it. I looked at her and shrugged my shoulders.

"That's very nice, Dave. Are you sure it wouldn't be too much trouble?"

I was already regretting my burst of familiarity, but there was no way to extricate myself. What the heck was I supposed to say, 'Yes, as a matter of fact it will be a hell of a lot of trouble, so just forget I asked'?

"No, of course not," I lied. "It's no trouble at all."

"Well, all right," he said. "I'll bring a bottle of wine and see you about six-thirty. Is that okay?"

"Sure, Sarge, that will be fine." I was about to hang up and then added quickly, "Wait a minute, you don't know where we live."

"Of course I do. You gave me your address the night I had you picked up to talk to Shawn, remember?" He was right: the notebook. Our address must be in there along with everything else Watkins had ever seen or heard. I wondered for a moment whether he kept all of that information or simply threw it away as each case ended. Knowing Watkins, I was sure he kept everything. Somewhere he must have a whole wall full of notebooks.

"We'll see you at six-thirty," I replied.

"Barbara was getting dressed as I hung up the receiver.

84

"I don't think we've ever had someone from your work join us for supper," she said with a margin of surprise in her voice.

"Do you mind?" I asked. "I don't know what got into me. You know, I don't know the first thing about him. I don't know if he's married . . . nothing."

"Of course I don't mind, Darling,' she replied as she blew me a kiss. "But I think you should put some clothes on before your friend gets here."

"Barbara I know this case has kind of gotten to me. If I've been ignoring you, it hasn't been intentional."

"You haven't been ignoring me, Lover. I'm going to get to work in the kitchen. It would be nice to relax with a few snacks before supper, don't you agree?"

Watkins arrived promptly at six-thirty wearing a casual shirt and slacks, and carrying two bottles of wine: red and white. "I didn't know what was on the menu, so I took no chances," he explained.

I relieved him of his burden and attempted to make the introductions. "Sarge, this is my wife, Barbara. Barb, this is . . . Sergeant Watkins . . . What the heck is your first name, anyway?"

"Clive. Clive Watkins. It's a pleasure to meet you, Mrs. Bradley," he said, taking Barb's hand. I had never seen Sarge try to act charming before, and I was surprised that he carried it off so well.

"Clive is a splendid name, Sergeant. General Clive of India, wasn't it?" Barb's British heritage was showing.

"Yes, well, it didn't make it any easier growing up with that moniker back in New Jersey."

That took care of the 'charm,' I thought. Now we could get back to Hoboken.

"Well, I've found that most people dislike their own first names even when they're perfectly delightful," Barb replied.

"Please come in. I thought we could chat on the patio while David starts a fire in the grill."

I don't know what Sergeant Clive Watkins of the Calusa County Sheriff's Office thought he was going to get, but the menu was grilled swordfish. Ever since my brush with mortality, Barb decreed we are a no-fat, no-cholesterol household. I doubt I would have had the will power to do it on my own, but I didn't have much of a choice in this situation. Besides, although I'd never admit it in front of her, I've found that a healthy lifestyle leaves a lot of extra energy for recreational pursuits. Like this afternoon.

"Are you married, Clive?" Maybe it's the accent – which I've noticed she can turn up for special occasions – but Barb can make even the most personal questions sound completely innocuous. She poured the wine while she set out a platter of stuffed mushrooms and low-fat cheese and I fiddled with the grill.

"Yes, well, that is, I was. My wife passed away a couple of years ago. Cancer. My daughter's back in New Jersey with her husband and their kids."

I was surprised, maybe I should say "ashamed" of myself. I had been working with this man for weeks, and I didn't know a thing about him. Now he was opening up to my blond wife and her cool Audrey Hepburn accent.

"You must be very lonely." You didn't have to be especially perceptive to hear the sympathy in Barb's voice.

"Nah. I have my job. And the weather's great. That's why we came down here ten years ago."

I couldn't keep quiet any longer. "What do you mean, 'ten years ago'?" I interjected. "I thought you've been doing this for twenty-five years."

"I have been, but the first fifteen were in Jersey. Is that fish ready yet? I could've caught it by this time."

It was obvious I didn't command the same kind of

respect that Barbara did. Maybe it was time to eat.

CHAPTER 6

After dinner Barb picked up the dishes and made herself scarce, claiming that she had to prepare a lesson plan. I knew it was an excuse. I silently thanked her and once again appreciated the fact that she had a lot of class.

"So tell me about this new witness," I said once she was gone.

"Not so fast," Watkins replied. "I think I'm entitled to an apology first."

"An apology? What for?"

"For thinking I was the leak, that's what for."

"Come on, Sarge." He looked at me and made a zipping motion across his lips. "Okay, I apologize. I was wrong. I'm sorry. Is that enough?"

"You better save some of that for my boss, too. 'Cause he's the one who got you your witness. I hope when the big shots come in from Tallahassee you can find a little room for him on the dais."

"For the Sheriff? What are you talking about?"

"I'm talking about the fact that I got this kid directly from Bear Harper."

Watkins still wasn't making any sense, and my confusion must have shown.

"After I left your office today," he continued, "I went back to the S.O. There was a message on my desk that the Sheriff wanted to see me as soon as I came in, and I hustled my butt up to his office." Sarge's excitement increased and his hands became more animated as he told the story. "I'm telling you, Dave, I had no idea what he wanted, and I'm thinking up excuses while I'm going up there. When I got off the elevator his personal secretary tells me to go right in. He's waiting for me. It turns out he wants to talk about the Stempo case; only he doesn't want to know what I'm doing, he wants to give me the name of a witness."

"How the hell did the Sheriff come up with a witness?"

"Listen and I'll tell you. It seems that one of the gals who used to work in the office called him . . . called him personally, I mean. Get this: our boy Melwin had been shooting his mouth off to her son. The kid was flabbergasted. He held it in for a day or two and then went to his parents. And his Mom called Bear."

"Damn! What did Melwin tell him?"

"Everything!"

"Everything? What do you mean, 'everything'?"

"I mean 'everything.' Melwin told him how they all bought the gun, and how the old lady wanted Joe dead, and how he, Melwin, personally accommodated her by pulling the trigger."

"How good of a witness is this kid?"

"The best: straight arrow, no record. But there's something else."

I could tell by his expression that he was teasing me. Those slate gray eyes were dancing in his head, and he could barely keep from laughing.

"Come on, out with it, Sarge!"

"The kid as agreed to be wired for sound if we want it."

"Damn! Does Harcourt know about this?"

Watkins leaned over the table with the air of a member of the underground resistance. "There are exactly six people on earth who know about this," he said. He ticked off the names on his fingers as he went down the list. "The kid, his mother, his stepfather, Bear Harper, me, and now you. That's it."

"We've got to tell Harcourt."

"Why?" Watkins exploded. "What if he's the leak? Why should we tell him anything?"

"What if he's not the leak?"

"Well goddamn it . . ." I shushed him and told him to keep his voice down. "Well," he continued more softly, ". . . you said yourself it had to be somebody on the inside who called the Journal. If it wasn't you, and it wasn't me, and it wasn't the Sheriff, that sort of cuts down on the number suspects, don't it?"

"It doesn't leave many options, that's for sure," I agreed. "But look at it this way: if we set up things with this kid quickly enough . . . say tomorrow . . . we can get up to Orlando and get an indictment before the leak matters."

"I still say we do our own investigation and run our own wire. These guys from Tallahassee aren't the only ones with fancy equipment. We've got all that crap at the S.O. too, you know."

"It isn't a question of equipment," I reminded him. "The people in Tally are the ones who sign my checks, and I have to do it their way." I tried to explain my predicament without getting into the political agenda. "Sarge, whether you like it or not . . . hell, whether I like it or not . . . Jim Harcourt has to be in on this all the way."

"Well I say he's the leak and he's going to blow the

whole thing."

"He may be the leak, but there's no way he or anybody else can blow it if we keep it moving fast enough. Now tell me about this kid and his parents. Does he have a name?"

"Jason. Jason Bonafidie. His mother's name is Lillian Davies. Like I said, Lillian used to work in the front office. Her son is a good kid; I guess she had a few problems with him after she got remarried, but they seem to have straightened them out."

I thought for a minute about Barb and Tori, and the changes that came into their lives when I entered the picture. Tori was in her last year of high school and her mind was already at F.S.U., and I suppose that made things a little easier. But no matter how hard we tried, there was always a certain tension in the air that first year. We really didn't become a "family" until she spent a month with her mother while I was in the hospital. By then she was about to graduate and had already been accepted for pre-med at Florida State University. She appointed herself my personal caregiver. If she someday becomes a world-famous cardiologist she'll have me to thank. And with me safely tucked away in Intensive Care, she and Barb had time to talk, and Tori learned the depth of commitment her mother and I had for each other. As I listened to Watkins talk about Jason Bonafidie, I wondered how a younger kid, someone with less maturity, would react under similar circumstances.

"Jason had some problems with his stepfather after his mother remarried, and he wound up moving out of the house for a few months. Part of that time he lived with the Stempo's. I guess Melwin picked the wrong guy when he decided to shoot off his mouth."

"Is he living at home now?"

"Everything's all patched up," he replied. "At least it's as patched up as it ever is when a teenage boy and a new stepfather are living under the same roof."

"When can I meet him?"

"I told them to be in your office tomorrow morning at nine. You do get in that early, don't you?"

I informed him that I regularly 'got in' a lot earlier than nine, and I wanted to talk to these people as soon as possible. But there was still no question about the fact that Jim Harcourt would have to be contacted and brought in immediately. I didn't want a report going to the General that said the F.D.L.E. had been cut out of a critical part of the investigation. Besides, I could not accept the idea that Jim was responsible for the leak to the press: not when he had been sent here by my boss who wanted complete secrecy until after the indictments came down. Anyway, it no longer mattered. With this kind of evidence we would have an indictment well within the seven-day time limit I had agreed to with Sylvia Mendez. The issue of who the leak was and who was responsible for giving information to the press was little more than an intellectual exercise.

Watkins looked at his watch. "Holy cats, look at the time," he said. "I'm wearing out my welcome. I'll say goodbye to your wife on my way out."

We stood up together. "Sarge, I just want you to know that I'm going to call Jim Harcourt as soon as you leave."

"I figured you would. Christ, David, how are you ever going to make it as a lawyer if you're so damn honest with everybody . . . even me?"

"That's the only way I've ever done it, Sarge. I don't know any other way."

"Well do me one favor, okay? Tell him I called you and I'm bringing in another witness tomorrow morning, but you don't know any details. As far as you know, it might all be bullshit. Think you can be that dishonest?"

I smiled. "Yeah, I can be that dishonest."

"Good. Try it sometime," he said, taking my hand. "It's good for the soul. It gives you something to ask forgiveness for."

Watkins was barely out the door before I was on the telephone calling Harcourt's hotel room. As agreed, I told him that all I knew was Sarge was bringing in a witness. I didn't know who he had, I said, but just to be on the safe side I asked Jim to bring his transmitting equipment. I could hardly wait to get to my office the next morning and arrived half an hour before my usual 8:30 starting time. Harcourt came in full of questions about fifteen minutes later. I didn't add anything to the scanty details I had given him the night before, and said we would both have to wait until Watkins showed up with whoever he was bringing. Sarge blew in shortly after 9:00 o'clock with Lillian Davies and her husband and son in tow. This was his show; I let him play it. Mary Ellen ushered them all into the conference room where Harcourt and I joined them.

Mrs. Davies was an attractive woman in spite of a stern expression that masked her face. I wondered whether the severe look was a permanent condition or the result of being dragged down to the Attorney General's Office so that her son could provide information in a first-degree murder investigation. Her husband said little, and I got the impression that while he was there for emotional support, Jason was Lillian's son and she would be the one making the decisions.

Jason, too, looked like he would rather be someplace else. He was an ordinary-looking kid whose dark hair and eyes contrasted with his mother's fairer complexion. There was an almost physical coldness between him and his stepfather, and I wondered if it might have helped ignite the fuse that resulted in the family explosion that sent him

– temporarily at least – to the Stempo's.

Watkins made the introductions and asked Jason to tell us what Melwin told him. Before the young man could speak, his mother interrupted with a question of her own.

"Before we get to that, Mr. Bradley, can you tell us why the Attorney General is doing this instead of the State Attorney?" Her expression had not softened any from the minute she walked in. I wondered what her political connection might be with Deke Stoner. A friend? A political supporter? Maybe even an enemy with a score to settle? Whatever the answer, I probably was not going to find out, so it was better to remain non-committal.

"There was a problem with the original investigation, Mrs. Davies. This case was cleared as a suicide. It was felt that our office should come in at this point because of the possible conflict of interest." It was pure bullshit, of course, but she appeared to buy it. I've always been surprised by the fact that when you say "*the* conflict of interest" nobody ever asks, "What the hell conflict of interest are you talking about?" It must have something to do with the perception of morality. Nobody wants to appear less ethical that anybody else, so when somebody says "*the*" conflict of interest, everybody else just assumes there is one and is ashamed to admit they don't see it. I'm not saying it's the right explanation for the phenomenon, or even that it's a good one, but at least it's plausible. In any event, it worked on Mrs. Davies. At least she didn't ask any more questions.

"Jason, I'm sure you've already spoken to Sergeant Watkins," I said, directing the conversation to the matter at hand without tipping off Harcourt to the fact that I knew what was coming, "but Agent Harcourt and I are still in the dark. What do you know about Joe Stempo's death?" The young man looked at his mother who nodded her head.

Apparently it was the only encouragement he needed.

"See, a few days ago I was at my friend Chris' house. We were just hangin' out, and I guess we started talkin' about it . . . you know . . . about Joe and everything. And all of a sudden, Melwin and Anita pull up in Joe's car. I guess it's Mel's car now. They said they needed to get tires and asked me if I wanted to go along for a ride. I go, 'Why not?' an' I got in the back seat."

"How about your friend Chris?" I asked.

"No, Chris stayed home."

"So we're driving to the tire store, you know? And Melwin and Anita are laughing . . . hysterically laughing. And I go, 'What's so funny?' and Mel said it was funny that Joe was dead, and that's why he and Anita were laughing. I asked again what was so funny about it, but I never got a straight answer, just more laughing. It was the following day when I found out what really happened."

"What *did* happen, Jason?" It was the first time Harcourt had said anything since they arrived.

"The next day we went to the movies, a bunch of us. Chris, his sister, his girlfriend, Melwin and me, we all went. At one point Mel and me were in the men's room, and I just asked him straight out how Joe died, and he told me."

"Told you what, Jason?" I asked.

The young man looked down at the floor for a moment as if he didn't want to say it; then he looked up and said, "He told me he shot him."

"That's the way he told you? That's how he told you he killed somebody?" Harcourt asked.

"Yeah, that's how he told me. It was really weird."

"Did he say it in a joking way, or something?" I asked.

"Yeah, it was kind of in a joking way but serious enough for me to believe that he shot him. We both knew it; I could tell by his expression."

"What did you say after he told you?" Harcourt asked.

"I just shook my head. I was in shock. I was mummified. I really didn't say anything to anybody for the rest of the night. I was numb. In fact, I didn't even go back into the movie theater. I just stayed in the lobby and played video games until the movie ended."

"Then what happened?" I asked.

Once again his mother interrupted. "Then he told me."

"Yeah, then I told my Mom. Well, not right away. I thought about it for a day or so, but you know, I kept thinking about Joe, and I just couldn't get it out of my head."

"How well did you know Joe, Jason?" Harcourt asked.

"Well, you know I stayed there for a couple of months when my Dad, well . . ." I glanced at Mr. Davies who looked vaguely embarrassed as Jason continued, "Anyway Joe was a real quiet guy. If he did have a problem, he usually would keep it to himself. He was real quiet and to himself. He would come home. He loved food, liked to cook. Sometimes Grace . . . Mrs. Stempo . . . would cook, but not all the time. He would eat and he liked to watch the news. He pretty much watched baseball and nature shows. He was into nature shows. He really could get into those." The room was silent for a minute before he added, "You know, I never paid Joe room and board while I was living there. I said I would, but he just said we'd talk about it after I got a job. He was really kind to me."

The room fell silent again. I'm not a mind reader, so I won't pretend to know what the others were thinking. My own thoughts were of some working stiff who came home every night, had dinner and plunked himself down in front of a TV. And for that his family murdered him. Was that the only reason? Could there be some dark family secret, or was the motive nothing more than ordinary, everyday frustration that built up over the years until the pressure was released by a single gunshot?

Harcourt let out a long breath. "Jason, would you be willing to wear a listening device and try to Melwin to talk to you again?

"Sergeant Watkins asked me about that. Yeah, I'll do it. I mean, I've thought about it and everything. You know, Joe was a pretty decent guy. They didn't have to kill him and everything."

"Just how dangerous will this be?" the boy's mother asked.

"It's not dangerous at all, Ma'am. If he knows where Melwin is, I'll wire him up right now." He turned back to the young man. "Do you have any idea where he might be this morning?"

"He usually hangs out at his house . . . Anita's house . . . you know, Joe's house. He doesn't have a job or nothing."

Harcourt and Watkins exchanged a knowing glance. "It's worth a shot," Watkins concluded.

Harcourt opened his briefcase. "Jason, this is a Unitel listening device," he said. "I'm going to tape it to your body. Take off your shirt."

"You mean right now?" A look of hesitation flickered across the kid's face; he wasn't ready for this.

"Now's as good a time as any," Watkins replied.

Jason looked as if he wanted to think this over a little longer, but Harcourt wasn't about to let that happen. At a nod from Mrs. Davies the young man stood up and stripped to the waist. In a moment Harcourt got down on his knees and was positioning the transmitter in the small of the kid's back. He asked Watkins for the surgical tape in his briefcase.

"We're going to tape you up real good, Jason," Jim explained as he and Watkins wrapped the tape around his body. "There won't be any chance of the unit slipping." A ripping sound filled the conference room as they continued to pull tape off the roll and apply it to his body. "All right, put your shirt on," Harcourt said when they were finished. He went to his briefcase where he deposited what was left of the tape and took out a wire with a miniature microphone on one end.

"Now, Jason," Harcourt continued, showing him the microphone, "I'm going to put this on the inside of your shirt where it can't be seen. The wire here – Jim worked as he talked – "will go around to the Unitel on your back. I could tape it to you, but I'd rather let it hang loose so that it doesn't pull on the shirt at all. How does that feel?"

"Fine, I guess." Jason flexed his shoulders and moved his arms. "Yeah, it feels fine."

"Okay, now the secret is to just act perfectly natural. Melwin's talked to you about this before, so you shouldn't be raising his suspicions by mentioning the subject again."

"What should I ask him?" Jason looked nervous and I began to question his ability to bring the thing off.

"Don't ask him anything. Just bring it up in conversation. You know, you can't believe what he told you at the movies the other night. How it must have been a real tough thing to do. Play up what guts he must have. Nobody but a real man could do a thing like, right? Then let him do the talking."

"How do I know when to stop?"

Harcourt looked at Watkins and thought for a second. "Sergeant Watkins and I will be in my car. We'll be listening to everything you say. When we've heard enough we'll come in and make the bust."

"Hold it, Jim," I said quickly. "That won't go. We're doing this by secret indictment. Nobody's going to get arrested today. He's just going in there for information."

Harcourt hesitated. We hadn't had time to work out a plan. Watkins came up with the solution. "Mrs. Davies, do you know the telephone number at the Stempo house?" he asked.

"I should. I've called it enough," she said.

Sarge laid out his idea. "Okay, Jim and I will be in the car listening. When we've heard enough, Jim radios his office and tells them to call Mr. Bradley at the Attorney General's Office and advise him the papers are ready to be picked up. David, as soon as you get that call here, Jason's mother telephones the house and asks if her son is there. When they say he is, she raises hell and tells him to get his rear end home right away because his father is having a fit about chores or something. Jason hightails it out of there and we pick him up right where we left him off."

Harcourt nodded his approval. "It'll work. It'll work just fine."

Now it was Mrs. Davies' turn to have second thoughts. "Are you absolutely certain this is safe?"

"Aw, Mom. You heard him. He said it'll work." The young man sounded as if he had overcome his fear and was anxious to play real life cops-and-robbers.

"Not to worry, Mrs. Davies," Harcourt responded. He directed the rest of his remarks to Jason, but he was obviously making them here in the conference room for the mother's benefit. "We'll let you off a block or so away from the house. I want you to talk to me to the Unitel at all times when you are alone."

"What do you mean?"

"Talk. Talk out loud. Say things like 'I'm walking up the driveway,' 'I'm going inside.' We'll hear whatever you say. If things go bad for any reason, just say you need help and we'll be there in seconds."

"Nothing's going to go bad, Jason," Watkins added.

"This is a piece of cake. Come on, let's take a ride."

Mrs. Davies, her husband and I all stood up. She hugged her son tightly, and her voice trembled a little. "You be careful, young man. Your father and I will be waiting right here when you get back."

"Don't worry, Mom. This will be really cool."

With that last comment, the boy who had volunteered for a man's mission left with two experienced police officers. I knew – and I'm sure everyone else knew – that in spite of what Harcourt and Watkins told him, when he was talking to Melwin Fanchie he would be very much alone. And even though the officers would be nearby, if Jason's secret were discovered there would be long and anxious moments during which he would be entirely at the mercy of a self-proclaimed killer.

I suggested Mr. and Mrs. Davies would be more comfortable in my office. When we got there, I opened the custom-made cabinet Barbara had given me and took out a bottle of Scotch and three glasses.

"Is this kind of thing permitted in State offices?" Mrs. Davies inquired. I couldn't tell if she was trying to be funny or if she was the type who would call Tally on me. At the moment I didn't care.

"No it isn't," I confirmed. "And even though it's too early, right now I need a drink and both of you do too." I asked Mary Ellen to bring some ice cubes from the break room and I poured three stiff drinks. Mrs. Davies made no further inquiry and accepted the glass gratefully. Her husband took a sip and said softly, "You know, that kid's got a lot of guts. He's got a lot more guts that I had at his age."

"He's got a lot more guts than most people have at any age, Mr. Davies."

He looked at me. "The name's 'Bill'," he said lifting the

glass to his lips again. "And my wife and I both appreciate your . . . hospitality."

We sat quietly for a long time before Mrs. Davies broke the silence. "You know, Jason was always a daredevil, even as a child. One day he and the little boy next door found some wood scraps and they built a ramp so they could jump their bicycles over the neighbor's rose bushes."

"What happened?"

"Jason went first and he didn't make it. Boy, he was a mess. He was covered with cuts and scratches for weeks."

"He doesn't seem to be any the worse for wear," I observed.

"No they heal up pretty quickly when they're children," she replied.

The conversation died away and left an awkward silence behind. Whether or not Mrs. Davies approved of liquor in a State building she didn't hesitate to take a sip from her glass now and then as the three of us sat together waiting for Mary Ellen's voice on the intercom. Suddenly it happened.

"Mr. Bradley you have a call on line one." This was much too soon. Something must have gone wrong. I grabbed for the receiver.

"Who is it?" I demanded.

"Cheryl Goodlander from the Public Defender's Office wants to talk to you about the Court's new policy on extensions of time."

"Mary Ellen, we're waiting for a very, very important call from the F.D.L.E. When it comes in, get me immediately. No matter what I'm doing, make sure I'm interrupted, okay?"

"Certainly. Do you want to talk to Cheryl?"

What the hell, I thought: anything to kill the time. I took a deep breath. "Okay, put her on. But if that call from

F.D.L.E. comes in, interrupt me immediately."

"You already said that."

"I know. And I'm saying it again, Mary Ellen. Interrupt me immediately."

Cheryl's call was unnecessarily long and generally irrelevant. She was composing a letter to the new chief judge of our appellate court, protesting his recent policy changes on extensions of time for appellate briefs. The way I saw it, the chief judge was going to do whatever the chief judge wanted to do, and if either of our offices protested the matter would be "taken under advisement" and we would politely be told to go piss up a pipe. Of course Cheryl didn't see it that way and she went on to explain at length why this should be a joint letter, blah, blah, blah. The call must have lasted even longer than it seemed, because she was still talking when Mary Ellen appeared at my door announcing a call from the Florida Department of Law Enforcement on line two.

I told Cheryl that I had an emergency call from Tally, hung up without another word and picked up the flashing line. The conversation was very short.

"David Bradley."

"Mr. Bradley, Agent Harcourt just radioed in and said your papers are ready and can be picked up at any time."

I flashed an "okay" sign to the two people on the other side of my desk, thanked the dispatcher and hung up.

"You're on, Mrs. Davies," I said, handing her the phone. "Get him out of there."

Her hand trembled slightly as she punched the numbers and drummed her fingers on my desk while she waited for someone to answer.

"Hello, this is Mrs. Davies . . . Jason's mother. Is he there?"

There was a short pause, then, "Well he's going to be in

big trouble if he's not home in ten minutes!"

Whoever answered must have called Jason to the phone, because a few seconds later she was apparently talking directly to her son.

"Jason! Your father and I want you home right now!"

She held the receiver away from her ear so that we could hear Jason putting up a fight. The kid deserved an Academy Award.

"I don't care what you're doing!" his mother shouted into the receiver. "If you're not home in ten minutes you'll be grounded for the entire year!"

That must have done it because she hung up. Her hands shook violently as she brought them up to her face. Suddenly she began to cry. Her husband moved closer and wrapped his arms around her.

"Hey, come on," he said softly. "It's all over now. They're getting him out right now. He's probably already in the car."

"I know."

"So why are you crying?"

"I don't know," she sobbed into the tissue she took from her purse. "This has been the worst day of my life."

"I thought the worst day of your life was the day you met me," he joked.

She smiled through her tears. It was the first time I had seen her smile and as her features softened I had to admit that although she was not a cover girl, Mrs. Davies was an attractive woman. "No," she said, "the day I met you is now only the second worst day."

He husband smiled back at her and looked at me. "Do you have children, Dave?"

"One stepchild, just like you."

"It isn't easy, is it?"

"No, it isn't. And I was lucky. Mine was getting ready for

college when I came into the picture."

"Boy or girl?"

"Girl."

"I think boys are harder," he suggested.

"It's tough having two men in the same house, especially when one of them comes in later," I replied.

Bill Davies looked at me for a minute. I hoped he understood what I was driving at. I didn't know much about their family situation, but Jason had been there first. Maybe he needed someone who was less of a father and more of a friend. "I guess he's older than I thought," Bill Davies finally said.

It wasn't too long before we heard Jason laughing with Harcourt and Watkins as they approached my door.

"You should have been there, Dave; it was beautiful," Watkins laughed as they entered the office.

Mrs. Davies embraced her son and held him for a long time. Jason looked thoroughly embarrassed. When she released him, his stepfather moved in and extended his hand. As the boy took it, Bill slapped him on the back and said, "Good Job, Jason. Damn good job. We're real proud of you." And then he added as he hugged the boy's neck, "I'm real proud of you."

Watkins and Harcourt gave me a quick rundown of what was on the tape. Melwin had been outside, working on Joe's car. Jason acted like he was just passing by, and he casually walked up the driveway and began talking to him. And Melwin fell right into the trap.

I turned to the Davies family. "Folks, there's just one more thing. We're going to need Jason in Orlando tomorrow afternoon. He'll have to testify before the Statewide Grand Jury. I'll be able to supply you with a hotel room and at least two airline tickets, but . . ."

"Don't bother with the tickets, Dave," Bill Davies

replied. "We'll drive up."

"Are you sure? That's three or four hours on the road."

"We need some family time together. Besides, what do I care about the time?" He put his arm around his stepson. "My partner's going to be doing most of the driving."

CHAPTER 7

Orlando, 1985. The Orange County Civil Courthouse was a ten-story red brick building that was known as the Angebilt Hotel before the county bought it and turned it into additional court space. The interior looked like it had been laid out by an unknown architect who got bored with the contract and ended up designing a bunch of cookie-cutter boxes finished in vinyl wall covering. Space requirements and existing walls forced long-forgotten work crews to shoehorn the courtrooms into both wings of the existing hotel, so the only windows faced each other across a narrow airshaft. Overall, the place fairly shouted out the fact that it was an old, unwanted building that somebody converted for public use. There are a lot of buildings like it in Florida where government has a hard time keeping up with population growth.

The Statewide Grand Jury was meeting there in an unoccupied courtroom on one of the upper floors. Shawn, Mollie, her mother, and Jason and his parents all sat in a waiting room while I went over my notes in the attorney's conference room.

The concept of the grand jury has been around for a

long time – ever since King Henry II, the great-grandson of William the Conqueror, held the Assize at a town called Clarendon in 1166. Around six hundred years later, people like James Madison incorporated it into the United States Constitution as a way of preventing an arrogant sovereign from prosecuting innocent citizens on a whim. The idea is the State has to present its evidence to a body of disinterested people who then decide whether there is enough evidence to subject some poor bastard to the rigor of a trial. If the grand jurors find there is sufficient "probable cause," they issue a "True Bill" or indictment; the defendant is arrested and the process begins. Even the secrecy that is so detested by defense lawyers was meant to safeguard the citizen: if the grand jurors find no probable cause, they issue a "No Bill" and, presumably, the reputation of an innocent person has not been sullied by the investigation.

That's the theory. The reality is different. Because there is no "other side of the story" in the grand jury room, it's pretty tough for a prosecutor to walk away empty-handed. You put your witnesses on the stand and lead them through their testimony. There is no defense lawyer to object to the form of your questions and no judge to rule on relevancy. After your witnesses tell the stories you have rehearsed a dozen times or more, you turn to the grand jurors and ask if they have any questions. There are always one or two people who want to play lawyer. They'll ask a couple of questions and nod sagaciously at the answers. Then you leave the room while the jurors vote. A Florida grand jury is made up of eighteen people, none of whom may be a public official. Fifteen jurors constitute a quorum; the State needs twelve votes for an indictment. Generally speaking, the testimony goes pretty quickly. It has to – it's all one-sided.

My plan was simple: call Shawn first to talk about the gun, then Mollie to explain how it got into Joe Stempo's room, and finally Jason to tie the whole thing up. My only fear was that the case against Melwin was so good it might inadvertently focus the jurors' attention on him and away from the two women who were equally guilty. I wanted three good, clean first-degree murder indictments, not some pseudo-lawyer getting his or her fellow jurors off the track by discussing vicarious liability and chasing arguments that were nothing but swamp gas.

Statewide Prosecutor Helene Hizer wore a gray business suit over a white silk blouse; it was an outfit entirely consistent with her office. I had told her it that wouldn't be necessary for her to be here; that I was perfectly capable of making a grand jury presentation without her assistance. Either she didn't believe me or she didn't trust me. In any event, she didn't want anybody messing with her grand jurors; she would make the presentation and I would sit at the counsel table.

"Haven't seen you since the last N.A.A.G. meeting, Dave," she said as she extended her hand. She was right; it had been a while. The National Association of Attorneys General had met in Fort Lauderdale the previous year, and Barbara and I ran into Helene at one of the cocktail parties. Frankly, I had completely forgotten the incident until she reminded me.

"It's been a while, Helene," I said, taking her hand.

"Are your people ready?"

"Ready and willing."

"Who am I calling first?"

I ran through my game plan, and pointed out the potential problems of the jurors focusing too much on Melwin and getting sidetracked when it came to the women.

"The 'principal statute' will take care of that," she said, flipping through my notes on the yellow legal pad.

"Do you have a copy of it?" I asked. She gave me a "drop dead" look that needed no words. "I meant, 'handy,'" I added, recovering nicely I thought. "Do you have a copy of it handy?"

"We have a set of statutes inside. When it comes to sticking points I prefer to have them look things up themselves . . . with a little guidance. It gives them a chance to play lawyer without getting out of control."

Getting out of control is one of the dangers of the grand jury system. Few grand jurors know it, but they are the ultimate power in the system. If they choose to grab the ball and run with it, there's nothing a prosecutor can do to stop them. They have the authority to subpoena witnesses and conduct their investigations without us. Sometimes it happens. It's called a "runaway grand jury," and because there's no telling where it will end up, it's the nightmare of every prosecuting attorney. It was pretty clear that Helene Hizer was not going to let it happen to her.

I reminded her about the lack of a clear-cut "statewide" issue in this case. A perceptive juror might raise hell about it.

"Yeah, I'm a little worried about that myself. I'm really not too crazy about using this jury for a political vendetta."

"We do have a murder, Helene," I reminded her.

She gave me another "drop dead" look and said, "Yeah, that's why we're taking it away from Deke Stoner, right?"

"Helene, I only work here."

Her expression did not soften as she examined me. "This is your case, isn't it? You're the one who brought it into the office?"

"Okay, it's my case. But all I wanted out of it was to get back into some trial work. It's a simple little murder case.

And maybe I am stretching jurisdiction a little bit to get my own way. But 'my own way' only involves getting back into the courtroom. I don't have a secret agenda."

She looked at me carefully. I couldn't tell if she believed me or not, but if I had to bet it would have been on the negative. "I'll introduce you and you can do a brief opening statement so they know what's coming. I'll examine the witness and answer any questions the jurors have. And I'll advise them on the law. Agreed?"

"It's your grand jury, Helene."

She looked at me for a moment as if she was about to say something, and then seemed to think better of it. It occurred to me that just as I didn't know how tightly she was wired in Tally, she didn't know much about me, either. In theory, at least, she reported directly to the General while I reported to somebody two steps removed. But in the arcane world of Tallahassee politics anything was possible. Right now she might be thinking that I was one of the inner circle with clandestine designs on her job. Perhaps she had already said too much.

"Well, we're all on the same team, right?" she said with a slight smile that might have been genuine. "Let's get to work."

The minimum fifteen statewide grand jurors were present in the jury box for the afternoon session. Considering the fact that we needed twelve votes for an indictment, we only had room for three nays. As we took our places across from them, I tried to pick out who the dissenters might be, and I found myself wondering if these people knew they were part of a process that began with the great-grandson of William the Conqueror. Did they take this public service seriously or was the grand jury just the rubber stamp defense lawyers always said it was? We would soon find out.

"Ladies and gentlemen, this is David Bradley," Helene said, motioning in my direction as I stood behind the counsel table. "Mr. Bradley is an Assistant Attorney General in our Bonita Office. He's here on special assignment and will assist me in presenting a murder case involving the Twenty-first and Twenty-fourth Judicial Circuits of Florida. I've asked him to give you a little background on this case before I begin calling witnesses. Mr. Bradley."

I briefly outlined the facts of the murder case as we had developed them. I explained that officers from the Sabal Palms Police Department had been called to the scene of a shooting, but they had concluded the case was a suicide. Later, our office was made aware of the fact – I conveniently left out the "how" – that the gun used in the shooting had been stolen in Cypress County, which is in another judicial circuit. We questioned the person who stole it, I explained, and learned that it had been purchased by a woman, the woman's daughter, and the daughter's boyfriend, for the specific purpose of killing the woman's husband. We also found out that the boyfriend was member of a gang that had members in several counties, and that he had taken the gun from its location in the daughter's bedroom minutes before the shooting. And finally, we had a tape recording of the boyfriend in which he admitted to his role in the killing. I looked at Helene and she nodded; it was time for me to sit down.

She called Shawn to the stand and led him through everything he told Watkins and me that fateful night at the Sheriff's Office. As he spoke, I thought of that first meeting. Even then I knew that jurisdiction would be the big hang-up. The Statewide Prosecutor is charged by law with "prosecuting matters which transpire or have significance in two or more judicial circuits." The idea is to go after criminal enterprises that are beyond the reach of any one state attorney. I wanted so badly to get back into things that I stretched a point. And, yes, even though I had no particular ax to grind with Deke Stoner, I admit I knew it would be easy to sell my idea to the upper echelons of our office. I could understand why Helene Hizer was not particularly amiable towards me.

Shawn's testimony ended after an interminable recitation of sentences that began with "I go" and "He goes." Helene asked if there were any questions of the witness. There weren't any. Maybe the jurors were just as tired of him as I was.

Next up was Mollie Sussman. She still looked incredibly frightened, but thankfully she did not cry. I had two tickets to Disney World in my pocket; they were a little surprise give to Mollie and her mother from Barbara and me. I intended to give them to her when we met in the waiting room later, and I had already arranged for the office to pick up the hotel tab for an extra day. Besides being the decent thing to do, I argued, keeping her in Orlando for an extra day would guarantee she'd be out of the way when we arrested her friends. Mollie was a good kid who had gotten caught up with a bunch of strange people. To this day I can't figure out why they allowed her to be in the house on the night of the murder.

Our next witness was Jason Bonafidie. Helene kept his testimony short, confining it to Melwin's admission and the role Jason played in making the tape we were about to hear. As I looked at the confident young man on the witness stand, I sincerely hoped that he and his stepfather would find some way to settle their differences. There was already enough animosity in the world, especially when a daughter could help plan the murder of her own father. We didn't need any more hatred. Maybe Jason and his stepfather could find some common ground, and at the same time give each other the space people need to grow in at any age. I thought I detected the beginnings of that in my office the previous day. If I was right, it was ironic that the same murder that was about to destroy one family might also build another one.

Our last witness was Jim Harcourt. Cool and deliberate, Jim described his role in the investigation and played the tape for the jurors. I could see their expressions change as they leaned forward and concentrated. This was much more real than listening to witnesses. Here was a person telling someone how he, personally, had committed a murder. Even though I had heard the tape in my office before coming to Orlando, I still got a cold feeling when Melwin described how he put the gun to Joe Stempo's head and pulled the trigger.

Helene excused the last witness and asked the jury to indict Grace Stempo, Anita Stempo, and Melwin Fanchie for a violation of Florida Statute 782.04(1)(a), Murder in the First Degree. This time a number of hands went up. Helene recognized one of the women who asked how they could indict everyone when only Melwin pulled the trigger.

"Principals in the first degree are defined in Florida law," Helene began. It was the question she anticipated, but she would not give them the answer. They would have to find it. "I believe it's somewhere around section seven hundred seventy-six or seventy-seven."

"Here it is!" another woman said, holding open a statute book. "'Principal in the first degree — Whoever commits a criminal offense against the state, whether felony or misdemeanor, or aids, abets, counsels, hires, or otherwise procures such offense to be committed, and such offense is committed or attempted to be committed, is a principal in the first degree and may be charged, convicted and punished as such, whether he is or is not actually or constructively present at the commission of the offense.' So the other two didn't have to be there," she concluded proudly.

A number of heads nodded. An abrupt answer from Helene might have started a game of "let's beat the lawyer." Instead one of their own jurors had done the legal research and they were satisfied with her answer. I guess Helene really did know her jurors.

One of the men spoke up. "I don't know. Why should we be fooling around with a murder?"

"They shot the woman's husband, for cryin' out loud!" another retorted.

"I know that. But we're supposed to be dealing with cases . . . cases where there's evidence of a conspiracy."

"So murder's not big enough? And this isn't a conspiracy?" another man said.

Helene raised her hand and motioned for silence. Ladies and gentlemen, it's your decision. I'm only here to present what evidence we have and advise you on the law. It's not appropriate for me to be in here while you discuss the case. Are there any other questions?" No one moved. "All right, since there are no further questions, Mr. Bradley and I will wait outside until you reach a decision."

I began to have doubts as we waited outside the door. If you had asked me earlier in the day I would have said that it was damn near impossible for a prosecutor to lose a case before a grand jury. Now I wasn't so sure. "Who the hell is that guy?" I asked as Helene and I compared notes.

"Howard Garner, land surveyor and general pain-in-the-ass. He prides himself on thinking nothing gets past him. Thinks he's smarter than any lawyer."

"He sure as hell picked up on the jurisdiction problem."

"Relax. The others will shout him down. They always

do. Howard has the ability to piss off everybody. Now tell me how you're going to get past a motion to dismiss in the trial court."

"One step at a time, Helene."

She hesitated for a minute. "Listen, Dave, what I said about not wanting to use this office for political purposes . . . I wasn't trying to second-guess anybody."

"Don't worry about it, Helene. I know exactly how you feel, and I don't talk to anybody, either."

There was a knock at the door. We re-entered the room and were told that the Statewide Grand Jury had voted to issue three first-degree murder indictments. The foreman formally asked Helene to prepare the papers and said he would sign them as soon as they were ready. We thanked them and I went back to the waiting room to release my witnesses and make plans for the arrests.

I rode back with Jim Harcourt that evening. As we rocketed south on Interstate 75 with his stick-on blue light flashing on the top of his car, we planned the rest of our strategy. We now had the legal authority to arrest Grace, Anita and Melwin. The question was, in which order should we do it? In spite of the audiotape, Jim was not convinced Melwin was the actual shooter. He wanted to pick up Grace first and try to sweat the truth out of her. I hesitated. Once any one of the trio was arrested, the odds were that Deke Stoner would get wind of it and the cat would be out of the political bag. I pointed out the other two might make a run for it, and, even if they didn't, they were sure to "lawyer up" and would be advised to remain silent at all costs.

"Where the hell are they going to run to?" Jim asked in response to my first objection. This isn't the Old West. There's no place in this country where people like Anita and Melwin can hide for very long."

"And how about the attorney problem?"

"We don't need statements from either one of them. We've got Melwin on tape and an eyeball witness on Anita at the time the shot was fired."

"So why don't we pick up all three of them and see if we can play them against each other?"

"That's not a bad idea, but what are you going to give up in return for a statement?"

"The electric chair, Jim. We can always give up the death penalty."

"The chair? David, you couldn't get the death penalty in this case. Even if you did get it the sentence would never be upheld on appeal."

"I know that. The question is, do they know it?"

Jim Harcourt nodded his head and a smile crept across his face. "David, you're starting to think like a police officer."

The discussion next turned to timing. Harcourt wanted to move on the defendants immediately – tonight if possible. I wanted to be in on the bust, and I figured Barbara would have a fit if I told her that I would be out until all hours of the morning. I argued for a noontime raid.

"Sorry, Dave. This time we do it my way."

"But why? Why should we kill ourselves by staying up all night when we can bust them in the middle of the day?"

"Psychological advantage. Can you imagine how it feels to be dragged out of your house late at night? Who are you going to call? Getting processed and booking will take an hour if not more . . . and after than we're going to take statements. Do you know how shitty you feel at feel at midnight or one in the morning? Think of how shitty they'll feel. You know what's coming; they don't. You can leave and go home; they can't. Believe me, Counselor, if you want to wear somebody down, bust them late at night."

His explanation made a lot of sense, but it also sounded vaguely unconstitutional.

"What do you mean, 'due process of law'?" he said when I voiced my objection. "We want to nail all of them at the same time for security reasons . . . 'officer safety.' We don't know anything about the living habits of these people. One or two of them might have jobs. The only time we can be sure of getting everyone in the same place at the same time is late at night." He looked over at me and added, "At least that's the explanation we'll give if anybody asks why."

Once again, I had to admit that the explanation was entirely plausible. But whisking people out of their homes in the middle of the night still smacked of fascism. On the other hand, guys like Jim Harcourt were the professionals when it came to arresting people. If I didn't want police officers telling me how to try the case, maybe I shouldn't be telling them how to make arrests. And besides, my major problem with a nighttime arrest was a personal one: I didn't want to admit to this experienced police officer that I was afraid my wife might not let me out of the house tonight.

"Anything you say, Jim," I conceded. "But tomorrow night would be a lot better for me. I just need to take care of a few things at home."

"Well, I'd really like to make our move tonight, but I'm not sure we'll have time to set up after we get back. Watkins is going to want to be in on it. He's entitled. The subjects will be F.D.L.E. prisoners; the county jails generally like to have a little advance notice when we're bringing them in. I guess we could just as easily stake out the place tonight and tomorrow, and then execute the warrants tomorrow night. Besides, that'll give us time to get a search warrant so we'll be able to do a thorough search for the gun at the same time."

I marveled at Jim's thought process. Always think ahead; always cover all the bases. And there was something else: ever since we got the indictments that afternoon, Grace, Anita and Melwin no longer had names. As far as he was concerned they were now simply "subjects." It seemed to be his way of neutralizing the situation. One might have pity for a woman named "Grace Stempo," but no feelings of any kind attached to a "subject."

"Tomorrow night then, Jim?" I was still thinking about home and hoping the delay would allow me to explain things to Barbara. Okay, so I know that makes me sound like a wimp, but her feelings are very important to me. And what the hell difference did it make to Fanchie and the Stempo's? With the way things were going they would be behind bars for a very long time.

"Hell, I don't guess Deke Stoner can outflank us now. We might as well set things up real careful and do it all tomorrow night," Harcourt said grudgingly.

The mention of Deke Stoner and a possible flanking maneuver led to thoughts of our nemesis Sylvia Mendez.

"How about the gal from The Journal, Jim?

"How about her?"

"I promised her an exclusive story."

"So give it to her; *after* we make the collars."

"Jim, I know you're not going to like this idea, but . . ."

"You're right. I don't like it."

"Come on, Jim. Be serious."

"Okay, let's hear what I'm not going to like."

"Suppose we call her tomorrow morning and take her along on the bust. It would make a hell of a story for her."

"David, I know you haven't been drinking. And I also know you haven't been sampling anything in the evidence vault. So I'm going to assume this idea is the result of some kind of prescription medication."

"Why is it such a crazy idea?"

"Because after we make the collars, I intend to squeeze Grace until she pops like an overripe mango. The last thing I want is some nosy reporter writing a lot of bleeding-heart crap about how I violated Grace's civil rights."

"Sylvia doesn't strike me as much of a bleeding heart. I think she's only interested in a good story."

"And if she can get a Pulitzer Prize by writing about how the big, ugly F.D.L.E. trampled on some lady's rights, she'll turn on us faster than a cornered gator. Don't do it, Dave. Please. Don't even think about it."

I wasn't about to overrule Harcourt on something he felt so strongly about, but I still thought it would make a hell of a story. At least my suggestion proved one thing: I could cross Jim off my list of "leak" suspects.

Even with an average speed of eighty miles an hour, it was after six o'clock when he dropped me off at my condo on the north side of town. "What are your plans for the night, Jim?" I asked as I opened the passenger door.

"Me? Are you kidding? I'm going to the F.D.L.E. office to make arrangements for a stakeout. We'll probably use a General Telephone Company truck . . . anything that can stay parked in a neighborhood all day without being noticed. I've got to get a hold of Watkins and tell him we're a 'go' for tomorrow night. Then I've got to write a bunch of reports and prepare an affidavit for a search warrant. I'll be lucky to get to my hotel by midnight."

"Are you going to stop by my office tomorrow?"

"No reason to. I'd rather get the search warrant myself. That keeps you and the Attorney General out of the picture. As far as planning . . . the planning is over, Counselor. In forty-eight hours I'll be on my way back home."

How true, I thought. As far as the police officers were concerned, this case was almost history. Now it was the lawyers' turn. Our work began when theirs ended. "So how am I going to meet up with you guys tomorrow night?"

He looked at me, with an expression of surprise. "Do you want to be there?"

"I wouldn't miss it for the world."

"Why don't you meet us at my office about eight o'clock. I'll send a car for you. Better yet, Watkins can pick you up on his way in."

"Good idea. Sarge can do it. He knows where I live." I extended my hand and Harcourt took it. "I'll see you tomorrow night, Jim."

Now I would have to face my final problem: explaining to my darling over-protective wife why I would be going out the following night and most likely would not be back for many hours. I could not even argue that it was necessary for the case. I had to admit that my presence at the scene of the arrest could do no good, and stemmed from nothing more than plain old-fashioned curiosity. I had come this far with the investigation and felt a proprietary interest in it. I wanted to see it through to its conclusion.

Barb met me at the door. "Well, how did it go?"

"Perfect. Three first-degree murder indictments. Of course it's still a big, deep-dark secret."

"I shan't tell a living soul. But I wonder how much the National Enquirer would pay for such heady information?"

I changed out of my lawyer suit and met her out on the patio. The heat of summer had finally broken, and the evening air was delightful. I poured us two glasses of wine and waited for the right opportunity to bring up the problem of tomorrow night.

"So, will your boyfriends be out rounding up the

varmints tonight?" she asked as she took a glass from me.

"Have we really been acting that juvenile?"

"Of course not, Darling. It's just that all boys love to play 'Cowboys and Outlaws'. And when they do, someone has to round up the varmints. That's one of the rules." "For your information, they'll be rounding up the varmints late tomorrow night."

"You'll want to be with them, I suppose."

"How did you know?"

"David, you *are* one of the Cowboys. It wouldn't be right for you to let the posse leave town without you."

"You don't mind?"

She stroked the side of my face lightly with her hand. "Of course I mind, Darling. I'm very worried about you. But I told you I wouldn't hold you back." She paused for a moment and added, "Let's have a light supper and get some rest. It appears tomorrow will be a long day.

CHAPTER 8

I could barely get through the next day. It was no use trying to read a transcript or write an appellate brief; my mind kept wandering away to what would happen that night. Would we be able to pull it off? Would any of the "subjects," as Harcourt called them, crack under the pressure and confess? Even better, would any one of them confess and implicate the other two? On the face if it, we had enough evidence for conviction, but I remembered the rule our old boss had drummed into Tom Julian and me when we were young prosecutors back in our early Bonita days: "You can never have too much evidence."

In those years I had never seen a case through from the very beginning of the investigation to the jury verdict. Back then people like Tom and I didn't have time for such luxury; instead, we spent most of our time counting "dispositions." We generally considered ourselves lucky if we got to talk to our witnesses for a few minutes in the hallway outside the courtroom immediately before they testified. It was seat-of-the-pants trial work, pure and simple. We learned a lot about thinking on our feet.

Mary Ellen said the secretaries took a vote and she was

ordered to drive me home at lunchtime. They didn't know what was going on, but they said I was driving everybody crazy pacing around the office. I guess I'm still a "Type A": I don't hide my emotions very well. I had to do something to keep busy, and by the time Barbara came home I had dinner ready and the table set on the patio.

"Well this is a pleasant surprise," she said after she changed out of her working clothes and joined me. "Perhaps you should indict a few more people."

"I even took a nap this afternoon," I lied. Well, actually, I did stretch out on the lounge and close my eyes. I even kind of drifted off for a couple of minutes. I guess I was worn out from the sleep I lost tossing and turning the previous night.

We sat down to chilled wine and salad before I surprised her with chicken breasts stuffed with herbed ricotta cheese.

"Is this on our diet?" she inquired with a lifted eyebrow.

"The cheese is made from nonfat milk."

"I don't believe you."

"Okay, so it's partially skimmed. Honest. I got it at Publix on the way home. The container is in the wastebasket."

She looked at me and smiled. "It seems he doth protest too much."

There was a long pause. I was thinking about how much I loved her. It took a special woman to put up with someone like me. After a minute she broke the silence.

"David, you will be careful tonight, won't you?"

"What do you mean? Of course I'll be careful. What are you so worried about?"

"There won't be any guns out there?"

"I doubt it. I mean, I'm sure Watkins and Harcourt have guns, but there won't be any shooting."

"Just promise me you'll be careful, all right?"

"Barbara, I will be very careful. I'm not going to louse up a relationship as good as ours by getting shot."

I had made espresso for dessert and drank two cups. I usually avoid even regular coffee in the evening, but I figured that tonight I would be awake far beyond my regular bedtime. At eight o'clock sharp Sergeant Watkins appeared at our door. He declined Barbara's offer to come inside.

"Some other time, Ma'am. Right now we're on a schedule."

"You will take care of him, won't you Clive? Don't let him get into any trouble."

I know she meant well, but it was embarrassing nonetheless. I gave her a perfunctory kiss and accompanied Watkins to his car. I was sure that I was going to hear about her "take care of him" comment for weeks to come. I was wrong.

"She really worries about you, doesn't she?" Sarge asked as we left the condominium grounds.

"Yeah, well, I guess it's a woman thing . . ."

"Don't put it down, Dave. It's kind of nice to have somebody worry about you." He reached under the seat. "Here," he said as he handed me a revolver.

"What am I supposed to do with this?"

"Stick it in your belt or something. You might need it. If anything happens I don't want you hanging around like a sitting duck."

"Sarge, I'm *not* an assistant *state* attorney. People in our office aren't authorized to carry concealed firearms."

"So who's going to arrest you, me or Harcourt? Put it in your belt. And if anything *does* happen, for chrissake stay out of the way."

I wondered how many times the late Mrs. Watkins pleaded with her husband to "be careful" and how many lonely hours she spent waiting for him to come home from a particularly dangerous assignment. Or was Sarge one of those men who never told the "little woman" anything? Would his wife have been one of those unfortunate women who got a call to come to a hospital one night when she thought her husband was working a desk job? There are all kinds of police officers; some thrive on danger and some avoid it. But they all have one thing in common: like it or not, they are engaged in a very dangerous profession. Any call might be their last. There is no mercy in the streets.

We arrived at the F.D.L.E. office a few minutes past eight-thirty. Harcourt was there, wearing his badge on his belt next to his pistol. "We've had a Florida Power Company truck parked across from the house all day," he reported.

"What happened to the phone company?" I asked.

"Turns out this office doesn't have a General Telephone vehicle. Can you believe it?" He appeared to be shocked that any F.D.L.E. office could exist without such an obvious necessity. "Anyway, Florida Power is better. They're always out replacing wires."

"What's the story on the Stempo's?"

"The three subjects have been in and out all day. It appears that none of them has a job. Latest report is that they're all home now."

"So let's do it," I suggested.

"We've got time. We'll move out at nine-thirty."

Harcourt was called away to the telephone leaving us with little to do besides sit around and feel the tension build. Watkins took a seat at one of the desks and I paced around the office that contained the standard collection of nondescript furniture. Florida has unique supplier for the stuff: prisons. Prisoners make most of the desks in state offices. There's a moral there somewhere, but I've never been able to put my finger on it.

There wasn't much to read other than bulletin boards, and I guess my pacing must have gotten to Watkins. "Sit down, Dave. You're going to wear out your shoes."

"How can you guys be so calm?"

"What's the big deal? We've got our warrants; we're going to collar two kids and a woman. Piece of cake."

"Why can't we go now?"

"It's Jim's show. We go when he says."

"About thirty minutes later, other agents filtered in, acting as cool and casual as Watkins. As far as they were concerned, it was just another day on the job. Harcourt called a meeting in the conference room. "Gentlemen, we have three first-degree murder warrants to execute tonight. The subjects are a middle-aged woman, her daughter and the daughter's boyfriend who is connected with a local gang known as the Jolly Boys. We've had the house under surveillance since last night, and we don't expect any trouble. I'll want at least one agent with each of the subjects at all times. After we make the arrests, we'll bring them back here for interrogation. Any questions?"

"Any weapons on the premises?" one of the agents asked.

"There might be at least one handgun on the premises, exact location unknown. We have a search warrant, and once the subjects are secured one of our jobs is to find it."

"Any history of violence?"

"The woman killed her husband and made it look like a suicide. Exercise caution."

"How about local support?"

"Sergeant Watkins here is our liaison with the Calusa County S.O.," Harcourt answered, motioning toward Sarge. "Other than that, this is strictly an F.D.L.E. operation." The mention of Watkins must have reminded him that I was in the room. "Oh, by the way," he added, "this is David Bradley from the Attorney General's Office. He'll be coming with us. Dave's a lawyer, but he's on our side, so don't shoot him."

Watkins and I shook hands all around, and I reminded the agents of what Harcourt said about not shooting the lawyer. Then it was time to go. Seven of us piled into three cars in the parking lot. Jim and another agent were in the first car; Watkins and I were in the second, and three more agents in the car behind us. There were no blue lights or sirens, only simple matter-of-fact efficiency. We were on our way to arrest three people for premeditated murder. Just another day in the life of a police officer.

Neither Sarge nor I spoke on our way to the Stempo house. There didn't seem to be much to say, and I didn't want to show my inexperience by asking stupid questions. Whenever the lighting was right, I could see Harcourt and his partner in the car ahead of us. They didn't appear to be talking either. Maybe we all just wanted to get this over with.

It took us about half an hour to get to the city of Sabal Palms and Harcourt led us into a residential area where he pulled into a driveway across from a Florida Power Company truck. We had arrived. Watkins pulled up on the swale in front of the house. As we got out of our cars, the door of a car parked across the street opened and two people ran toward us.

"Hey, Bradley! Remember me?" It was Sylvia Mendez.

Watkins looked like he was about to be sick. "Jesus Christ! What's she doing here?" he demanded.

"Sylvia, what the hell are you doing here?"

"Covering the news, David. Is that illegal?"

Harcourt veered away from the front door and came toward us. "What the hell's going on? Who the hell is she?"

"Newspaper reporter," Watkins replied.

Jim looked at me with a mixture of anger and contempt. "Just keep her the hell out of the way until we get everybody secured." He turned to the agents from the car behind us. "Don, you and Lou cover the back door and make sure nobody leaves. Hank, follow us in as backup."

Whether or not Harcourt thought I sold him out, I wasn't about to be left out now. "Please, Sylvia. I don't know how you found out about this, but just stay here, okay?"

"I'll give you five minutes, Bradley, and then my photographer and I are coming in. I want a picture of those handcuffs going on."

I took off after Harcourt, Watkins and the two agents who were already at the front door. "I didn't do it Jim! I didn't say anything!" Harcourt wasn't buying any of it. "Police! Open up!" he shouted as he pounded on the door.

A frightened-looking woman opened the door. She was middle-aged and overweight. Her hair may have been dark once, but it was now streaked with gray. She wore a shapeless housedress and bedroom slippers and answered to her name.

"Grace Stempo?"

"Yes?"

"You're under arrest for the murder of your husband."

The blood drained out of her face and her hands went up to her mouth. "Oh, my God! No!"

Watkins and the other agent brushed past her and into the house. A surprisingly attractive young woman with dark hair and eyes came out of a doorway as Harcourt turned Grace Stempo over to the agent he had called "Hank."

"Mom? What's going on? What happened?"

"Anita Stempo?" Harcourt demanded.

"Leave her alone! She had nothing to do with this!"

Grace screamed.

"What's going on?" the girl repeated.

"You're under arrest for the murder of your father."

The girl took a step backwards. "She didn't have nothing to do with it!" her mother screamed again.

"Mel's trying to get out the window!" Watkins' voice from a back room – possibly a bedroom – mingled with the sound of breaking glass and a scuffle. And at that moment Sylvia Mendez and her photographer came in the front door. The place was pure bedlam.

The confusion lasted a surprisingly short time. The agents got the three "subjects" herded into the living room where they were handcuffed. Grace's arms could not reach behind her, so the men linked two sets of cuffs together. That glitch out of the way, the agents searched the house for the gun and to make sure there was nobody else inside. Harcourt remained with the handcuffed "subjects" and advised them of their rights:

"You have the right to remain silent. Anything you say can and will be used against you. You have the right to have a lawyer present. If you want a lawyer but cannot afford one, one will be appointed for you. Do you understand those rights?"

Anita and Melwin nodded. "My daughter didn't have nothing to do with this," Grace insisted. Anita cut her off. "Ma, just don't say anything, all right?"

"Okay, we're going to take all of you down to our field office and book you, and then you'll be taken to the County Jail. You'll see a judge in the morning. The Statewide Grand Jury has indicted the three of you for first-degree murder, so right now there's no bail." Harcourt turned to the other agents. "Don, you and Lou take the female; Sergeant Watkins can take the male and I'll take the mother."

"Can we at least get dressed; put on better clothes?" Anita protested.

"They'll issue you clothes at the jail," Harcourt replied as his men and Watkins let her and Melwin to their cars. His voice was cold and matter-of-fact, and although in retrospect it sounds like an especially cruel statement, I'm sure it wasn't meant to be. I had come to know Jim; this was just another case. He didn't bear any particular animosity toward these people. They were simply "subjects."

The Journal photographer was still snapping pictures as the defendants were being taken away. "That man shouldn't be here," Harcourt protested.

"Agent Harcourt, I'm Sylvia Mendez from The Bonita Journal," Sylvia said, extending her hand.

Harcourt did not take it but looked at me instead. "She's not supposed to be here, either," he said as he and his partner took Mrs. Stempo out the door.

I caught up with him as he was closing his car door on his prisoner. "Jim, I know what you think, but I didn't call her."

"Well somebody did, and it wasn't me," he said severely.

I knew he didn't believe me. Why should he? I was the one who argued to hold off the arrest until tonight. Who in his right mind would believe I did it to placate my wife? "Jim, I know you don't believe me . . ."

"You're God damn right I don't!" That was not like Harcourt. He was really angry.

"Okay, you don't believe me. I accept that. Just tell me one thing: did you send a report to Tally last night?

"As a matter of fact, Counselor, I did fax a report. I faxed it to the Attorney General's Office very late last night . . . long after they closed. I plan to send them another report tonight. Do you have any other questions?"

"Then it has to be somebody up there, Jim! It wasn't me!"

"You can think what you want, Counselor. I've made my own conclusions." He got into the driver's seat, slammed the door and sped away.

Watkins was waiting for me back at his car with Melwin in the back seat. "He was pretty pissed off," Sarge observed. "You shouldn't have called that reporter, Dave."

"I didn't, for chrissake!"

"All right, so you didn't. Jim thinks you did. In another couple of hours he'll be out of town and this case will be all yours. What the hell difference does it make?"

"I don't like taking the rap for somebody else, all right?" I looked at him coldly. "Besides, how do I know it didn't come out of your office? You knew about tonight too."

With that Watkins gunned the engine and we took off. We hadn't gone far before Melwin started to talk.

"I don't know what you guys got, but I didn't pull the trigger."

Watkins ignored him.

"I said I didn't pull the fuckin' trigger," Melwin shouted.

"Melwin, Agent Harcourt read you your rights," I reminded him. "You might want to have a lawyer present before you say anything."

Watkins drove on, apparently oblivious to the conversation.

"Fuck my rights, man! I said I didn't pull no fuckin' trigger!"

Watkins finally spoke up. "Maybe you should have thought about that before you started running your mouth to all of your little friends."

"What did those motherfuckers say, man? Whatever it was, it was a lie 'cause I didn't pull no fuckin' trigger!"

Watkins goaded him. "Don't worry about 'those

motherfuckers' Melwin. You told us everything we needed to hear." Watkins chuckled as if he was a party to some private joke. "Didn't he, Dave?"

"I never talked to you guys, man!"

"You didn't know you did, *man*," Watkins taunted. "Now why don't you shut up before you get yourself into more trouble?"

Melwin shut up after that. I didn't understand what was happening here. I wouldn't mind hearing what Melwin had to say. As long as the statement was voluntary it couldn't hurt our case. But my police officer friend was preventing him from talking, not merely by advising him of his rights but by telling him to "shut up." I looked at Watkins who nodded toward the back seat and said, "He's a two-bit punk," loud enough for Melwin to hear.

Harcourt was waiting for us at the F.D.L.E. office. He looked like he was still upset about the Journal fiasco, but he had work to do and he was too much of a professional to let anything get in the way for the moment.

"Melwin's dying to talk," Watkins told him after two agents put our "subject" in an interrogation room. "I practically had to gag him to keep him quiet on the way down here."

"I don't doubt it. I told you he wasn't the shooter."

"I've got five bucks says he is," Sarge insisted.

"You're on. You want 'good cop' or 'bad cop'?"

"'Bad cop', Jim. I'm always the 'bad cop'."

The three of us walked into a room that was almost identical to the one in which I had talked to Shawn back when this whole thing started. How was it that all interrogation rooms looked alike? Were there special schools for police architecture? Even the hard wooden furniture was unchanged. Harcourt took a seat across the table from Melwin and once again read him his rights.

"Melwin, I'm agent Jim Harcourt from the Florida Department of Law Enforcement. This is Sergeant Watkins from the Calusa County Sheriff's Office and David Bradley from the Florida Attorney General's Office. Before you say anything, I want to read you your rights, understand?"

"I don't need 'rights', man. I just need you to understand I didn't shoot nobody, okay?"

"All right, listen. You have the right to remain silent. Do you understand that?"

Melwin nodded.

"Anything you say can and will be used against you in a court of law. Do you understand that?"

He nodded again.

"You have the right to have a lawyer present during any questioning. Do you understand that?"

Another nod.

"If you can't afford a lawyer, the court will appoint one for you. Do you understand that?"

Melwin nodded a fourth time. That was it, just like the United States Supreme Court said it should be done *in Miranda v. Arizona*. And after all that you would think that anybody would say, "I'm not saying anything; get me a lawyer." The Supreme Court said that's what anybody would say. Only in real life people *don't* say it; instead they *"explain."* Melwin didn't say it. He "explained."

"Like I said, fuck my rights, man. I didn't shoot nobody."

"Harcourt continued, "Having those rights in mind, do you want to talk to us now?"

"Yeah, I'll talk. I'll tell you what happened. Only I didn't pull the trigger, understand? It was the old lady; she done it. She wanted me to do it, but I wouldn't. Joe was a decent guy. I wasn't gonna shoot him or nothin'. It was Grace. She pulled the trigger."

Harcourt gave up some information and slowly drew him into a conversation. "Melwin, we have a witness who says you took the gun out of Anita's dresser and left her bedroom shortly before the shooting."

Melwin's eyes darted from Harcourt to Watkins and to me. "Yeah, okay, I knew where the gun was, but I still didn't kill him. I gave it to his old lady. She's the one who wanted it. Why would I want to kill him?"

"You're driving his car," Harcourt reminded him.

"Hey, man, I can buy a car. I don't need to kill a guy for a car."

"You're living with his daughter."

"So what? He knew it. He didn't stop us or nothin'."

"Maybe he didn't like it," Harcourt suggested cooly. "Maybe he wanted you to move out," Harcourt suggested.

"He didn't, man. He didn't say a word. Why would I want to kill him?" He almost sneered and added, "I don't have, you know, a motive."

At the sound of the word "motive" Watkins seemed to go berserk. "Fuck this guy, Jim. Tell him the truth." He hunched over the table and looked directly into Melwin's eyes. "Listen to me, you little son-of-a-bitch. We don't need to prove no motive because we got you on tape. You confessed the whole thing, you stupid bastard, and we were listening. Now do you want to talk about motive, you little piece of shit?"

Melwin looked like he had been shot. Harcourt grabbed Watkins and pulled him back from the table. "Take it easy, Sarge," he said quietly.

"Take it easy my ass," Watkins retorted. He pushed Harcourt out of the way and went back at Melwin. "Yeah, we got you on tape, Melwin. You were good. You were so good they're gonna give you your own radio show up at Raiford. You want to hear the tape?"

Melwin was breathing heavily, but Watkins wouldn't let him get a word in. Harcourt got physical and pushed Watkins away from the table again, more forcefully this time, and it looked like they might actually exchange blows in a minute. "Come on, Sarge. We don't do things like this anymore. Maybe he wants a lawyer. At least give him a chance to think about it."

Sarge fought his way past Harcourt again. "Give him a chance to think about it? Yeah, I'll give him a chance to think about it. Think about this, Melwin. Know what it's like in the Death House? Did you ever see somebody die in the electric chair? It's bad, Melwin. It's real bad. Their eyeballs pop out. And their skin turns black, fried from the electrodes. And sometimes they don't die right away. They just stiffen up but they're not dead, so they have to give 'em a couple more jolts." He looked at me and shouted, "Isn't that right, Dave?"

I froze. I had never witnessed an actual execution, but I had heard plenty of stories. I was in shock; I couldn't say anything.

"Yeah, that's right," Sarge continued, not missing a beat. "Sometimes they just sit there and quiver and shake, and it takes two . . . maybe three jolts to kill them. 'Couse it don't matter 'cause at that point they don't feel nothing. At least that's what the people up at Raiford say." Sarge got right down in the guy's face, smiled evilly and added, "You'll have a chance to find out for yourself, Melwin."

Melwin was trembling as if he had the chills. "Come on, Sarge. Take it easy," Harcourt protested.

"Take it easy? Sure, I'll take it easy. Know what happens when they see the chair, Melwin? They piss their pants, just like you're gonna do. Every time. All those big, rough, tough murderers. Four guards have to drag them into the room and they piss their pants when they see it. Some of them even crap in their pants when they get strapped in. They die sitting in their own shit, Melwin, just like you're gonna do."

It was too much for Melwin. He stood up, his body shaking violently. "Get him out of here, man," he said, pointing at Watkins. "He's an animal! I ain't talking with him in the room!"

Harcourt grabbed Watkins around the shoulders. "Come on, Sarge, leave him alone. Dave, take him outside and get him a cup of coffee or something, will you?"

I had never seen Watkins so completely out of control. He seemed to have developed a personal, deep-seated hatred for Melwin, and he took a sadistic pleasure in describing how he hoped he would die. I agreed with Harcourt that it would be best to get him out of the room, and I escorted him out.

"Not a bad piece of acting, huh?" he said as he straightened his shirt after I closed the door. "I should get some kind of award for that."

"What? You mean that was all an act?"

"Of course it was. You heard Jim ask me if I wanted to be the 'good cop' or the 'bad cop'."

"Well, yes, but . . ."

"I chose 'bad cop'. It's a lot easier, at least for me. Of course, I can play the 'good cop' too."

Watkins' talents never failed to surprise me. "What's the 'good cop'?" I couldn't stop a smile from creeping across my face.

"The 'good cop' is what Jim is doing in there right now. It goes like this: 'Look, Melwin, these local bastards are crazy . . . both of them. They won't be happy until they see you in the electric chair. Now, I can help you, but you have to level with me. Tell me what happened . . . what really happened . . . and I'll make a deal with Bradley's boss in

Tallahassee. But if you try to screw me, I'll walk out of here and leave you to the local yokels. Now what do you want to do?'"

"And you think that'll work?"

"I've got ten bucks says it does."

"You bet Harcourt five."

"Because I think he might be right. I'm not sure that Melwin pulled the trigger after all. I wanted Jim to have a little extra incentive to get the real story."

Harcourt began opening the door. Before he could say anything, I grabbed Watkins' arm. "Sarge, just tell me one thing . . . you guys couldn't possibly have rehearsed this. How did you know what to say?"

"It's like jazz, Dave. The good jazz players just feel it and know when to cut in. Hell, I even gave you a cue for a solo, but you didn't get it. You'll do better next time."

"He wants to make a statement, but only if Mr. Bradley is in here. Sergeant Watkins will have to wait outside," Harcourt said in a voice loud enough for Melwin to hear. Watkins slapped me on the back. "Do a good job. I'll be out here with the coffee."

I went back into the interrogation room, and once again Harcourt read Melwin his rights. This time there was a difference. Harcourt had a tape recorder running and he read the "rights" off a form that Melwin initialed. The rehearsal was over; it was time for the real show.

"Melwin, now that you've had your rights explained to you, and you've said that you understood them, do you still want to talk to us?"

"I ain't sayin' anything unless I know I ain't goin' to the electric chair."

Harcourt looked at me. "Melwin, I'm prosecuting this case. If you give us a statement detailing your involvement *and* if you agree to testify truthfully against everyone else involved, I give you my word that I will not seek the death penalty against you."

"Mr. Bradley says he won't send you to the chair, Melwin. But you've got to tell us what happened."

"His wife did it, man. She wanted him dead. She was always after me, sayin' 'I want him dead'. I checked out the gun, you know that, and I even went into his bedroom. But I couldn't pull the trigger. I had the gun right up against his head, man, but I couldn't pull the trigger. Joe never done nothin' to me." He looked back and forth between Harcourt and me, as though he expected us to praise him for his high moral character.

"So who pulled the trigger?"

"She did. Grace. Mrs. Stempo. She was in bed with him, man. He was asleep. So I come in with the gun, and I put it to his head, but I couldn't do it. So Grace takes the gun out of my hand and reaches over him and bang! She shoots him right in the head. And after she does it, she starts screamin' like she didn't know it was goin' to happen."

"Then what did she do?"

"Like I said, man, she went nuts. She was screamin' an' cryin' like she didn't think he was gonna die. An' she goes, 'He killed himself; right in my own bed, he killed himself!' An' she gets up and puts the gun in his hand, the hand that's hangin' off the bed, and she starts screamin', 'Call the police! Call the police!'"

"And?"

"I called the police, man. I figured no matter what happened, I didn't kill nobody. And the police come, and by this time both Grace and Anita are out of their heads, hysterical. An' the police talk to everybody, but I guess you know that, too. An' Grace says that she was asleep in bed with Joe when he woke up and shot himself. An' Anita's a wreck, too. An' I guess the cops just didn't want to deal with it, so they said, 'Okay, he shot himself.'"

It was time for Harcourt to play his trump card. "Okay, I understand that, Melwin. But, you see, the only problem is that you told Jason Bonafidie that you did it. You pulled the trigger. Watkins wasn't bullshitting when he said we have you on tape. We *do* have you on tape. So unless you can convince me otherwise, I'd have to say that everything you said is true *except* the part about Grace pulling the trigger."

It's *all true*, man. Every word of it. All right, I told Jason I did it, but I was bullshittin' him, man. I didn't pull the trigger. I'll take a lie detector. Anything. It's true, man."

Harcourt looked at me and then back at Melwin. "You just sit here for a minute, Melwin. I'll have one of the guys bring you some coffee." Melwin hung his head and nodded as Harcourt and I left the room.

CHAPTER 9

"**P**ay me, Sarge," Harcourt said as he closed the door. "Five bucks."

"Pay you, hell. I still say Melwin's the shooter."

"He said Grace did it."

"Sure. Next he'll say you did it. And then it'll be Santa Claus did it. Come on! Melwin was a killer; now he's a killer and a liar."

"All right. Grace is next. That'll settle it," Harcourt said.

"Good cop, bad cop?" Watkins offered.

"I don't think that'll be necessary. Let's see how it goes, first."

The three of us entered the interrogation room where Grace was being held. Once again Harcourt made the introductions and carefully explained Grace's rights to her. And once again a person who had no legal duty to speak apparently felt a moral compulsion to do so.

"Joe went to bed about 10:30 or so," she began. "I joined him about 11:00. The TV was on in the bedroom but he wasn't watching it. He had turned away from it. I thought he was asleep. About 11:15 . . . halfway through the news . . . he says, 'Are you going to keep that thing on all night?' and I said, 'No, as soon as the weather is over, I'll shut it off.' And I did. I shut it off a few minutes later and went to sleep."

"About two o'clock I woke up and made my usual trip to the bathroom; then back to bed. Anita had a friend over, and she was in her room. They had rented some videos or something, and I could hear them in the next room. I guess Melwin was on the couch in the living room."

"I heard a noise like a firecracker, and I yelled to Joe and put my hand out and pushed at him, like I usually do, to wake him up. He didn't move, so I got up and turned on the light on my side of the bed. Joe had the sheet part way over him and he was facing my side. I pulled the sheet, and his hand was on the pillow. And there was a gun, either in his hand or it or right near it . . . I can't say for sure."

"By this time, I heard someone up so I went right to the door and Mel was coming down the hallway and I told him to go in the room with the girls and stay there. At least that's what I think I did. Then I went to the kitchen phone. I don't remember whether I put the sheet back over him or not, but I went to the kitchen phone and I called 911. They kept me on the phone until the police arrived or the ambulance arrived. I don't remember which one of them got there first."

"When they got there, I went to Anita's bedroom and brought her to the kitchen to be with me, because I knew the other two would stay in the room. But knowing my daughter, I didn't want her to go in the bedroom and see him like that. So I went and got her and made her stay with me for the rest of the time that the police and paramedics were there."

Grace ended her story and placed her hands on her ample lap. It was a nice, cogent story; one she undoubtedly thought covered all of the gaps in the mystery of Joe

Stempo's death. Now it was time for Jim Harcourt to start punching holes in it. If he could trap her in enough inconsistencies, she might realize the game was up and make a clean breast of it. In the give and take of questioning, her need to explain would overcome her common sense; she would forget about her right to remain silent and simply dig herself in deeper. I had seen the process played out in transcripts; now I was about to witness it in action.

"When you went to bed at eleven, was Joe still awake?" It was a safe, innocuous question. No need to panic and ask for a lawyer.

"He was sort of awake. You know, not really awake and not really asleep." She was explaining herself already. Answers like that could eventually bury her under an avalanche of contradictory details.

"How about when you woke up at two o'clock? Was he asleep then?"

"I don't know. I wasn't paying much attention."

"Did you hear him snoring?"

"I don't think so. I don't remember him snoring."

"That's funny, because I just talked to Melwin and he said that he could hear Joe snoring from the living room." Melwin had not said that of course, but I could see the flicker of emotion race across Grace's eyes. She thought she had been caught in a lie, and now she had to make up for it with another explanation.

"Joe snores . . . Joe snored when he was awake," she said with an innocent smile.

"Really?" Harcourt acted like he had been taken in by her charm. He was her friend.

"He can lay on the sofa in the living room and he has got one of his programs on TV, those nature programs, and his eyes are closed and he's snoring. And if you try and change the channel he says, 'I was watching that,' and he makes you put it back."

"I do that all the time with baseball games," Harcourt responded. He was truly her friend now. They were exchanging personal anecdotes.

"Yeah, but do you know what's going on in the game? Joe always knew what was happening. But maybe that's because he had seen those shows ten million times." Another explanation; another little bit of information. Could she possibly have killed him because of his television habits?

"Well, at two o'clock in the morning, the lights are out and there's no TV on and I would just think that you'd know if he was snoring, that's all." Jim was back on the snoring again, but this time in an offhand, friendly way.

"Well, yeah, I guess I would."

"Because Melwin said that he heard him snoring, and that's from the living room. And with you right there next to him, I just thought it was kind of strange that you didn't hear it."

"Yeah, well, now that you mention it, I did hear him snoring. It was pretty loud, and I remember thinking that I was going to have trouble getting back to sleep."

Jim looked at me and in an instant I knew what he was thinking. She was lying. Either she heard him snoring or she didn't. Now she was changing her story to fit the one fact she thought Jim had. The snoring was irrelevant. It was only important because it was the first crack in her carefully-built wall.

"Okay," he said. "When you went to bed, was there any type of arguing? Did you two have any type of argument or anything? Any problems?"

"No, we never fought. He wouldn't fight. I got mad at him sometimes, but he wouldn't fight."

Nonsense. Everybody fights. Barbara and I have has some knock-down drag-outs that had us making up for days afterwards. Every married couple fights.

Harcourt didn't say anything and waited for Grace's need to explain kick in. It did. "Well, you know," she said, "we fought sometimes, but it was nothing serious. We had our times." Jim remained impassive and waited. Finally, she added, "A year ago I even thought I wanted a divorce. But we worked it out."

"That's a pretty serious step, divorce," Jim agreed. "My sister just got divorced. It was bad." I wasn't sure Jim had a sister, but if he did I was willing to bet she had not been divorced. "What happened," Jim said.

"I don't know; I guess it was me. I wanted out. Twenty-seven yeas of being dominated. I just wanted out."

"I meant, how did you work it out?" Jim asked.

"He said, 'no', so it was no," Grace said.

"Yeah, but usually if one party wants a divorce . . ."

This time Grace's explanation came even before Jim finished his question. "I couldn't see calling the police to get him out of the house," she said, "which is the way I would have had to do it. I couldn't see . . . as much as I hated the guy, I loved the guy. You know, it was a love/hate relationship . . . but, you know, if I really wanted something . . . if he thought it was right, he'd give it to me. If he thought it was wrong . . . forget it. No matter what temper tantrums I pulled . . . forget it. And I always gave in because he was always right. Twenty-seven years of trying to prove a guy wrong, you can't prove him wrong; you learn to do what he says."

"That's what I keep telling my wife," Harcourt said with a chuckle. A motive was starting to emerge; before the atmosphere in the room got too tense, Jim broke the mood with a joke. "I've never been wrong, either."

"Maybe she's not as good as me," Grace suggested. "She doesn't understand as well . . . I don't know."

"Maybe you should talk to her." Harcourt was still trying to lighten up the atmosphere, but now Grace was falling apart and would have none of it.

"Maybe I'm just weak," she said. "I have seen too many times when he has been unreasonable in refusing something, but turned out it's a damn good thing he did. He said he has psychic abilities and I have seen . . . I have seen it happen a few times."

"But in the meantime, the last twenty . . . you been married twenty-seven years?"

"Twenty-seven," she said flatly. There was a deep undertone of regret in her voice.

"I guess the last few weren't very enjoyable," Jim suggested.

"No, because he got very depressed and very pessimistic. Extremely so."

"Do you consider yourself . . . there are a lot of ways to be abused," Jim observed. "There is physical abuse and mental abuse. Would you consider yourself abused?" He was giving her a moral way out; telling her she could confess to killing her husband and he would understand.

"Mentally. Mentally. I went through a lot of mental abuse with him. You don't know. Nobody knows. I even went through counseling."

"You must have suffered a lot."

"It was a nervous breakdown, in plain English. The doctor put me in the hospital for acute depression."

"Was this recently??

"No, it was a long time ago; about ten years ago. But I got over it, and I became a lot stronger within myself. After that, I could take a lot of his mental abuse because he was very domineering. I just let it wash over my head, you know? Before, I would take it to heart."

"Didn't you ever get to the point where you just said, 'To hell with it . . . I can't take it'?" Jim had become the confidant, the psychologist. He was on her side. She would hear no moral rebuke from him.

"Yeah, yeah, a lot of times. But it's kind of my personality, too, because I graduated high school and went to nursing school and I quit after three months. And that was a big thing with my father, 'You never finish anything that you start.' So went I got married and was divorced . . . I mean, what do you call it? . . . annulled . . . I got an annulment. And then Joe came along and we got married, I says, I don't give a shit what the hell happens, 'till death do us part. I'll learn to cope with any situation that I can't handle. I'll get help. I'll do whatever I have to do, but this one I'm going to finish."

"And that feeling was so strong, you know, that I was going to prove to my father that I could finish something I started. I was going to stay no matter what."

She looked at Jim for approval. He nodded and she continued, "Like I said, last year I wanted to go for a divorce. He says, 'no;' he didn't want to move out and this and that. So all things considered, I says . . . well, we sat down and had a long talk and I says, 'Okay, you go your way, I'll go mine. You know, we'll live together.' That didn't last long. It went back to the same thing as before. It's not that it was bad, it's just that . . . you know . . ."

"Your life could have been a lot more enjoyable?" Jim asked.

"A lot more. My daughters would say, 'Ma, put it behind you. He did it for a reason,' Well everybody does things for a reason. That don't make it easier to take. You don't hurt any less because somebody did something for a reason."

"It must have been very hard on Anita." Jim wasn't

asking questions anymore, just directing the flow of her conversation. Grace had been very protective of her daughter back at the house when they were arrested. Now we would see how far that protection would extend.

"Very hard. Extremely hard. She was the youngest of the three. He was very domineering, extremely mean to all of them, but the worst was with her. He never showed her any affection when she was a kid. Up 'till she was about two years old, he played with her and showed her some affection, but after that, 'close it off; lock it up,'" – she made a cutting motion with her hand across her own throat; it was the first time she had shown any animation – "You know, I mean, he was good to her, but there was never any emotion. She was at a time . . . don't get me wrong, most teenagers go through a stage when they hate their parents. She was beginning to hate him because he was so strict with her. She got in with the wrong crowd of kids. But it was his fault. I told him, 'It's your fault because you don't show her any love, any affection.' He was constantly on her."

"You know, I've seen situations like this where people do things that are pretty drastic," Jim left the "people" undefined. He might be talking about Joe; he might be talking about Grace; he might even be talking about Anita. Grace's response would determine the direction the conversation would take from here.

"You know what I think?" she said. "I think he killed himself because he was miserable. He was following in his father's footsteps. His father had emphysema real bad, and Joe was afraid it was going to happen to him, too. I think Joe just didn't want to put up with it anymore."

Grace had brought the conversation back to the shooting of her husband. I could see that whether she knew it or not, she needed to confess, and her subconscious was pushing her in that direction.

Jim picked up on it immediately. "Yeah, well, see, that's what we're trying to figure out. You know, that's one of the parts of this job, to get the details straight. We can be a little bit more analytical because we're not personally involved." He conveniently left out the fact that we had already indicted and arrested her for first-degree murder. This was still only a conversation.

"I know," she said quietly.

"See, we check everything out and make sure, and to be honest with you there are a lot of things about this situation that are a little bit inconsistent."

"Inconsistent? That was Joe all over."

"Well I understand that, but see, one of the things that doesn't make sense is when he decided to do it. I mean, with you sleeping right there next to him. That floored me."

"It was his way of telling me this was my fault. He was telling me he was doing it because of me."

"But he could have done it in the bathroom and given you the same message, couldn't he?"

"Yes, but . . . why block up the bathroom? Joe could be overly practical at times. I could see him saying, 'Why block up the bathroom when I can give her the same message right here?'"

"Well, I tell you another thing I can't understand. Maybe you can help me. If a person is going to kill himself, once he decided to do it, I can't figure out why he would lay in bed for six hours before he did it. Now, a little while ago you said that you heard him snoring."

"Yeah. I don't know. I'm not sure."

"Can you imagine a person who is going to kill himself . . . goes to sleep first?"

"Well he may not have been asleep," she said, retreating

from her earlier story.

"Okay, but to be laying down for six hours? Usually people plan it a little bit more. I mean, maybe not a complete plan in every detail, but it's something that you only do once. They go out on the porch, or in the car. There are so many things he could have done, so many questions we would like to have answered. Your hands, for example. The Sabal Palms police checked your hands for gunpowder, and that was negative. But see, they also checked Joe's hands and they were negative too."

I looked at Harcourt. He was lying to her, plain and simple. We both knew that nobody ever checked Joe's hands. It was one of the weak points in our case. Did she know that? Would she take the bait?

"There was nothing on them?"

"There was nothing on Joe's hands."

"Maybe he was holding the gun in the sheet or something."

"The sheet wasn't in his hand. There would have been powder burns on the sheet."

"That's what I saying. They might be on the sheet instead of on his hand."

It was an implausible idea, but one that provided her with a temporary refuge. Jim dropped the powder gambit and moved in from another direction.

Yeah, but see, Grace, you told me that Joe shot himself when he was laying next to you in bed."

The woman nodded her affirmance.

"Well I read the report that the paramedics filed, and they said he was laying on his side. Was he laying on his side, Grace?"

She nodded again.

"I don't want to upset you, but according to the medical examiner the bullet went right through his brain. He was dead instantly. There was blood because the heart was pumping, but he was dead instantly. Now when something like that happens, that gun should have fallen straight down. But, see, the paramedics said it was still in his hand."

Grace did not answer.

"And, see, the position he was laying, he shot himself with his left hand."

"Joe was . . . what do you call it? . . . ambidextrous." She had him on that one, and seemed to relax for a moment.

"Okay, but even if he was ambidextrous, people who do things like that, they don't usually do it when they laying on their sides. They put the gun in their mouths or under their chins. Isn't that right?"

"I don't know. I don't know if there's a right way to kill yourself." Grace seemed to be gaining ground for the moment. A few minutes ago I would have given odds that she was about to crack. Now she was scoring points on Jim.

"Well you don't follow a certain set of rules," he said. "There's no handbook that says if you do it, you have to do it this way or that way. But I've seen a lot of suicides, and they generally fall into a pattern. This one doesn't fit the pattern and that's what I'm concerned about."

"Joe didn't fit anybody's pattern, that's for sure." She was getting stronger; at this rate she would soon take over the conversation.

"Grace, the fact is that after we looked at all of the evidence, it's pretty clear that the gun was placed in his hand after the shot was fired."

"Well, what I told you is the way it happened, and if you don't want to believe it, I can't . . . I can't say anything else."

That last sentence set off alarm bells in my head. Grace was dangerously close to invoking her constitutional right to remain silent. The momentum of the conversation had turned. She was no longer on the defensive.

"I thought it was you, Grace. I thought you shot him. I couldn't understand how you wouldn't have any power on your hands, and then when I talked to Melwin I thought maybe he did it."

"He wasn't in the room," she insisted. "When I put the light on, it was just Joe and me in that room."

"No, Grace. Melwin says he was in the room. He just made a full confession explaining how he took the gun from Anita's room and took it into your room. He said Anita was going to kill Joe but he decided to do it instead. And he also said that he couldn't go through with it and you took the gun from him and you shot Joe."

Grace did not respond verbally. Instead she put her head down in her hands and began to weep. Joe would not let up.

"Grace, we know what happened; we have known it for some time. You know, I don't know what makes a person do something. I know there must have been a lot of torture, there must have been a lot going through your mind. I know that you had a reason in your own mind to do whatever you did . . . and believe me, I'm not second-guessing you. I'm not passing judgment. But there had to be a better way . . . talking it out . . . divorce."

He paused for a moment and then he said softly, "You had a pair of gloves on, and you shot him. And afterwards Anita took the gloves and got rid of them. She got rid of them to protect you. Am I right? Grace?"

The woman continued to sob into her hands, louder than before. She would not respond, would not answer; and now Jim began to press harder.

"Grace? Look at me, Grace. Can I get you some water? Were things that bad? Were they?"

Still no response.

"Couldn't you have come up with some better way? I mean, wouldn't you have been better off living in a rented room? Grace? Grace, look at me."

The woman began to rock from side to side as she sobbed. She looked at no one.

"Grace?" Jim demanded. "Look at me. Everything I said, is that accurate? Is that what happened? Grace?"

The woman continued to sob bitterly with her face in her hands. But now the side to side rocking stopped and she nodded her head up and down, although I couldn't honestly say it was in answer to Jim's questions.

"You want to talk about it, Grace?"

The side to side rocking began again.

"Answer me this, please, Grace: Was this your idea all along?"

"The side to side rocking stopped and the nodding began again.

"It was? From the time you considered divorce or was it just in the last couple of weeks?"

She removed her hands from her face and wiped her nose on the back of her wrist as she stared down at the floor. "For a long time. For a long, long time. You can put me in jail; you can kill me. I don't care. But I'll never say 'I'm sorry'. Never. Twenty-seven years without love. Twenty-seven years of hell. I'll never say 'I'm sorry.'"

"Let me tell you something, Grace. You may think I'm sitting here without compassion. Believe me, you don't know how badly I feel about this. I really wish we weren't doing this right now."

Harcourt looked up at Watkins and me. Neither Sarge nor I had said a word throughout the entire interview. I couldn't speak for him, but I was drenched with sweat and had a pounding headache. I could only guess how Grace

Stempo felt. Right now if she thought about the death penalty at all, it would have sounded like a relief. Watkins and I got up to leave and Harcourt spoke to his prisoner again.

"Grace?" Her eyes were locked on the floor, and if she heard him she gave no clue. "Grace, I'm going to send one of the boys in with some coffee. How do you want it?"

"With cream." She did not look up as she said it.

"I'll have one of them bring in some coffee with cream."

Harcourt, Watkins and I left the room and went outside. The Florida night air was fragrant and refreshing; so different from the tension that hung like an oppressive stench in the interrogation rooms. Harcourt collapsed onto the edge of a concrete planter and carefully unwrapped a stick of chewing gum.

"I'm sorry I couldn't get a better admission for you, Dave. She wouldn't crack."

He had to be upset with himself to apologize to me like that so soon after the reporter incident. He felt that he was – that we were – entitled to a complete confession from Grace's own mouth. Anything less was failure as far as he was concerned. No wonder he was so upset when Sylvia showed up at the scene of the arrest. Jim knew only one way: his way. Anything else was unacceptable.

"Don't worry about it, Jim. I'm sure a jury won't have any trouble getting the message."

"Are we going to talk to Anita?" Watkins asked.

Harcourt chewed slowly. "What for? We know what she was doing."

"Give me a chance to talk to her. Maybe she can fill in some gaps. I'd really like to know what makes these people tick."

"Help yourself, Sarge," he replied. "I'll wait out here. I've heard enough about what makes them tick for one night."

"Coming Dave?"

I felt as exhausted as Harcourt looked, but like Watkins, curiosity got the better of me. "Yeah," I said, getting up from the planter. "I never miss a final act."

Watkins and I went back inside. Two of the F.D.L.E. agents had taken Melwin to a holding cell and brought Anita to the interrogation room he had vacated. The place looked exactly the same as it had earlier, except the smell of guilt hung even heavier in the air.

"Anita, I'm Sergeant Watkins from the Calusa County Sheriff's Office," Sarge began. "This is Mr. Bradley. He's from the Attorney General's Office. I'd like to ask you a few questions."

"I've got nothing to say. I want a lawyer."

That was it. Legally, the interrogation was over. We were now obligated to provide her with a lawyer. I knew it, and I knew Sarge knew it. That's why I was surprised when he didn't move.

"Anita, I don't want you to answer any questions. And I'm not going to advise you of your rights, so we won't be able to use anything you say to us, understand? I'm going to tell you what we know. If you want to add anything after you hear it, you let me know and I'll get you a lawyer right away if you still want one, okay?"

Anita nodded. "I got nothin' to say to you. If you want to say something to me that's your business, I guess."

"Anita, we know that you, Melwin and your mother bought a gun about a month before your father was killed. We know that you paid twenty-five dollars for it, and that your mother cashed a check to pay for it. I have a copy of the check. We know that you tried to use that gun on your father a couple of weeks before his death, but you couldn't go through with it. We know that his death wasn't a suicide. Melwin and your mother murdered him. On the night of the murder, Melwin took the gun out of your dresser drawer and went into your parents' bedroom. He put the gun to your father's head just like you had done a couple of weeks earlier, but he couldn't do it, either. Melwin couldn't pull the trigger. We know that your mother put on a pair of gloves, took the gun from Melwin, put it to your father's head and pulled the trigger. And we know that after she did it, she put the gun in his hand and disposed of the gloves. Now, is there anything you want to add to that?"

Anita Stempo stared straight ahead and did not move. Her impassive face gave no hint of her emotions. We waited for what seemed like an eternity, but she did not say a word. Finally, Watkins admitted defeat.

"All right, Anita. I understand." We got up to go and reached the door before the girl broke her silence.

"There's something you don't know, Sergeant. There's a lot you don't know. My father, my wonderful, God-fearing father . . . was a pig. He was a child abuser. He liked to beat up on little girls, Sergeant. And he liked to have little girls play with his dick." Her expression changed to pure hatred as she looked at Watkins and continued. "And you know how I know that? I know it because me and my sisters . . . we were the little girls."

"I'm really sorry to hear that, Anita," Watkins replied.

"I'll tell you something else, Sergeant. And I don't care if you use it against me or not. You know what I regret most? I regret that I didn't have the guts to do it when I had the chance. I should have blown his brains out and then turned the gun on myself. I could have put both of us out of our misery. But because I was too weak, my mother and Melwin will have to suffer for it." She looked at us with an expression of utter calm. "That's all. You can write that down in your little black book or whatever Sergeants do. My only regret is that I didn't kill him when I had the chance."

Watkins sighed heavily. "I'll see that you get a lawyer, Anita. They're going to take you down to the County Jail in a few minutes. You'll have to spend the night there."

Anita nodded without emotion. "That's okay. I understand."

We left the room and Watkins closed the door behind us. "What the hell kind of world is this?" he demanded. "Guys screwing around with their daughters, wives killing their husbands; I'm too old for this shit, Dave."

"Come on, Sarge, this is nothing new. Things like this have been going on for centuries."

"Maybe. I don't know. But it's creeping up on us; you know what I mean? Maybe it used to go on before, but it was always the degenerates, the bottom of the barrel. These people are too much like us; too much like you and me."

"Yeah, or maybe people like us did it before, too, but nobody talked about it, I suggested."

"Christ, I hope not. Come on, I'll drive you home. Your wife is probably worried sick."

I glanced at my watch. It was two o'clock in the morning. I thought about calling, but I hoped Barb would be asleep and I didn't want to wake her. "Yeah, I guess we'd better go," I replied.

Barb was very much awake when we got home. She invited Sarge in for herbal tea, but I think we were both grateful when he refused. Barb poured two cups at the kitchen counter after he left. "How was it?" she asked.

"Do you really want to know or are you just being polite?"

"A little of both."

"It was horrible, Barb. I've heard stories like that in the

courtroom. Heck, I've heard everything in the courtroom. But I've never been to where the people lived, at least not while they were still living there. Do you know what I'm trying to say?"

"You never saw them as human beings, only case files."

"I guess that's it. Tonight these people looked so . . . I don't know, so ordinary."

"Most people *are* ordinary, Darling."

"But these people committed premeditated murder."

"Yes, but you said it was just an ordinary little murder, didn't you? Perhaps that's what most of them are . . . ordinary. Now finish your tea and let's go to bed. We both have to get up early tomorrow."

CHAPTER 10

I didn't sleep well that night. I spend most of the night trying the case of State of Florida versus Anita Stempo; and the only good arguments I could think of were on the defense side. I finally dropped off around 4:30. When the alarm went off two and a half hours later, I felt like a truck had hit me. I dragged myself out of bed when the snooze alarm went off for the second time. Barbara was already in the kitchen. I put on a robe and went to the front door for the morning paper. What I saw on the front page didn't make me feel any better: it was a full-color picture of Jim Harcourt reading Grace, Anita and Melwin their rights while they sat handcuffed on the couch in the Stempo living room. I was standing next to Jim looking very somber. And, just in case there was any doubt about who I was, the caption identified me as "David J. Bradley, Assistant Attorney General in charge of the Bonita Office." As I padded into the kitchen in my bedroom slippers, I wondered how Deke Stoner was choking down his breakfast.

"What's in the news," Barb asked brightly.

"It looks like we made the front page," I said as I

handed her the paper.

"Well at least your hair was combed."

"Barbara, this is not funny."

"I didn't say it was, Darling."

"This is it; the fat's in the fire. There's no turning back." I don't know if I was trying to explain the situation to her or drilling it into my own head. She put down the teapot and studied me.

"David, you must have known that the story would break once the Stempo's were arrested. How can you complain now?"

Of course, she was right. I knew all along that the crap would hit the fan as soon as the F.D.L.E. made the arrests. I guess I was just ignoring the problem, hoping it would go away; or maybe I was hoping the news would leak out slowly rather than having it blasted all over the front page. Not that it mattered, of course. Sooner or later Stoner would find out and know that our office was after his ass. Now it was out in the open; at least he wouldn't hear about it through a rumor.

My first stop was the county courtroom at the Calusa County Jail. The building is located on Terrapin Road in Bonita. The massive utilitarian structure was visible long before I got to the parking lot. The complex houses the Sheriff's Office, Jail, and a courtroom that is used for first appearances of prisoners. Normally, a young Assistant State Attorney represents the State out there. But this wasn't a normal case; it was one that had been brought by the Attorney General of the State of Florida. The State Attorney was not involved and even less welcome. "First Appearance" duty fell to the prosecutor who was responsible for the indictment: today that was me.

Everyone who is arrested in the State of Florida must be brought before a judge within twenty-four hours. These "first appearances" take place seven days a week, 365 days a year. They are a defendant's first contact with the judiciary; the hearing at which charges are read, bail is set and a public defender appointed if necessary.

There are two ways of being charged with a crime in our State. The first is by being arrested: the police take the initiative by making the arrest and filling out a "probable cause affidavit" which explains to the court why they did what they did. The suspect is brought before a judge and advised of the "nature of the charge" against him. The State Attorney then has thirty days to file a formal charge known as an "information." If he does, the defendant is brought back into court for an "arraignment," the proceeding at which the poor bastard is given the bad news that a formal charge has been laid.

The other route is the one we had taken: the criminal charge – in this case the Grand Jury indictment – is filed first. The police merely execute an arrest warrant or "capias"; there is no probable cause affidavit because the police have merely performed a ministerial duty. Using this method, the State cuts out one step, and the first appearance is actually the arraignment. It's a small technicality, but one that I knew would not be lost on Judge Bill Bellingham. In spite of all his country boy charm, Bill is a very good lawyer.

Judge Bellingham handles all first appearances in Calusa County – all of them, that is, except for the ones that occur on weekends and holidays when a rotating "duty judge" fills in. The system favors Bill in two ways: he gets most of his weekends off, and his judicial brethren are constantly reminded that they would never, ever want his job.

Bill was one of the good old boys in the Bonita State Attorney's Office when I was there. He's a real Florida cracker who always said he only went to law school because he couldn't get into his chosen profession: being a professional fishing guide. Bill and I worked together in the office before I got divorced and moved to Palm Beach, and he stayed on for a couple of years with the Deke Stoner administration after Tom Julian was fired. His ticket out of there came when the governor was looking for someone to appoint to the Calusa County Court bench. Bill was a natural choice: a good, practical lawyer with a brilliant mind and a winning personality. As a new judge, Bill drew the bottom of the barrel – first appearances. He threw himself into the assignment with characteristic gusto and with his innate practicality and street-sense, not to mention down-home Southern drawl, he was able to talk to even the most hardened criminals on a level they understood. His courtroom became a model of efficiency if not decorum. Before long, "Judge Bill" was on his way to becoming a local legend, dispensing rough justice from his jailhouse courtroom. He carved out a kingdom few could handle and even fewer wanted. Everyone agreed Bill had guaranteed himself a lifetime position.

Security at the Terrapin Road courtroom is tight. It has to be; at any given time defendants outnumber court personnel by about four to one, and the law permits only the most serious security risks to be brought into the courtroom in manacles. The deputies who swap fishing stories with Judge Bellingham consider him one of their own and protect him with the same fierce loyalty the Swiss Guards reserve for the Holy Father. Their day starts early; the parking lot was already full when I got there at 8:30. Assistant Attorneys General don't get out here very much, so no one ever thought of reserving a parking space for people like me. I had to fight my way into the visitor's lot and walk across black top that was already beginning to absorb the heat of the Florida sun. Two deputies stopped me inside the front door. I was an unknown quantity, and in spite of my credentials from the State capital I had to wait in line to go through the metal detector.

Once inside the courtroom, I headed for one of the counsel tables and was stopped by another deputy. He politely explained that the front tables were reserved for "state attorneys and public defenders" and I just as politely explained that I was from the Attorney General's Office and was here on assignment from the Office of Statewide Prosecution. After checking my credentials – again – he escorted me to the front of the room, probably to make sure I would sit where he could keep an eye on me.

Bill came out shortly before nine, looking very judicial in his black robe. He began what sounded like a well-rehearsed speech, informing the defendants in the front rows as well as the spectators – mostly family members, I guessed – in the back exactly what would and what would not happen this morning. In most cases, bail would be set and attorneys would be assigned to those who were indigent. Minor offenses for which informations had been filed could be disposed of by a quick plea of guilty and short sentence. Many would receive "time served" which is legalese for "Okay, we caught you. You spent some time in jail. Now get the hell out of here and don't let us see you again . . . at least not until next payday when you'll most likely get into another drunken brawl."

Bill scanned the courtroom while he talked. His face registered surprise when he saw me, and when he ended his prepared remarks he addressed me by name.

"Mr. Bradley, does the Attorney General have something before the Court his morning?"

"Yes, Your Honor. I'm here representing the Office of Statewide Prosecution. We have three defendants who have been indicted for first-degree murder."

"That's the case in this morning's Journal, I'll bet."

"The same, Judge."

"All right, we might as well get you out of here first. What are their names?"

"Grace Stempo, Anita Stempo and Melwin Fanchie, Your Honor."

He turned to one of the deputies. "Do we have anyone here who can get the females down for us?"

"No, Judge."

"Well, see if we can get somebody. We can't have the Attorney General sitting around all morning."

I appreciated his concern, but actually I would be quite happy to sit around his courtroom all morning. My office was probably a madhouse by now. No doubt every half-assed political shark in Calusa County had seen the Journal was trying to figure out what was happening between the General and Deke Stoner. Many of those people would be calling me, trying to act friendly and not incidentally getting a handle on the political situation. Like atheists who go to church for "insurance," they wanted their names on the list— just in case. That way, if our side happened to win whatever pissing contest we were in, at least they could say they had called early and often.

I didn't recognize Melwin until his name was called. He was wearing the jail-issue blue jumpsuit and was seated with the rest of the prisoners. Bill Bellingham took a look at the file and told him to have a seat until the women were brought down. It was a small example of Bellingham efficiency: don't have three arraignments when one will do. It took a while but eventually Grace Stempo and her daughter were brought in, both looking like they were still in shock. They, too, were wearing "Calusa County Blue" as Bill called it; only instead of jumpsuits their clothing consisted of formless smocks in the same color. The two women did not speak to each other. That struck me as unusual, especially since it was unlikely they were being held in the same cellblock. They had probably not seen each other since last night. On the other hand, what did I expect them to say? "How's Dad?" Their names were called and the deputies motioned the three defendants toward the bench and took their places behind them.

"Grace Stempo, Anita Stempo and Melwin Fanchie, each of you has been indicted by the Grand Jury of the State of Florida for murder in the first degree," Judge Bellingham began. "You have the right to remain silent . . ."

Another repetition of "rights" began. This will give the guys in Melwin's cell block something to talk about, I thought. Whenever people are locked up together, the ones charged with first-degree murder go to the top of the social heap. It might be the only time in Melwin's life when his contemporaries actually looked up to him. I wondered whether the same held true for the other two. I didn't know much about the social structure of women behind bars. Were they any more sympathetic than men in the same situation? I doubted it. People behind bars are people behind bars, regardless of their gender. They're macho, or scared, or bored, or crazy, or all of the above. A surprising number take a sudden interest in religion, claiming they have "found Jesus" as if this was the place where He had been living all along, only nobody realized it. Most people in my business don't think jailhouse conversions are real. I disagree. They're real all right. The problem is they don't last past the parole hearing. But as long as they're locked up, most of the converts study their bibles with a ferocity that would put a Southern Baptist to shame.

Grace, Anita and Melwin all said they needed lawyers and did not have funds to hire them. This is the part of the process that always gets me. Consider this: if you were charged with a serious crime and had spent the night in jail, would you want a lawyer? Damn right, you would. Could you afford a lawyer if you really, really needed one and there was no free one to be had? Damn right, you could. It might involve doing some things you wouldn't want to do: things like selling your car or putting the bite on relatives, but if you really, really had to do it, you could. Almost anybody could.

Now put yourself in the position of a prisoner who is asked, "Can you afford a lawyer, or do you want me to appoint one for you for free?" That's a lot like saying, "Hey, can you afford to pay your taxes, or would you rather just skip it this year?" Is it any wonder that the public defenders' offices are the fastest growing government bureaucracies in this country? We've created a great system. Somebody commits a crime and the public pays the cost of investigation, prosecution and punishment. The same public also pays the cost of defense and appeal. It's your tax dollars at work.

"Judge, we'll have a conflict of interest representing all three of these defendants. Two of them will need assigned counsel." A young Assistant Public Defender earning somewhere around thirty thousand dollars a year made an instant decision that would cost the taxpayers of Calusa County – myself included – an extra hundred grand or so. The Public Defender couldn't possibly defend all three of these people. Goodness gracious no! Why, they might have mutually exclusive interests: they might all want to play against each other, for example. One "law firm" couldn't possibly do that! We need to get specially-appointed private counsel in here. Never mind the fact that the P.D.'s office has fifty or more perfectly capable criminal lawyers on its staff, most of whom don't even know each other much less speak to each other. Never mind that there are strict rules of ethics that prohibit talking about a client's case to anyone. Never mind that the P.D.'s — just like the rest of us — are officers of the Court and could be ordered to refrain from discussing the case with each other. The "appearance of impropriety" is what counts. So let's appoint the P.D. for one defendant and get two assigned lawyers — at fifty or a hundred bucks an hour each — for the other two. Calusa County will pay.

I knew Bill Bellingham didn't like the situation any better than I did. Hell, I'd heard the speech from him any number of times back in the old days when we were prosecuting cases together. But rules are rules, and Bill would be looking for an instant reversal and maybe a censure from the appellate court if he didn't follow them. Grace Stempo got the Public Defender; Anita got Paul Berman, and Melwin got a young lawyer by the name of Todd Francesco whom I had never met.

"First degree murder is a capital offense, so there's no bail," Bill explained. "We'll get hold of your assigned attorneys and have them meet you here at the jail. Does anybody have any questions?"

"Can I call my sisters?" Anita asked. Her voice sounded almost hopeful. It was the only time she showed any emotion.

"Sure." He turned to one of the deputies. "Let her call her sisters." Then back to Anita. "How many have you got?"

"Two."

"Okay. Usually they make you call collect, but I guess the county can afford fifty cents." He turned to the deputies. "See that she gets two phone calls — and I mean actually connect. None of this 'leave a message on the machine' business. Got that?"

"We'll pass the word, Judge. She'll get through twice."

"Okay, anything else?" Bill asked the defendants. No one responded.

"I'm going to set this case down for a status check with counsel in two weeks. You all should have been arraigned in the Circuit Court by then. If you have been, that's okay, but I'm going to set a date here anyway so y'all don't get lost in the system someplace. Once I know you've been arraigned with lawyers in the Circuit Court, I'll step aside."

It was typical Bill Bellingham. Leave nothing to chance. Don't let any case, big or small, fall through the cracks. Any lawyer can tell you stories of some poor bastard who wound up spending nine months in the county jail before anybody took the time to listen to him and figure out that he should have been out after thirty days. It happens. Bill was not about to let it happen in his court. A male deputy and two matrons led Grace, Anita and Melwin away, and I turned to go.

"Mr. Bradley, if you're satisfied that things are moving along over there, there's no need for you to come back for another arraignment."

"I understand, Judge."

"I just don't want anybody getting lost on my watch."

It would have been nice to stay and chat, but it would have been completely improper, and besides Bill looked like he had enough to keep him busy for a month. And he would have to somehow plow through all of it before the end of the day. Tomorrow would bring a new day and a new onslaught of defendants. Besides which, I had to get to my office and face whatever music was playing there.

A ton of messages were waiting for me, but only two of them needed a return call. The first was from Rusty Zylka who was Deke Stoner's Chief Assistant; the other was from Sylvia Mendez. I know whatever Zylka wanted wouldn't be good, so I called Sylvia first.

"Hey, Bradley, I made you a star. Can my photographer take good pictures or what?"

"He takes great pictures, Sylvia. I'm returning your call."

"So what do I want, right?"

"Well, since you put it so bluntly . . ."

"I'm a reporter, Bradley. Got to keep the questions short and to the point."

"Okay, so what's the point?"

"My exclusive. What, did you forget already? We had a deal, remember?"

"Sylvia, you knew you that we were investigating the Stempo's for first degree murder, and you managed to get yourself on the scene when we made the arrests. What else do you want?"

"I want my exclusive. I want to know what tipped you off. I want to know if Grace had any gunpowder on her hands. I want to know where they got the gun."

"In other words, you want to know everything."

"Basically, yes."

"All right, Sylvia, a deal is a deal. Come over today and I tell you as much as I can . . . but it won't be everything."

We made an appointment for two-thirty, and I hung up and called Rusty Zylka. I did not expect the conversation to be pleasant. I was right.

"David, so nice to hear from you," he began. I could feel the insincere political smile through the telephone line. It occurred to me that Rusty was the kind of rat who would think nothing of taping a telephone conversation even though that happened to be a felony in our State.

"Nice to hear from you, Rusty. It's been a long time." That was a nice non-committal statement. Let the son-of-a-bitch use that against me if he could.

"So I see your office is going into criminal prosecution.

That's a little unusual, isn't it?"

"Office of Statewide Prosecution, Rusty. Nothing unusual at all."

"Well it's unusual because the Statewide Prosecutor generally pays a courtesy call on the local State Attorney."

"Things like that are policy decisions, Rusty. They're way above my pay grade. I don't have anything to say about them."

"I see." He made that aggravating clicking sound with his mouth that some people do when they're thinking on the telephone. I kept quiet, and that forced him to carry the conversation forward. "So are you going to be handling the case?" he finally asked.

The question now was whether to tell him the truth or stall. It couldn't do any harm to tell the truth, but why should I give this obnoxious jerk any information? On the other hand, if I lied and he already knew the truth, I would be caught and look like a horse's ass. What were the chances that he knew the inner workings of the Attorney General's Office? Sylvia Mendez apparently knew them well enough to stake out our arrest. Zylka might be trading at the same window. I decided on a compromise answer.

"I am for now, Rusty. At least until Helene Hizer replaces me with somebody else."

"Well it's nice to know somebody local is in charge. Why don't you stop by some day and we'll talk? Maybe our office can be of assistance."

"We're out on Palm Lakes Boulevard, Rusty. I don't get downtown too often." Piss on him. There was no way I was going to play in his ballpark. If he wanted to talk to me, he could do it on my field.

"Right. Sure, David. I understand. Why don't I give you a call early next week? Maybe we can do lunch or something."

"Anytime, Rusty. Always anxious to meet with a fellow prosecutor."

We exchanged a few more pleasantries and hung up. The first round went to the Attorney General. It was obvious that Zylka and his boss had been bowled over by the Journal photo, and they were scratching and grabbing for information. The only thing I had given him was to confirm that I was handling the case. Otherwise he was as much in the dark as he was thirty seconds after he opened the morning paper. I could picture Stoner's staff scurrying around their library, trying to do some last-ditch research and come up with a way to screw up our indictment of Joe Stempo's killers.

Back when I was in law school, in prehistoric times, we learned that the body of the law is divided into two great categories: substantive and adjective. Substantive law is the law that says what you can and can't do – kind of like the Ten Commandments. "Thou shalt not kill" is a good example of substantive law. Adjective law is procedural. It's all about how things work, about how the substantive law is put into practice. This morning in Bill Bellingham's courtroom: the formal entry of a plea, the assignment of a lawyer; those things are procedural and are part of the "adjective law."

Good lawyers—make that "really good lawyers"—can kill you with procedure before you ever get up to bat. The "exclusionary rule" is the ultimate example of this kind of thing; the triumph of procedure over substance. It drives most non-lawyers crazy and is the subject of endless radio talk shows. Here's how it works: Let's say that when Jim Harcourt got his search warrant for the Stempo house he had made some mistake; the warrant actually described the house next door, for example. Okay, the warrant is no good. So, the argument goes, the search is illegal. Now let's say Jim's troops found the murder weapon in Anita's dresser drawer. What happens? Nothing. The evidence is "excluded" because of the procedural error. So even though the gun in fact exists, the jury will never know about it.

Any kind of evidence is subject to the exclusionary rule: physical evidence found during a search; statements made when a defendant was not advised of his or her rights; even eyewitness identification; all may be "suppressed" at a hearing before the trial begins. It's one of the reasons trial lawyers take so much time selecting jurors who know nothing about the case. What people hear on the street or see in the newspapers may be nothing like the evidence that finally makes it into the courtroom.

I expected to get bombarded with pre-trial suppression motions because so much of our case depended on self-incriminatory statements. If the defense could get those statements excluded for any reason, our side would lose the ability to tie everything up for the jury at the end of the case. Any ballplayer knows its no use winning the early innings if you don't have a "closer" waiting in the bullpen. It wouldn't hurt me to spend a few hours in the library reading some case law, and that's where Sylvia Mendez found me.

"Must be a tough case if you're hitting the books already." Her words sounded like she was trying to needle me, but her smile betrayed her.

"How did you get in here? Mary Ellen should have called me."

"We investigative reporters have our ways, David."

"Oh, it's 'investigative reporter' now? Is that all in capital letters, or just with a capital 'I' and a capital 'R'?" I smiled back when I said it. Sylvia was okay, but I wouldn't want to get on the wrong side of her. She ignored my remark and perched demurely on a corner of the library table, her long legs replacing the books that had previously occupied all my attention.

"Okay, so what have you got for me?" she said in a way that left open any number of answers.

"So why is the Attorney General involved?" she added.

I looked at her and kept my mouth firmly shut.

"I need something to print, Bradley."

Again I did not respond.

"You want me to print the truth?" she demanded.

"And what might that be?"

"That the Attorney General wants to make Deke Stoner look stupid because Stoner had the balls to run against him in the last primary."

I tried to protest, but she ran right over me.

"*And* if he can make Stoner look really bad, maybe it will knock him out of next year's primary – and eliminate him politically. I'm sure you know he's already threatened to switch parties and run in the general election if he doesn't get the party's nomination."

"Sylvia, you've been reading too many political novels. The Attorney General is in this case because it involves two judicial circuits. It's a case of Statewide Prosecution, pure and simple."

"That's your quote?"

"That's my quote."

"I'll bet Stoner has a different version."

"Why don't you ask him?"

"I will, this afternoon at his press conference."

"At his what?"

"Haven't you heard?" she said, batting her big green eyes. "State Attorney Deke Stoner is having a press conference in the parking lot of the courthouse at four o'clock today. Just in time for the early news."

CHAPTER 11

Barbara left her studio and picked me up before quitting time so we could catch the early news at home. Once there, we broke one of the immutable laws of our household: we kept the television on while we prepared dinner and then ate as she called it "American Fashion" – in front of the TV. Deke Stoner's press conference was the lead story at 5:30. We switched channels at 6:00, and there he was again, at a different angle this time. At 6:30 he even got a spot on the national news. The message was always the same.

"The City of Sabal Palms is about twenty miles in that direction," Deke said as he squinted into the afternoon sun and gestured with his left hand. "And Tallahassee is about four hundred miles north." Right hand gesture this time, as he turned slightly toward the capital. "Now, if the Attorney General of this State thinks he can do a better job from four hundred and twenty miles away than I can do right here on the scene, let him try. My office relied on the findings of our local medical examiner and our local police department when we said Joe Stempo's death was a suicide. I have a great deal of faith in our local officials, and I intend to support them every step of the way in this case."

"So it's to be "Us Against Them," is it?" Barb asked as she refilled our wine glasses.

"What did you expect?"

"I don't know; professionalism, perhaps; possibly even cooperation. Do you think he's worried?"

"I didn't think so at first," I replied. "But after seeing him for the third time, I'm not so sure. It could be a great political move: 'I'm supportin' my boys, and if they're wrong, well, by Gawd, I intend to stick by 'em come hell 'er high water.' I can see that kind of gambit working for Deke regardless of how the trial turns out."

"So you don't think he'll try to sabotage your case?"

"Try, maybe. But I can't see how he can legally block us. No, I'd say that tonight makes it official: Deke Stoner is going to take on the Attorney General in the court of public opinion."

"Come on, let's do the washing up," she said, ending the conversation and moving into the kitchen. Obviously she did not understand – or care for – the finer points of local politics.

'Doing the washing up' means 'doing the dishes' in American English, and it isn't much of a chore at our place. It means stacking the plates in the dishwasher. It's really just an excuse to share a project and spend a little time together. Some very serious subjects get discussed during the 'washing up.' I was in that kind of mood tonight.

"Barb, do you think it's possible for people's attitudes to change?"

"Oh, I very much doubt it. Most people I know are pretty well set in their ways. I would be very surprised if any of them exhibited any real change."

"How about if a person went through a real crisis, a life-threatening crisis, do you think that might make a change?"

She put down the plate she was holding and looked at me suspiciously. "Who are we talking about, David?"

"What was I going to tell her, that we were talking about me? My attitudes? That I wasn't so sure about my chosen profession anymore? That I had begun to think that maybe Anita Stempo was at least morally justified in killing her father? And did I really believe that? Was she justified? Even if she was telling the truth; even if he raped her – not that she ever said he did – but, even then, would she be morally justified in killing him in cold blood many years later? Isn't that "law," the "law of the vendetta," one of the very things our society was created to prevent? I had been wrestling with that problem ever since the night of the arrest, and what bothered me more than the dilemma itself was the fact that this kind of second-guessing wasn't like me. I had always been so sure of the answers: present the State's case; leave the rest to the judge and jury. Now I had begun to wonder if that was an acceptable philosophy, or just another cop-out. "We have an adversarial system," I used to say whenever someone cornered me at a cocktail party. "I didn't create it; I only work in it. If I don't represent my client to the best of my ability, the system will break down. It won't function." It was the standard law school speech, but now I was having trouble selling it to myself. I smiled at Barbara. She was still looking at me as if I had just announced I was born on another planet. "We're not talking about anyone in particular," I said innocently. "I was just making conversation."

I could tell that answer didn't satisfy her. Fortunately it didn't matter because she had other things on her mind. "Well I'm going to give you a highly sensuous back rub with some scented oil I've been saving," she said, pressing her body against mine. "You've been much too tense lately, and it will help you relax."

"Are you sure you're not trying to get a little relaxed yourself?" I asked, nuzzling her neck. I loved kissing her there. She always smelled so good.

"There may be some ancillary benefit to me, I supposed. We'll just have to see what comes up," she said with a playful smile.

I wasn't about to respond to that last line; it was too perfect the way it was. The dishes didn't take long to finish, especially since I knew what she had in mind. That's what's so great about labor-saving appliances. They save time and energy for more important things.

I headed to the shower. It felt incredibly good to have the hot water pounding the back of my neck. I knew Barb was right; I was too tense. The strange thing was, this wasn't the way I remembered it. I had always been the star of the show, the actor who paced the courtroom and ran a hand along the rail of the jury box. It was always a show, just a show. It struck me as strange that as I stood there under the streaming water, I was able to recall only bits and pieces of trials – not the whole of any one in particular. I could not remember more than one or two defendants; their names faces, anything. And the only ones I could remember were the ones whom I felt should not have been convicted – even though they were guilty as hell. Those few still bothered me, and I had to remind myself that it was the jury, not me, who had sealed their fates.

The shower door slid open and Barbara stepped in with me.

"Mind if I join you?" She looked delicious as the steamy water cascaded over her creamy skin. The triangular patch she had shaved off in Tallahassee had begun to grow back in. It wasn't yet dense enough to hide the delicious fold where her legs met, and instead of concealing her charms it served as focus for my attention.

She pressed up against me and my hands roamed down her back to where the curvature of her rump began. "What are you thinking about?" she asked.

"Just thinking how wonderful nature is."

"David, you haven't been yourself since this case began."

"I know. I guess I've been ignoring you."

"It's not me that I'm worried about. When I first met you, trials were a big turn-on. Whenever you were in trial you always acted like you were on some kind of narcotic. Now it seems you spend most of your time lost in thought. Wouldn't it be better to give this case to Tom?"

"No. Not at all," I protested. "I'm fine. It's just that well . . . if you must know, it's just that sometimes I worry if I still know how." That wasn't what I was worried about. Hell, trying a lawsuit is like riding a bicycle; you never forget "how." Ben Cardin, my old section partner in the State Attorney's Office used to say that being a prosecutor was like being a bus driver: you could walk into any city in the United States and get a job. I smiled at Barbara, and she wrapped her arms around my neck as the hot water streamed down my back and the steam swirled around us.

"You're not telling me the truth, are you?"

"Yes, I am," I responded lamely. "I really am, Barb. I guess I'm just out of practice a little bit."

"And you won't consider giving this case to Tom?"

I looked at her and shook my head.

"Come on," she said as she reached behind me and shut off the faucets, "our utility bills are high enough. We have to pay for all this water, you know.

Barb had two large towels waiting for us, but it was my idea to use them on each other. Whenever I toweled myself off after a shower, she always complained that I never finished the job and climbed into bed wet. I would blame it on the humidity but the truth was that I was in a hurry to join her. Besides, I don't get much of a thrill out of touching myself. Now with her, it was a different story. I caressed every part of her body with that soft towel. Doing each other was a much better idea; I didn't mind spending as much time as necessary to get every square inch of her skin dry.

We moved to the bedroom where I sprawled face down on the bed and waited for the soft caress of her hands. She began by lighting a candle and warming the special oil. The scent of jasmine filled the room. It recalled tropical nights on the French side of St. Maarten where we had spent our honeymoon, walking on the beach in the moonlight and making love under the stars next to the night-flowering shrubs outside our bungalow. After my little health problem and the depression that followed it a few years ago, thoughts of St. Maarten were often the only things that kept me from doing myself in. I kept promising myself that someday we would return there – and possibly stay forever.

Barb poured the warm oil between my shoulders. The feeling made me shiver involuntarily. I knew what was coming, and the thought of her touch was almost as exquisite as the reality that followed moments later.

"Isn't that better?" she asked as she kneaded my flesh at the base of my neck. I moaned in response. Speaking might break the spell. If this was a dream, I didn't want to wake up.

She spread the oil to my shoulders and then moved down my right arm to a troublesome spot that I attribute to my college baseball days; too much throwing or something. My genius cousin "the Doctor" examined it and says there's nothing wrong with me, but I'm the one who sometimes stays awake at night because of the pain. Barbara has heard me complain about it often enough, and now as she worked on that spot I began to forget everything else and drift off. Maybe I'm getting old, but the feeling of her fingers pressing into my upper arm was better than an orgasm.

The room was dark when I woke up: dark and empty. I heard a sound coming from the other end of our apartment and I got up to investigate. Barbara was asleep on the couch while an old movie flickered on the television screen. She woke up when I kissed her softly. "Hey? Are you going to spend the night out here?" I asked.

"Huh? Oh, I'm sorry. You fell asleep and I didn't want to disturb you," she replied.

"I don't remember anything that happened after you got to my arm."

"Perhaps that's because nothing happened," she said with a sleepy smile.

"Then I'm the one who's sorry."

"Nonsense," she said. "You've been under a lot of stress. I'm glad you were able to get some rest. Come on, let's go to bed."

We acted on her suggestion and although she cuddled against me, I just couldn't get into the mood. And that bothered me. It was the first time in our marriage that I thought of a bed primarily for the purpose of sleeping, but I was too tired to worry about it at the moment and I fell back into a dreamless sleep within minutes.

I felt crummy about it at breakfast. It's strange, isn't it? Sometimes you do it and feel crummy in the morning, and sometimes you don't do it and feel crummy in the morning. I guess it all depends on who wakes up with you. Anyway, crummy was the word of the moment. I pushed around my Grape-Nuts in silence while Barb busied herself with making a bowl of fresh fruit and mixing it with yogurt.

"I'm sorry about last night," I said, breaking the silence.

"David, don't be silly. You were just tired, that's all.

Don't worry about it."

"I am worried about it, Barbara. That's always been an important part of my life . . . our lives" – she looked at me as if to say something, but I beat her to it – "okay, maybe too important. But I'm not willing to give it up just yet."

"David, you were tired. You fell asleep," she said sternly. "Don't let's make more out of it than that."

She was right, of course. But that didn't make me feel any better. I was going to say something – probably something completely idiotic about how important performance is to the male ego – when the doorbell rang. It was Walter VanDiale, our across-the-hall neighbor, self-appointed overseer of the public good and condo commando extraordinaire.

"Listen, I hope you know what you were doing, having those fellas work on your mailbox like that," Walter began, assuming as usual that I knew what he was talking about and gave a royal damn.

"I don't have the foggiest idea what you're talking about, Walter."

"Those young fellas. Said you were having your mailbox wired for a burglar alarm. Not that it's a bad idea, but work like that is supposed to be okayed by the Board first, and we gotta make sure they're licensed."

Barbara had joined me at the door while Walter was still performing his monologue. "David, what is he talking about?" she asked. I detected something like the sound of fear in her voice.

"Walter, I didn't hire anyone to do anything to my mailbox," I said, putting an arm around my wife and trying to calm her.

"Well there were two fellas out there yesterday afternoon. Didn't you pick up your mail? You always pick it up when you come home at night."

What else did he keep track of? I wondered if he kept an ear to our door when we were making love. Still, at the moment it sounded like an extra pair of ears – and eyes – might be working to our advantage. "I . . . we were in a hurry when we got home last night . . ." I began to explain, and then I cut myself off. What we did and when we did it was none of his damn business. "We didn't pick up the mail last night."

Barbara was holding me now. "David, call Clive Watkins," she begged.

I knew what she was thinking: the bomb in the mailbox bit. It was a mainstay in the plot of every cop/lawyer show and two-bit novel. Only it never happens in real life, and I wasn't about to get caught up that kind of nonsense. I was prosecuting a garden-variety murder for chrissake. Let's not get all melodramatic.

"Stay here. I'm going to see what this is all about," I said in my best macho-man voice. I promised myself that when I got to the office I was going to call our condo manager and raise hell about our so-called security people in the guardhouse. What the hell was the sense of living in a gated community if every wasteoid in Calusa County could get into the place?

"David, please. Call Clive." It was Barbara, trying to hold me back and again begging me to call Watkins. Yeah. Right. Call him and ask him to open my mailbox because my picture had appeared on the front page of the newspaper. Let's see if I could live that one down when this was all over.

"Barbara, say here." I meant it this time, and I tried to convey that message by the tone of my voice. I guess she didn't get the message.

"I will not!" she insisted. "I'm coming with you!"

Of course it would have been far too much to expect

Walter mind-everybody's-business VanDiale to stay behind. He didn't. In a minute the three of us were packed into the elevator and heading down to the mailboxes on the first floor.

"Now, damn it, stay here," I shouted at both of them before I headed across the open area in front of the elevator to the wall that held the mailboxes for our building. Maybe the tone of my voice got to them, or maybe they were held back by some sense of self-preservation that many people seem to have. Whatever it was, they stayed behind. I tried not to think about what I was doing while I strode over to the wall and slipped the key into the mailbox. At that moment I suddenly had the same sense. If the damn thing was wired it might be set to go off when I turned the key. But if I backed down, Barbara would know that I gave some credence to her fears and she would really freak out. I decided to put up a good show and hope the whole thing was some kind of stupid mistake. I held my breath and turned the key, half expecting to feel an explosion rip my guts out. Nothing happened. I drew a deep breath and was about to yank the damn door open when I got a prickly feeling on the back of my neck. This little game might not be over. Just because I got lucky once was not reason to go for a double play.

"All right, keep back," I repeated to my two escorts. I flattened myself against the wall, took out my trusty Swiss army penknife and used the blade to flip open the door.

A quart-size plastic bottle fell out and rolled across the Chattahoochee floor. Something told me to cover up and just as I was bringing my arm up and turning my face aside the thing went off with a roar that could have been heard out at the front gate. It slammed me hard against the wall; the air was ripped out of my lungs and my skin felt like a million needles were flailing it. I remember hearing Barbara scream. And then I didn't hear anything.

I don't know what happened next, but I awoke to the sound of thousands of crickets all chirping inside my head at the same time. And I was in a lot of pain – crushing, nauseating pain; more pain than I ever felt from a heart attack. I used to think nitro headaches were bad; they were a pleasure compared to the way my head felt at that moment. It took me a couple of minutes to figure out where I was. In spite of the cricket noise I knew I wasn't outside. I was in the kind of narrow bed with side rails and white sheets that could only mean a hospital, and the goldfish bowl type room meant intensive care. I wondered through blurred eyes how I got there.

Barb was sitting in a chair nearby. She grabbed my hand when I opened my eyes. "Clive, he's coming around," were the first words I heard through the noise of the crickets.

Sure enough, Sarge was there, looking older and a little grayer. Jim Harcourt was in another corner of the room. I was sure they were sidestepping hospital regulations about the number of visitors in the room, and I hoped they didn't expect me to discuss the progress of our case.

"You scared the crap out of us, Dave," Watkins said. "Do you know you're supposed to call the police for things like that?"

I tried to ask him what happened, but my voice wasn't working too well, and my head hurt too much to lift it off the pillow.

Harcourt moved closer to the bed. "It was a pretty crude bomb, Dave. Any kid could have made it." Leave it to Jim to give me an official analysis when my head was pounding like a pile driver. "Pool cleaner and tinfoil," he explained. "Set the thing up so that it falls over and they mix together. It'll give you a hell of a bang."

"It did," I managed to croak out from between caked lips. The mention of pool cleaner drew my attention to the throbbing in my chest and left arm. I hoped the pain wasn't caused by acid burns, but the way I felt made me suspect it would be a long time before those areas would again be ready for Barbara's soothing touch.

"I've got some of my men running checks on Melwin's Jolly Boys. We'll find out who did it.

"What makes you think it's them?" If I squeezed my eyes shut hard enough I could block out a little of the pain.

"Are you joking? Can you see any of Grace's friends pulling something like this?" Jim replied.

If it was the Jolly Boys, I wanted to ask him how he was going to keep them from taking another shot at me, or maybe hurting Barbara. Watkins anticipated my question.

"Looks like I'm gonna be your house guest for a while, Dave. I hope we can have meatloaf every now and then."

"Clive gave me a little device that starts the car from a block away, Darling," Barbara added, holding up a small box. "I'll be perfectly safe." She smiled bravely, but I knew she didn't like this situation any better than I did. I wanted to apologize to her and tell her that I loved her. This mess was all my fault. I wanted to try a simple little murder case, not get involved in something where I put her life in danger.

"How long am I going to be here?" I croaked. My mouth tasted like I had eaten gravel for breakfast, and my voice sounded like most of the gravel had gotten stuck in my throat.

"Doctor says you'll be out of intensive care tomorrow or the day after" Barb replied. "And he hopes to have you home in a week."

"I'm not going to give up," I warned her.

"We'll talk about it after you're home." She leaned over

and kissed my forehead. It was nice to know I still had one. "Clive and I are going out for supper; we'll be back for the evening visit."

"Evening? What time is it?"

"Nurse is here with your injection, Darling," Barbara replied. "We have to leave." She kissed my forehead again. "We'll be back soon."

Before I could protest a nurse was sticking a hypodermic needle into a tube that went from a bag of clear liquid to somewhere in the back of my right hand. I saw her push the plunger, and a minute or two later the crickets stopped chirping and I didn't care what time it was. I wanted to think of St. Maarten, but the only images that came to mind were of my grandparents' house in Sandusky. I fell asleep thinking I was there.

My recovery was pretty boring. It consisting mostly of being moved to a private room, having dressings changed three times a day and being bored stiff by moronic daytime television. The crickets slowly died away, but I was left with a ringing in one ear and a hearing loss that may or may not be permanent. Doctor Ventura was true to his word; I went home in a week. What he didn't tell me until I was discharged was that just because I went home didn't mean I was allowed to leave our condo. I spent another three weeks bouncing off the walls and walking around the grounds with Clive Watkins when he wasn't chauffeuring me to twice-a-week appointments where the good doctor checked on my progress. And needless to say, the security at our condo guard gate was greatly improved.

I was more worried about Barbara than myself. If the Jolly Boys planted a bomb and were nuts enough to try to blow me away, there was no reason to believe they'd stay away from her. The Sheriff's Office had increased its patrols on Bonita Key, but Barb insisted that Bear Harper's offer of a full-time officer at her studio would be bad for what she called her "upscale image," and whoever was running the show in Tallahassee never got around to approving my request for 'round the clock undercover surveillance. Without that approval, Jim Harcourt's hands were tied. He reminded me that was on a special assignment; he didn't have the authority to pull local agents off their cases to keep an eye on her.

There was something else that bothered me. It was kind of nice having Clive Watkins around; he provided a much-needed feeling of security. But good old Ben Franklin once said that "Fish and visitors stink after three days," and we were going on three weeks. Barbara and I were used to a lot of privacy. No matter how much Sarge tried to mind his own business and stay out of the way, he was still there: underfoot, so to speak. Even though it was for our own good, it was one more stressor that we didn't need at the moment. Something was bound to give, and I was afraid it might be my marriage.

I tried to talk to Sarge about it out on the patio one afternoon after we returned from the doctor's office. He caught the drift of my conversation right away.

"I don't like this any better than you do, Counselor," he reminded me as he put a fresh glass of soda water down next to my lounge chair. "I'm just here to keep you from getting your rear-end blown off until the trial is over."

"Sarge, it's not that we don't appreciate what you're doing," I tried to explain.

"I know. I know. You just like to have a little afternoon delight every now and then. Jesus Christ, Dave, can't you think about anything else? Someday that dick of yours is going to get somebody killed."

"It's not that, Sarge, it's just that . . ." He looked at me and I broke off. What the hell was I supposed to tell him?

That Barbara enjoyed running around in a thong bikini? Or less? That we didn't always fit the image of a staid, professional couple? I wasn't about to get into a discussion of our personal lives with him. "It's just a little hard getting used to someone else in the house, that's all," I suggested rather lamely.

"Yeah, well like I said, I'm not any crazier about it than you are. We're just going to have to put up with each other until the trial's over."

"And then what? If it *is* the Jolly Boys, and they're as bad as you say, do you think they're going to give up just because Melwin's in prison?"

He looked at me seriously. "You can always move back to Palm Beach," he said without a trace of humor in his voice.

I was about to tell him what he could do with that idea when the telephone rang. It was Barbara. Her voice was trembling with fear. For a brief instant the thought flashed through my mind that she had been kidnapped, that the Jolly Boys were holding her somewhere, forcing her to make this call while they put a gun to her head.

"David . . ."

"Barbara! Are you all right?"

"David . . . there's been another explosion. Deanna is dead!"

Deanna Tracy. Barbara's partner in the studio. The woman who befriended her when we moved to Bonita two years ago. "Are you all right?" I demanded again. I couldn't sort out all my feelings at the moment, but it was a relief to hear Barbara's voice.

"I'm fine . . . I . . ." She began sobbing. "Deanna took my keys when I wasn't looking . . . my car . . ." she sobbed, "my car must have been blocking hers . . ."

"Are the police there?"

"They're here right now . . . and the fire brigade is putting out the fire in the street. Deanna's body is . . . still . . ."

"Are you inside the studio?"

"Yes," she sobbed.

"And the police are with you right now?"

"Yes . . . that's right." Her voice was trembling; she was obviously in shock.

"Stay right there. Don't let them leave. Clive and I will be right over."

Sarge had heard enough of my end of the conversation to know something was drastically wrong. "Another bomb," I said as I slammed down the phone. "This one killed her partner."

"Dave, you shouldn't be going out . . ." he protested. He had to know I wouldn't listen. "All right, I'll drive," he conceded before I could tell him to stuff it.

The studio was located in the village of Calkins Harbor, more or less in the center of Bonita Key. Calkins Harbor is a little Florida backwater that time forgot. If history was any guide, the tourists and snowbirds soon would find about it and turn it into an upscale-quaint-artsy-fartsy place where the locals couldn't afford to live. Barbara and Deanna had located their studio there in hopes of riding that wave. Sarge and I were across the bridge to the island in minutes. The firefighters were finishing up on the smoldering hulk of what had once been my Thunderbird; I tried not to look at what was in the front seat as I jumped out of Sarge's unmarked car and dashed inside. Barb was talking to a uniformed officer, holding herself with her arms across her chest and one hand up to her head. I ran over to her and she huddled in my arms.

"It's all my fault," she sobbed. "I didn't tell her about the starting device because I didn't want to frighten her. And now she's dead." She buried her head in my chest. "It's all my fault," she sobbed again.

"It's not your fault," I told her. "And everything is going to be okay," I added as I stroked her hair.

"No, it's not going to be 'okay,' David! I'm leaving! I'm going back to Palm Beach. I'm leaving tonight."

"You're just upset right now," I tried to reason with her.

She pulled away angrily. "I am not 'just upset right now'!" she screamed as Sarge walked in. "My best friend is dead. My dream of a quiet upscale studio is finished! And I'm worn out! I'm tired of needing to start our car with electronic devices!" she shouted, venting the pent-up anger and frustration this case had caused. "I'm tired of having my flesh crawl every time the telephone rings!" She caught sight of Sarge. "And I'm tired of living with people underfoot!" she added, looking at him while she was screaming at me. She looked at me again, exhausted from her outburst. "I want my life back, David. I want our quiet suppers on the patio and moonlight walks on the beach. If you love me you'll want those things too, and you'll come with me."

"I can't do that," I said quietly.

"Why not? Why can't you give up this horrid case?" she sobbed, pulling her hands through her blond hair.

"Barbara, I love you more than anything, but there's one thing I won't do and that's run away from a fight."

"But it's not running away, don't you see?" she pleaded with tears in her eyes. "This isn't your job. It was never supposed to be your job. It's just some horrid case you've gotten yourself involved in for no reason." She ran to me and held me close. "Come back with me, David. We can go back to Palm Beach and have things the way they were. Please."

I shook my head. I wanted to say yes; I really did. But

whoever was doing this had made it a personal matter. And I was going to see the son-of-a-bitch pay for it.

"Why can't you come with me?" she insisted. "Why can't you give this case to Tom and come with me?"

"It won't stop them, Barbara. If they're after me, I'll just draw them to you. It's better for both of us if I stay here and fight it out. I can join you in Palm Beach once we get the bastards convicted." Actually, I wasn't sure about that. Whoever they were – if it was a "they" – might well have the power to follow us across the state. The only solution to the problem was to fight them out on their home turf and keep them so busy they didn't have time to launch an offense. Besides, I wasn't about to turn tail and let the assholes win.

Clive Watkins was taking in the whole conversation. He didn't say anything, but he had to know I was right. It was a lot easier for him to protect one person than two, and if Jim Harcourt was right – if it was the beginning of a drug gang takeover in what had always been a quiet Florida community – the time to crush it was now before it got too powerful. Clive put a reassuring hand on Barbara's arm. "Maybe it would be best if you left, just for a while," he suggested. "He can join you over there in a few weeks when this is finished."

Barb nodded her head in defeat. "Please drive me home so I can get my things," she said quietly.

CHAPTER 12

It was a long, bitter night. Our minds were made up, and each of us was too stubborn to change. In spite of Barb's desire to get away from Bonita as soon as possible, she couldn't get a flight to Palm Beach until almost noon the next day. There wasn't any cheerful banter in the car as Clive Watkins drove us to the airport. We sat in the back seat, and after a while Barb sneaked her hand across to mine. I squeezed hers back. I was sorry it had come to this, but I wasn't going to run out now. Besides, she was better off, out of harm's way. At least I wouldn't have to worry about her. After it was all over, we could try to put things back together.

We walked wordlessly to the gate, each of us lost in our own thoughts while Sarge gallantly followed with her small carry-on bag.

"Promise me you'll be careful," she said in a small voice when we reached the gate.

"I'll be careful," I groused.

"And you'll take your medication every day?"

"Barbara, I'm an adult. I'm perfectly capable . . ." I was cut off by the boarding announcement.

"David, perhaps I should stay . . ." she offered.

"The plans have been made," I protested. "Alan and Monique are waiting for you in Palm Beach. You can stay with them for now." I hugged her without much emotion. "I'll be along in a few weeks." I wondered if I was lying when I said it.

The gate attendant repeated the boarding announcement. There were only a few passengers for the short hop across the state, and everybody else was on the plane. I tried to kiss Barb gently, but she suddenly held me tight, and I got the sickening feeling that I might not see her again. "Let's not make a scene," I whispered, appealing to her stiff-upper-lip, ever-so-proper British genes.

"Appearances be damned," she cried. "Hold me for a minute."

The attendant announced the flight one more time. It was painfully obvious now that she was directing her attention to only one passenger: the one in my arms.

"Come on, Barb, the plane is waiting," I said quietly.

She nodded her head, let go and walked out onto the tarmac. I watched her carefully as she climbed the steps to the plane. She didn't look back.

Clive Watkins put his hand on my shoulder as the aircraft taxied away from the terminal. "Come on," he said, "let's grab some lunch."

"Where are we going?" I asked as I followed him outside to his unmarked car.

"There's a place over on Coacoochee Boulevard called Vasilli's," he replied.

"I'm not in the mood for Italian food," I muttered. The truth was I wasn't in the mood for anything other than a good stiff drink; in fact, I was in the mood for several of them.

"It's Greek," he replied. "Besides, we're not going for

the food. Mollie Sussman works there. She's got a part-time job. I figured a little old-fashioned police work would get your mind off your own problems."

"How do you get these leads, Sarge?" I asked as he drove out of the airport parking lot.

"I just keep my ears open, Counselor. I ask a few questions and keep my ears open."

If Vasilli's had an architectural style it would have to be called Greek Art Deco. Its new-made-to-look-old appearance was a function of its reclaimed brick exterior and arched windows. We entered through an arbor of artificial grapes and a small glass lobby containing the inevitable statute of Venus di Milo. Once inside we walked past a counter until a chunky blonde and a "Hostess Will Seat You" sign stopped us. Sarge said something about Mollie to the woman who greeted him. She smiled, escorted us to a table flanked by two captain's chairs with red vinyl seats and handed us red and yellow menus that were only slightly smaller than the Bonita Journal. This was the kind of place where once upon a time I would have come for a barbequed pork sandwich and French fries smothered with gravy. And now you know at least one of the reasons why I had a heart attack so early in life.

"I told her I was Mollie's uncle," Sarge said after the hostess left, "so she we got one of her tables."

The object of our expedition soon appeared at our table dressed in a flouncy white blouse and black skirt that must have been the uniform of the place. She hesitated when she recognized her newest customers.

"Oh, hi," she said to Sarge, trying not to look at my bandaged left arm.

"Hello, Mollie," I interjected. Her eyes finally left Watkins and she looked at me.

"Oh, hello, Mr. Bradley." She almost sighed with relief

when I didn't hand her a subpoena. "I really want to thank you for those tickets to Disney World. Me and my Mom had a great time."

"It was my pleasure, Mollie. Maybe we can all get together when this case is over and go back there or something."

"Yeah, I guess."

"Mollie, we need a little more help," Watkins bulldozed his way into the conversation. "Somebody tried to kill Mr. Bradley's wife yesterday." The girl looked at him with a shocked expression but she said nothing. "We think it might have something to do with Melwin and the Jolly Boys." Still no answer from our young waitress. "Do you know anybody who might know anything about that, Mollie?"

The girl bit her lower lip. "Gosh, no. I . . . well, I don't guess I'd know anything about any Jolly Boys. Who are they, anyway?"

I held her eyes and explained quietly, "We didn't think you knew any of them, Mollie; we just thought maybe you had heard of somebody who had. You can understand that, can't you?" I didn't want the kid to think we were trying to implicate her.

"Sure, I understand," she said. "But, like, not any of the kids I know would do anything like that."

"If it's not the Jolly Boys, if it's somebody we don't know, then I guess we might have an even bigger problem," I said.

She glanced around the dining room with a worried look and said that she better take our order. Sarge ordered a bacon cheeseburger with lettuce, tomato and extra mayo, and readily accepted her suggestion of fries. I stuck to a salad and iced tea.

"You know you're going to kill yourself with that kind of

diet," I lectured after she left.

"Hey, knock it off. You're the one with the bad heart. I've been eating like this my whole life and I never felt better."

"Maybe that says something about the difference in stress levels between policemen and lawyers," I suggested. "Do you think she knows anything?"

"She's thinkin' about it. That was a nice little speech you gave her, about going back to Disney."

"I meant it. Mollie's a good kid who deserves a break."

Sarge didn't answer. I looked around the dining room that was made of the same reclaimed brick as the outside of the building. A few notches here and there held ersatz Grecian busts that carried out the theme of the place and softened the monotony of the walls and quarry tile floor. The rest of the décor consisted of potted plants suspended from the ceiling.

"Don't tell me; I'll bet this place is open twenty-four-seven, right?"

His expression answered my question.

"What does reclaimed brick have to do with Greece?"

Sarge shrugged. "You'll have to ask Vasilli. He had the place built right around his original diner. Never missed a day. The brick and statues were his idea. Anyway he's got a gold mine here. The food's decent, the prices are right, and he's always open."

"Which makes it perfect for people in your line of work," I observed.

He shrugged. "Here . . . Jersey . . . it's the same all over, Dave. Cops and Greek restaurants: they feed off each other just like lawyers and those crummy courthouse coffee shops the disabled folks run."

I had never thought about it in terms of a symbiotic relationship, but I had to admit he was right. I don't think

I've ever been in a courthouse that didn't have the kind of coffee shop he was talking about.

The arrival of Mollie and our lunch cut off further discussion. She didn't have anything to add to our earlier conversation, and I didn't push it. Even if the kid knew something, I didn't want Watkins to sweat any more information out of her; she had been through enough. I had pretty much given up hope of getting anything more out of her when she returned and handed us our checks.

"Thanks, Mollie. Lunch was great," I said as she looked down at her hands. Her eyes did not move.

"Mr. Bradley, I . . . well, I don't know anything about Jolly Boys, but I do know something else about that gun."

"I'd really like to hear anything you know, Mollie."

"One of the kids at school, I mean, who goes to our school, well, he's sort of a friend of me and Anita. And I guess she showed him the gun one day and even let him shoot it. That's really all I know about it. Honest."

"What's this boy's name?" I asked.

"Ian. Ian Highsmith. I'm not real sure where he lives."

"That's okay, Mollie. I really appreciate you taking the time to think about this."

"I'm not going to get him in trouble too, am I?"

"Mollie, you didn't get anyone in trouble. We found out about Anita because Melwin started shooting off his mouth. And Ian's not in any trouble at all."

"You won't tell him I told you?"

"I promise."

She smiled for the first time. "Thanks, Mr. Bradley. And thanks again for Disney World."

"Mollie, what I said about getting together and going back there . . . I meant that."

"Okay, sure. I'll tell my Mom."

Watkins raised his eyebrows when he saw me leave a

ten-dollar tip. Hell, the kid needed it, I explained. It was comforting to know there were a few decent kids left who were trying to get ahead in the world. Out in the lobby we checked the directory at the pay phone that was conveniently located between Venus di Milo and the last of the plastic grapes. There were three Highsmith's in the area, but only one of them was near Anita Stempo's school. Maybe I should have asked Sarge or Jim Harcourt or to investigate this lead, but we both knew I needed something to do. Sarge didn't object when I suggested that he drive down to Oakland Beach to find out what Ian knew about our case.

The town where the Highsmith's live is older than the adjoining city of Sabal Palms which was built right over the line in Cypress County. Their town, Oakland Beach, is one of many that got caught in the boom-and-bust cycle of Florida real estate. Places like this sprang up in the Fifties, filled with two-bedroom, one-bath and three-bedroom, two-bath houses built of concrete block and stucco. They're so common that "2/1", "3/2" and "CBS" have become part of the argot of South Florida just like "Tamiami Trail" and "Dixie Highway." Developers built these places and sold them for peanuts, and the people who bought them were astonished to learn they could get forty or fifty thousand dollars for them when they sold out in the Sixties and early Seventies. And that wasn't the end of the story. The people who bought them found that by the late Eighties real estate brokers were mentioning numbers like ninety and a hundred thousand dollars for the very same houses. Some people got out; many did not, waiting for prices to go even higher. Today the litany of many a Florida household begins with the words, "If only I had . . ."

The Highsmith house was one of those. One-story CBS, two-car carport with half of it converted into a storage shed. That meant either they had one car or one of two cars stayed outside and got baked by the sun. A woman dressed in shorts and a tee shirt came to the door. She looked to be around forty, with short hair and a pleasant face, and she spoke to Watkins and me through the screen.

"Can I help you?"

"Mrs. Highsmith?" She nodded and Sarge took out his badge. "I'm Sergeant Watkins from the Calusa County Sheriff's Office. This is Mr. Bradley from the Attorney General's Office. We'd like to talk to you for a minute if we may."

Her jaw tightened. "What's wrong?"

"Nothing's wrong, Mrs. Highsmith," I replied, attempting to reassure her. "We're working on a case and we think your son Ian might have some information.

"Has he done something?" Her face hardened more.

"No," I said quickly. "He hasn't done anything. We just think he might be a witness to something. We'd really like to talk to him if that's all right."

"My husband's not home," she protested.

"This will only take a minute."

"My son is mentally challenged; some people might even call him retarded, Mister . . ."

"Bradley. David Bradley. I'm very sorry to hear that."

"And I think it would be better if you talked to him when his father is home."

"I understand, Mrs. Highsmith."

"No, I'm afraid you don't understand, Mr. Bradley. Physically my son is eighteen; mentally he's half that age. He's old enough to hang around with other kids and get into trouble with them, but not always old enough to know why he's in trouble. He'll never get married; never have children. Ian will always be a child himself. You don't understand at all, Mr. Bradley."

"We can come back later." I didn't mind being polite but I didn't want her to think she had any choice in the matter. "What would be a good time?"

She reluctantly agreed to a seven-thirty appointment, which meant another evening of overtime for me. It didn't matter anymore. I didn't have anything better to do and, besides, I wouldn't have to hear one of Barbara's lectures about stress and my heart. And I sure as hell wasn't going to let Watkins come out here alone and talk to some retarded kid. Sarge was a nice guy, but his years of police work left him a little heavy-handed in the question and answer department. I wanted to do this job myself. Besides, I really needed to evaluate just how "retarded" Ian was if I was going to call him as a witness.

Sarge and I picked up our dinner at the Publix deli on the way home and ate on TV tables while watching the hated you-know-what. Doing the dishes consisted of throwing away the plastic plates and utensils. I had been a bachelor for less than twelve hours and already was starting to hate my new life.

We arrived at the Highsmith house a few minutes before our scheduled seven-thirty time. The front door was open with only the screen door standing in the way of visitors. Either these folks didn't have central air-conditioning or they were attempting to save on electric bills. I knocked on the edge of the screen door and a man came to answer it.

"Mr. Bradley? I'm Jules Highsmith," he began. I introduced Sergeant Watkins and the man of the house invited us inside.

"My wife has Ian in the family room. I wanted to talk to you first. I don't know what you think my boy's done . . ."

"We don't think he's done anything, Mr. Highsmith. He might have some information about a crime, and at worst he might possibly be a witness, but that's all."

"That's impossible. Ian always comes right home after school, and he tells us everything about his day." Mr. Highsmith smiled and added, "Sometimes we have a hard time shutting him up. I don't know how he could be involved in anything without us knowing about it . . . especially anything as serious as what was in the paper."

"Your son's not in any kind of trouble, Mr. Highsmith. But if he knows something . . . anything . . . about the murder of Joe Stempo, Sergeant Watkins and I sure would like to hear about it."

"I think I would too," Jules Highsmith replied. "But, please, take it easy with him. Ian's a little . . . slow. He goes to school with the other kids but he's a little . . . childish, if you know what I mean."

As Ian's father led us through the house and into the family room, I wondered what I would be facing. How slow is "slow"? This afternoon his mother implied he had the mental capacity of a nine-year-old. Was that anywhere near accurate? And what kind of mental capacity did nine-year-olds have? I hadn't met very many of them. Would I be able to question him? Did he have a reason to conceal anything?

Ian was sitting on the floor in front of the television set. His mother sat close by in a chair, flipping through a magazine and looking like people look in a dentist's waiting room.

"Ian, there are some men here to see you," his father announced.

The boy looked up. I could see the fear in his eyes almost immediately.

"Hi, Ian. Do you know who I am?" I asked, smiling at him.

He scooted over closer to his mother's legs. "You're the man in the newspaper," he said defensively.

"He saw your picture in the Bonita Journal when the Stempo girl was arrested," the father explained.

"Are you gonna arrest me?" Ian asked, moving closer still to his mother.

I sat down on the floor with him. "Arrest you? No, I can't arrest anybody, Ian. I'm only a lawyer. Besides, you didn't do anything to get arrested for, right?"

"I guess so."

"So, what are you doing?"

"Watchin' tee vee."

"Anything interesting on?"

"No."

The boy would not move away from his mother. I desperately needed a way to gain his confidence. If only I could find some common ground with him, maybe I could start a meaningful conversation. I looked around the room, hoping to see something that would serve as a way into his world. My eyes fell on a plaque above the television set. I don't think I've ever been happier to see the famous trefoil emblazoned with an eagle that had been such a great part of my own youth.

"Are you a Boy Scout, Ian?"

"Yeah." His eyes brightened, just for a second.

I stood up, examined the plaque and read the words out loud. "'Special Achievement Award, Troop 139, Ian Highsmith' . . . Hey, that's you!"

"Yeah!" He was smiling from ear to ear. I had found the doorway into his world. Now I had to gain his trust.

"That's quite an honor. You should be very proud of it."

He stood up and inched away from his mother's side. "Want to see my uniform?"

"I sure would."

The kid was out of the room like a rocket. "He outgrew three uniforms," his mother explained. Thank God the Boy

Scouts make them in adult sizes."

"Scoutmasters need something to wear too," I told her with a smile.

"Ian loves Scouting, but I'm afraid that award isn't all that much," she said apologetically. "They had an awards banquet and all the other boys got together and insisted that Ian get something too, so their Scoutmaster made up an award."

It struck me as a particularly lousy thing to say, putting your own kid down like that. "Awards from your peers are the best kind, Mrs. Highsmith," I reminded her. "Anybody can set up a tent, but not everybody can touch people's lives enough to make them create a special award for you."

Ian flew back into the room, tucking his shirt into his pants and putting on his beret. "Do I look good?" he asked.

"You look great, Ian. Of course, when I was a Scout, we didn't have berets. We had what they called a garrison cap; your father might know about that."

The kid's eyes widened. "You were a Scout?"

"Sure was."

"How far did you go?"

"All the way up to Eagle."

The kid's eyes were saucers now. "You were an Eagle Scout?"

I held up three fingers. "Scout's honor."

"Scouts don't lie, right?" he confirmed.

"No, we don't. We never lie. Do you know the Scout Motto?"

"Be Prepared."

"How about the Scout Oath?" I asked as I returned to my seat on the floor and he followed me. He knew the oath, and he knew the Scout Law, too. It was strange, sitting on the floor, listening to this man in boy's clothing recite the words of my own boyhood. Memorizing the words of the oath, not to mention the twelve precepts of the Scout Law was no easy feat; I was impressed with his dedication and I told him so. As the bond grew between us, I began to sense something of his mother's frustration. Ian was safe as long as his parents were here to take care of him, but he could not be a Boy Scout all his life. Who would fill their place in his world when they got too old, or when they passed on? He was too bright for an institution, but he would never be mature enough to live on his own. Instead he would live his life in eternal twilight, a member of society but not a part of it.

We talked for quite a while. He told me about a camporee he had attended and showed me his merit badges, one of which was for Rifle Shooting. It was time to turn the conversation to the purpose of my visit.

"Do you like guns, Ian?"

"Guns? Yeah."

"You're a pretty good shot, huh?"

"Yeah."

"Of course, sometimes guns can hurt people if you're not careful," I said.

"Yeah. Sometimes people get killed," he agreed.

"You know, Ian, right now I'm working on a case where a man got killed."

The smile on his face began to falter. "That's why you were in the newspaper, right?"

"That's right. The man who got killed in that case was Mr. Stempo: Anita's father."

"Anita is my friend." He wasn't smiling any longer.

"Is she a good friend?"

"She's a good friend. At school. She's always nice to me. And she's pretty."

"Yes, she is," I agreed. "You know about the gun that

Anita had, right?"

"It's a secret. She made me promise not to tell." He held up three fingers. "Scout's Honor."

I sighed heavily. How the hell was I going to explain to him that sometimes secrets could not be kept, even promises that had been backed up with Scout's Honor? I looked at Ian's father who started to say something. I stopped him with a wave of my hand. I was the Eagle Scout; I had to explain this one.

"Ian, sometimes we make promises we can't keep because later we find out they were bad promises. Understand?" He began to scowl. I had to be careful here; I could lose him in an instant. "That doesn't mean we were bad for making the promise, it just means that when we made it, we didn't know everything about it. Like the person who made us promise didn't tell us something. See? Sometimes we find out later that if we knew something before, we wouldn't have promised."

"Like goin' in Jimmy's pool?"

I looked at his father again. This time I really did need help.

"One of the neighbor kids," the man explained. "He had a big pool party one weekend when his parents were away. He didn't bother to tell the kids that he didn't have permission for a party."

I understood and I was happy that Ian made the connection. "Right. Just like Jimmy's pool. You wouldn't have gone in if you knew his parents didn't let him have that party, right?"

"No," the boy said, shaking his head severely.

"Of course not. Because you're a Good Scout. And you wouldn't have promised Anita anything about the gun if you knew it was going to be used to kill her father, right?"

"I guess not," he said, looking at the floor.

"Ian," I said quietly, "I know Anita is your friend, but I don't think she should have asked you to keep a secret about a gun that was used to kill somebody. That's not a good promise."

I couldn't think of anything else to say. Either the kid would tell me what he knew or he wouldn't; I couldn't imagine what else I could do to convince him that his loyalty was misplaced. There was a long pause while Ian mulled things over.

"She showed me the gun, an' she let me shoot it," he finally admitted. "I shot it into a pillow, like in the movies. An' then I found the bullet, an' she let me keep it. But she made me promise not to tell. Not to tell nobody." There were tears in his eyes and I felt like crap for making him break his promise.

"Do you still have the bullet, Ian?" I asked gently.

The kid nodded. "Uh-huh. I got it hidden in a secret place in my room."

Score one for Ian. He might be slow, but he knew how to find secret places in his room that even his mother didn't know about.

"Would you loan it to me for a while if I promise to give it back?"

The boy got up. He barely took his eyes off the floor as he left the room. Mrs. Highsmith's hand trembled a little as she ran it over her eyes, and I wondered how many more households were going to be affected by Joe Stempo's death.

Ian came back into the room holding something. Tears were streaming down his cheeks. "You can have it," he said, placing the small lump of lead into my hand. "I don't want anything that made somebody die."

I held the bullet between my fingers and looked at it for a minute. It amazed me that something so small could do so much damage to so many lives.

"Ian, do you know what fingerprints are?" I asked quietly.

"Uh-huh. That's the way they can find out if you touched something."

"That's right. Are your fingerprints on that gun?"

"Un-uh." He shook his head vigorously from side to side.

"Why not?"

"Anita made me wear . . ." he ran his hands over each other . . . "gloves."

I could feel Sarge's eyebrows arch before I even glanced at him. If we needed any additional proof of premeditation, this was it.

"Anita made you wear gloves when you shot the gun?"

"Yeah."

"Did she say why?"

"Yeah." He hesitated for a moment before continuing. "She said she didn't want no fingerprints on it in case somethin' happened." His face clouded over again.

"Something like what, Ian?"

There was a long pause while Ian stared at his shoes. Finally he looked up at me and said, "In case somebody got killed with it."

CHAPTER 13

The Circuit Court arraignment took place in the Calusa County Courthouse, an amalgamated structure that had grown like topsy over half a century. The stately granite courthouse that had served the county so well in the Twenties was overwhelmed by the South Florida population explosion. In the Sixties the old courthouse was expanded and "modernized" by the addition of a four-story wraparound structure that swallowed the older building whole but failed to digest it. The result was windowless offices that appeared more like bomb shelters, and a strange mixture of courtrooms: some built of dignified marble and cypress, and some of airport-waiting-lounge vinyl and plastic.

Howard Westbroke was a former probate court judge who had recently been reassigned to the criminal division thanks to a lunk-headed decision of the Florida Supreme Court that judges should be "rotated" to get experience in all phases of the law. Personally, I was relieved when I heard that he had drawn our case. I didn't know much about Judge Westbroke, but I suspected his former duties had likewise insulated him from Deke Stoner's influence.

That insulation would more than make up for any lack of criminal law experience on his part.

Because of his recent arrival on the criminal bench, Judge Westbroke was assigned to one of the old courtrooms deep in the interior of the building. It was one of the courtrooms I had been assigned to regularly back in my long-ago days in the State Attorney's Office – before the breakup of my first marriage and my escape to Palm Beach – and for some reason the nostalgia made Barbara's absence all the more painful.

An arraignment is the formal proceeding at which a defendant is read the charge – although the formal "reading" is almost always waived – and enters a plea. We had done it once at the jail on Terrapin Road; now we would do it again in Circuit Court with defense attorneys present. A date would be set for discovery and any motions the defense might wish to make. In all, I was prepared for a very short court appearance at which nothing much would happen. Nothing usually does; but this had stopped being a usual case.

Things began to get unusual right away. I had just shaken hands with young Todd Francesco, Melwin's assigned lawyer, when Bobby Greenburg came blowing into the courtroom.

Robert J. 'Bobby' Greenburg: he was short, squat, with a bulbous nose and out-of-style pompadour haircut that accentuated his bulldog appearance; he was known as 'Bobby' to his friends, enemies and clients; and he was a longtime criminal lawyer and pariah of the Calusa County Bar.

All trial lawyers have a personal style: some use the elegant, white-starched handkerchief in the pocket approach, and some the down-home, practiced-rumpled look. Bobby's style was pure bull-in-the-china-shop. He attacked everybody: the prosecutor, the witnesses, the judge – as far as Bobby was concerned every criminal case is nothing but a big conspiracy on the part of the state to put his poor, helpless client in jail. His style is good for publicity, and he gets more than his fair share of big cases, although he never fails to antagonize everyone around him. That fact either doesn't register or doesn't bother the new clients who seek out his services.

Bobby's ability to capture new business in spite of his personality and his track record was a constant source of amazement to many of us in the Bonita State Attorney's Office years ago, and it provided a generation of young prosecutors with fodder for lunchtime conversations. Bill Bellingham finally came up with the most plausible explanation of Bobby's success. "Hell," Bill said in his comfortable Southern drawl, "it's easy to figure out. All of these sons-of-bitches know they're guilty as hell. So once they get convicted and sent to Raiford, they're sittin' around talkin', an' one of them says, 'You know, that Bobby Greenburg, why he came in an' yelled at the prosecutor, an' he shook his finger in the judge's face, an' he slammed his fist down on the jury rail. You know, if I hadn't 'a been guilty, he'd 'a got me off!' That's all they're lookin' for is the show," Bill concluded. "That's why good lawyers don't impress those people. Good lawyers do all their work behind the scenes and get a better result. But since the best result is usually some kind of plea, the clients don't get a show and they're pissed off at the lawyer."

Bobby's clients always got the full show; they always got a jury trial. I was about to ask him what he was doing here when the bailiff called for everyone to rise and Judge Westbroke came out on the bench. A pained expression crossed his face when he saw his courtroom full of defense attorneys and their seedy-looking clients.

"Robert Greenburg for the defendant Melwin Fanchie, Your Honor." Bobby immediately took the offensive when the judge asked the attorneys to note their appearances for the record.

"Your Honor, my name is Todd Francesco," the young lawyer said tentatively. "It's my understanding that I was assigned to represent Mr. Fanchie."

"My client doesn't need an assigned attorney, Judge," Bobby interjected. "I have been privately retained to represent him."

Judge Westbroke looked around for guidance and found none. "How about you, Mr. Fanchie?" he finally asked. "Do you know which of these gentlemen is your lawyer?"

"Well, Bobby Greenburg was over to see me yesterday and said that he had been hired . . ."

"Retained, Your Honor," Bobby interjected, cutting off his client. "I have been privately retained on this case and I hereby enter a plea of 'Not Guilty' on behalf of my client."

Judge Westbroke still looked flustered, but he knew better than to keep an assigned, taxpayer-paid lawyer on the case when a privately retained one was standing next to him. "Mr. Francesco, is it?" the Judge asked. "Perhaps it would be better if you would submit a bill for any services you've performed including today and I'll approve it and then relieve you."

The young man looked crushed, but there was nothing anyone could do. He thanked the judge, closed his still-unscarred attaché case and quietly left the courtroom.

That little mix-up out of the way, Judge Westbroke asked Bobby Greenburg, Paul Berman and a young Assistant Public Defender how their clients would plead. One after the other they stood up and responded, "Not guilty, Your Honor," before Anita Stempo spoke up. "Your Honor," she said, raising her hand as if she were in a classroom, "I want to plead guilty."

If you've ever been to a ball game and seen an unsuspecting patron get hit by a foul ball, you know how poor Paul Berman looked at that moment. Judge Westbroke didn't look any better.

"You want to do what?" the Judge asked as if he couldn't believe anything else could go wrong that morning.

"Plead guilty, Your Honor. I want to plead guilty."

"You can't plead guilty to a first-degree murder indictment," Westbroke responded.

"Why not? I'm guilty and I want to plead guilty."

The judge looked at Paul. "Counselor, would you please explain things to your client?"

While the deputies took her mother and Melwin back to the holding cells and the judge went on with the arraignment of other defendants who had been assigned to his division, Anita huddled with Paul at the counsel table. It did not look like a pleasant discussion; Anita kept shaking her head, and Paul waved his hands a lot. There were many other cases, and Judge Westbroke ignored the two of them for as long as he could. Finally he took off his glasses and rubbed the back of his hand across his forehead. "Making any progress, Mr. Berman?"

"I'm afraid not, Your Honor. She still says she wants to plead guilty to the charge."

"Well she's not going to do it, not in my courtroom anyway, so just tell her to forget it."

"Why can't I plead guilty if I'm guilty?" Anita was on her feet and becoming adamant. The courtroom deputies began inching over toward her, preparing for trouble.

"Do you understand there might be the death penalty involved here?" the judge asked.

"I understand that."

"If I allowed you to plead guilty to the charge, it would be like me helping you to commit suicide."

"But I'm guilty. Why can't I plead guilty if I'm guilty?"

"Because I'm not going to be reversed by the appellate courts on my very first day. Talk to her again, Mr. Berman."

"With all due respect, Your Honor," Paul responded as diplomatically as he could, "I *have* talked to her. I don't think I can change her mind."

It was a prosecutor's dream come true. Anita had been read her rights more times than I could remember, she had a lawyer standing next to her, and he she was making statements about her own guilt in open court. I kept my mouth shut and watched the unfolding drama. If she had any defense at all, she was destroying it by the minute.

"The Court will enter a plea of 'Not Guilty' on behalf of the defendant Anita Stempo," Judge Westbroke began.

"Can I say something?" Anita interrupted. "I'd really like to object or something."

"No, you can't say anything," the Judge responded. "I'm going to enter a 'not guilty' plea for you whether you like it or not. Your lawyer can talk to the State Attorney about where he wants to go from here. That's all for now."

I felt sorry for Westbroke. His first criminal trial hadn't started yet and already it was giving him more than his share of grief. He was so flustered he even forgot the State Attorney had nothing to do with his case; it was the Attorney General – and I didn't think it was a good time to remind him. We all knew what he meant: if Anita wanted to plead guilty her lawyer could damn well plea bargain just like everyone else.

Plea bargaining is the most misunderstood and wrongly maligned part of the criminal justice process. To the uninitiated the very words "plea bargaining" convey and impression of sleaziness, as if justice was somehow subject to market forces of supply and demand. Lawyers take an entirely different view. We *know* that justice is subject to those forces and we live with the reality of the situation.

Consider this: the year Grace Stempo was indicted, prosecutors in Calusa County filed approximately seven thousand criminal cases. That same year there were seven – count them, seven – judges assigned to the criminal division. That's one thousand cases per judge per year. Give each judge two weeks off for holidays, vacation, sick leave and the ever-popular judicial conferences (and that all adds up to a lot more than two weeks) and you're expecting each judge to dispose of a minimum of fifty cases per week. Think of that: ten trials a day.

No court in the world can hold ten felony trials a day and preserve any semblance of due process of law. There are two solutions: either the taxpayers vote for a several-thousand percent increase in the number of judges, courtrooms and court personnel, or we dispose of most of our cases by some other, non-trial method. That other method is plea-bargaining. The State gives up a conviction on a more serious charge and the longer prison sentence that goes with it in exchange for the certainty of a conviction. The defendant gives up the uncertainty of a trial and the possibility of a long sentence in return for a more lenient sentence. The Court gets to dispose of another case on a severely backlogged docket. Everybody wins, except the people who think it's a sleazy way to dole out justice. Maybe it is, but it's the only practical solution we've ever found.

Plea bargaining ordinarily starts later in the criminal justice process, after discovery depositions are completed. The game begins when the defense attorney puts in a call to the prosecutor. A prosecutor who takes the initiative and offers a reduced plea before one is requested does nothing but advertise that he or she has a weak case, so our side waits, much like the girl who sits by the phone in the weeks before the high school prom.

I waited for the defense attorneys to call me. They would have to do it even if their clients insisted on a trial in order to protect themselves against "ineffective assistance of counsel" claims if nothing else. Besides, a good defense lawyer knows that the strength of the State's case is inversely proportional to the possible plea. If one of the attorneys could get me down low enough, it would be an indication that I had a weak case, a fact that lawyer would lose no time in disclosing to the others.

I would be operating under one more handicap: the defense gets the final "at bat" in this game. The Rules of Ethics required the lawyer to report the results of our conversation to his client, but since it is the client who will plead guilty, he or she can pull the plug at any time. That means defense lawyers enter the process without knowing for sure if their clients will plead. They can use the process as a way of sizing up the prosecutor's case, and then squirm away at the last minute when their clients balk. My job would be to negotiate without giving away the ranch.

Because of what happened at the arraignment, I was not surprised when I got an early visit from Anita's lawyer, Paul Berman. Paul had the cleft chin and clean-cut good looks of an F.B.I. agent, which is what he was before he resigned from the Bureau to swim in the cesspool of criminal law with the rest of us.

"Paul, I didn't expect to see you this soon," I said, extending my hand and showing him into my office.

"This soon? After what went on at the arraignment. I thought about coming over here directly from the courtroom. But first tell me this: how are you feeling?"

Coming from anyone else it might have been insincere, but not from Paul. We knew each other from the old days. I respected him as one of the few remaining gentlemen of our profession, and I believe he thought the same thing of me. No bullshit, no game playing. We both knew why he was there and we would get down to business in a minute. Right now, we were going to chat.

"Fine, Paul. Real good."

"We all got wind of your little stunt over in Palm Beach. Getting carried out of a courtroom on a stretcher is bound to make lawyers talk."

"Don't worry about me, Paul. Everything is under control."

"Well just don't do it here, okay?" he said with a smile. There was a pause in our conversation while he looked around. "This is quite a nice set-up you've got here. Very impressive: it's close to the Mall; lots of parking. This is really very nice."

"The nicest part is that Tallahassee pays the rent," I reminded him.

"And the phone bill," he added with a smile.

"And the phone bill," I confirmed.

There was another pause in the conversation and his expression turned serious. "So what am I going to do with Anita?"

"I don't know, Paul."

"You know she didn't pull the trigger."

"I know that."

"Did you know he molested her?"

"I know that, too."

"So can I get a plea to manslaughter?"

"Paul! Your client's charged with first-degree murder! Do you really expect me to drop down four steps? You could at least have asked about third-degree."

"Nobody's ever been able to figure out the difference between third degree murder and manslaughter, David, you know that. Besides, what difference does it make? They're both second degree felonies."

"Murder sounds better. And if both carry the same penalty, what difference does it make to you?" I asked with a smile. I already knew what is answer would be.

"Manslaughter sounds better for me," he said, smiling in return. "And I need the publicity. Potential clients read the newspapers, and your boss is a shoo-in for re-election. Besides, manslaughter is only three steps. Count them," he said, holding up his fingers, "Murder second is one step down, murder third is two steps, and manslaughter is three steps." He dropped the smile and looked at me carefully. So you'll take a plea to murder third?"

"I didn't say that," I replied.

"Sure you did. You expressly implied you'd agree to a plea to murder third."

"What the hell does 'expressly implied' mean?"

"I don't know, but if I ever get a chance to teach at Bonita College, I'm going to use it," he said with a chuckle.

"Paul, this isn't entirely my case. I have to answer to people in Tallahassee. I don't think I can go as low as third degree unless I get something in return."

He tightened his lips and shook his head. "She won't testify. I know that already."

"Talk to her again. Tell her I'll sell Tally on a murder third plea and maybe won't oppose probation if she testifies truthfully against the other two defendants. Otherwise the best she's going to get is murder second and jail time." I was going on a limb and I knew it. Our office had gone through a hell of a lot of trouble to get this indictment. Any reduced plea could be interpreted as being soft on crime. Deke Stoner could rant on about this whole thing being a waste of taxpayers' money and we might be buried in the media. I thought for a moment about Sylvia Mendez and her nose for a story; and I wondered where she would stand if the chips were down. I tended to agree with Jim Harcourt: she was not likely to let anything get in the way of a good story.

But I needed proof of a conspiracy, and the best way to get it was from one of the conspirators. I might have problems using the statements of the other two against each other; but if I could get Anita to 'flip,' I could justify a much lighter sentence for her by using her testimony against both of them. And, besides, there was something gnawing inside of me about Anita. I couldn't stop thinking about the look on her face and the way she said, "That's okay, I understand," when Watkins told her she would be taken to jail. It was almost as though she wanted to be punished. It was the kind of response I would have expected from a person who had been made to feel worthless as a child; the kind of response I expected from a victim of abuse.

The plusses and minuses went through my mind faster than it takes to tell. I was squeezed between loyalty to my side and what I saw as the ends of justice in this case. I had gone as far as I could. Paul would have to make the decision.

He shook his head again, sadly this time. "I've talked to her, David. She won't testify against her mother. Maybe I can talk her into testifying against the boyfriend, but not the mother."

"Why don't you try the case, Paul? Let her testify about what the old man did to her. A thing like that could get her a jury pardon."

He knew what I was suggesting and looked at me with a shocked expression that I might have gotten if I had asked him for a job clerking at his law firm.

Florida courts have always recognized the "inherent power of a jury to pardon." The defense problem is that jurors never hear about that "power" during jury instructions; quite the opposite, they are repeatedly told they must follow the law with neither fear nor favor. But every once in a while a particular combination of a ballsy jury and an especially nasty case results in a verdict that everyone knows is right, regardless of the instructions. Some good ol' boys refer to it as an "N.K." for "Needed Killin'." The Double Jeopardy Clause of our Constitution prohibits the State from having a "re-do," and since there's nothing anyone can do about such a verdict, our appellate courts chalk it up to a "jury pardon." I was suggesting something like that might happen to Anita.

Paul shook his head for a third time. "Not in a first-degree case; not unless you don't leave me any other way out. You can't get the death penalty for her; we both know that. But a first-degree conviction means life without parole for twenty-five calendar years. She gets no gain time. I think I can do better than that for her with a plea even if it has to be to second degree." He stood up and extended his hand. "I'll talk to her, David, but I can't promise anything."

"Let me know, Paul," I replied. "I'm not going anywhere."

I watched him leave my office knowing that I was right about one thing: Paul and I were a lot alike — two dinosaurs marching toward extinction. We had learned our trade in the days when a lawyer's word was inviolate. We could attempt to do justice by laying things on the line without worrying about how our conversation might be used against us later. Paul was the kind of guy who would work his ass off for a client, cut your heart out in the courtroom, have dinner with you later, and always, *always* be friendly and polite. Things had changed now in 1985. The new people were all young, bright and obnoxiously aggressive. They knew every rule except the most important one: the one that said when the other side said "uncle" you were supposed to back off and seek justice. Not anymore. The current crop of practitioners fought every legal battle to the death from the moment discovery began.

Discovery is one of the things that took the fun out of lawyering. Discovery and billable hours turned a once-honorable profession into a business dominated by eager young nerds with sharp pencils and intense expressions. Florida law required me to turn over a complete list of my witnesses to the defense; they are supposed to do the same for me. Long before the trial, we would each depose – take court-reported statements from – the other side's witnesses. But the time we got around to the trial, there would be little we didn't know. Forget about those television lawyers and their last-minute witnesses. In the real world if you haven't disclosed the witness' name and given the other side a chance to depose, there's little chance of that person getting to the witness stand.

I was handing our witness list to Mary Ellen and asking her to mail it to the defense attorneys when the PVC hit. PVC is cardiac-ese for Post Ventricular Contraction. It meant my heart had missed a beat, and when it picked up again on the next one, the rhythm was off for a moment. It feels like a hiccup deep in your chest, and while it's not especially dangerous, it can scare the shit out of you. I hesitated in mid-sentence with the witness list still in my hand.

"Are you all right?" Even though she was new, Mary Ellen's age qualified her to be the mother hen of the office.

"All right? Yes, I'm fine," I replied as another PVC hit. This had happened before, and every time it did my cardiologist assured me it wasn't serious. And I assured him he would think it was a lot more serious if it was his heart skipping beats. I got another twinge. This had stopped being funny. I didn't like it at all. "Take care of this witness list, okay? I'll be in my office."

She was at my door ten seconds after I sat down. "David, are you sure you're all right?" Word of my wife's departure had spread through the office like a plague. It appeared Mary Ellen had decided she was going to be my health monitor for the time being.

"Yes, really. I'm fine," I said, dragging my hand across my forehead. I was sweating slightly; my chest felt a little constricted and a lump was forming in the back of my throat. I might be having symptoms of a heart attack, or I might just be having a case of overactive imagination.

"Shall I call Barbara?"

"No! God, don't do that! Not yet; I'll be fine." It didn't occur to me at the time that Mary Ellen shouldn't have any reason to know my wife's number in Palm Beach. I started looking for that damn little bottle of nitroglycerin pills that had been rolling around in my desk drawer since God-knew-when. Mary Ellen hadn't moved; she was watching me closely.

"There's nothing to worry about," I told her, tapping one of the tiny pills into my hand and trying to reassure her as much as myself. "I'm going to put one of these under my tongue. The problem is that after I do I'll have a splitting headache in about one minute. So please just turn out the light and hold all my calls." I put the tab under my tongue and waited. The instructions were to wait five minutes. If the chest pain didn't stop, take another. After another five minutes without relief take a third and get ready to call the hospital.

"Are you sure you don't want me to call someone?"

"No, please don't do that. Really, this is just . . . kind of normal. It hasn't happened for a while and it caught me off guard. But it's fairly normal." I looked at her and smiled. I was feeling better already. The nitro was kicking in.

She pushed down the light switch and gently closed the door as my head began to pound. Nitroglycerin is great stuff for constricted arteries. It relaxes them; they open instantly and the damaged heart doesn't have to work as hard to keep blood moving. The down side is that it also opens the arteries in the brain and the resulting headache is incredible. That's what was happening at the moment, and I closed my eyes and tried to drift back to my grandparents' house in Sandusky.

They had lived in a big, gray house on Prospect Street, close enough to Lake Erie so that you could hear the foghorn when the weather closed in. Whenever I think of that house I think of those foggy days. My grandfather was retired from the huge grain and iron ore ships the people up there call "lake boats." He used to say the fog was nothing more than a cloud that had touched the ground, and he would tell me stories of picking his way past the lighthouse called "Chinaman's Light" in Buffalo, at the other end of the great lake. He was gone now, of course, as was my grandmother and the house, but when I was having a difficult time in intensive care a couple of years ago, I would put myself to sleep by imagining myself walking through that house and studying every detail. I tilted my chair back and began again to see the front steps that canted slight to the right. I think I got through the front door and into the hall before I nodded off. It must have been a couple of hours, because Mary Ellen came in and told me Clive Watkins had arrived to take me home.

"What time is it?"

"It's only four o'clock," she answered, "but you're

entitled. You *are* the boss, and you've been putting in a lot of extra time. Are you sure you're all right?" she added with a suspicious scowl.

"I'm fine, Mary Ellen. Thank you for being so concerned."

"I hope I did the right thing," she said as she turned and walked away.

I thought about that last comment as I rode home with Sarge. I wondered more and more whether I was doing the right thing. Maybe I should turn the case over to Tom. I had gotten into this to prove to myself that I could still do it. Maybe I was finding out that I couldn't do it. My marriage was hanging by a thread; I hadn't even thought about nitro pills in at least a year, and now I was making a mental note to renew the prescription. Barb's answer was to get away: leave it all behind. But when I thought of doing that, I remembered the sight of that thing in the front seat of my burning car, and the horrific odor in the air. And I thought of my own time in the hospital following that mailbox stunt. If Melwin and his playmates really were responsible for all of it, I wanted somebody's ass in jail. Forever.

I telephoned Barbara when I got home. I hoped the sound of her voice would cheer me up, but knowing I was talking to her long distance only made things worse.

"I went up to Worth Avenue today," she told me. "I think I'll be able to get my old job back."

"I thought you hated that place," I replied. "You always wanted your own studio."

The conversation died as quickly as if I had poured ice water on it. Thoughts of her own studio must have reminded her of Deanna, and I was sorry I had mentioned it.

"So, how did everything go with you today?" she asked

when we resumed.

"Good. Fine. Same old stuff."

There was a long silence on the line. Finally she said, "Are you going to tell me about it?"

Mary Ellen must have called her after all. "I had a little episode at the office today, a couple of PVC's."

"Did you call Dr. Crandall?"

"He always said not to worry about them," I said, avoiding the direct "no" that would have been the proper answer.

"Anything else?"

"A little pain, a little sweating. I don't know, maybe I was imagining it. I took a nitro and it went away." The mention of nitroglycerin was bound to worry her, but she had a right to know about it. Besides, it might worry her enough to bring her home where she belonged. "Anyway, it doesn't matter," I continued, being brave and noble. "It went away."

"I wish you would give it up, David. You can get on a plane and be here in less than an hour."

"Planes fly both ways, Barbara."

"I can't live like that anymore. Don't let's talk about it. Please?"

I took a deep breath. This conversation was going nowhere except to an argument, which was the one thing I didn't need at the moment.

"Why don't we get together when it's all over?" I suggested. "Maybe somewhere halfway."

"I don't think there are many places halfway between us right now," she replied, and I wondered if she was referring only to geography.

"We'll find a place, Barbara. If we can't find one, we'll make one ourselves."

"Will you keep in touch and let me know how you're

doing?"

"Of course."

"I'll be waiting."

There wasn't anything more to say and we hung up. I went to the serving cart in the living room that doubled as our bar and poured myself a stiff drink. It wasn't the wisest thing to do in light of what had happened that day, but at the moment I didn't much care if I woke up the next morning or not.

CHAPTER 14

The pre-trial discovery process began with the defense lawyers issuing subpoenas to everybody on my witness list including Boy Scout Ian Highsmith. The parents of some of the kids were pretty unhappy about it, especially Susan Sussman, Mollie's mother. Watkins had assured her that no one would ever have to actually testify. Ms. Sussman was not amused when a process server appeared at her door.

"What the hell is this, Mr. Bradley?" she shouted over the telephone. "Some guy was just here and handed my daughter a subpoena. It says she's supposed to come downtown for some kind of deposition. That Sergeant Watkins of yours told us everyone would just plead guilty."

"It's not quite that simple, Ms. Sussman . . ."

"What do you mean, 'not that simple'?" she shouted. "They shot the old man; everybody knows they did it. Let them plead guilty. I'm not gonna have my daughter get mixed up in it anymore."

"Ms. Sussman, she's already mixed up in it because she's a witness. I had to include her on our witness list . . ."

"Well you can just go ahead and cross her name off your witness list. Mollie's not gonna get involved. That Sergeant Watkins said that all she had to do was give a statement. She gave it, and that's it."

"Sergeant Watkins doesn't have anything to do with it anymore . . ."

"Doesn't have anything to do with it anymore? That's a fine thing. He gives us his word and now you tell me he doesn't have anything to do with it anymore? Are you gonna decide Mollie did something after all? Maybe charge her with something?"

I could hear Mollie saying something in the background. She was obviously upset, and I felt responsible for the whole mess. I should have laid it on the line with both of them in my office; told them that Mollie was an important witness to a very serious crime and would likely be involved with the case for the duration. At least I should have told them what to expect. Frankly, with everything else going on, it just slipped my mind and now I was paying for it.

"Look, Ms. Sussman," I said, trying to use my most reasonable voice. "Mollie happened to be in the wrong place at the wrong time. She didn't do anything, but unfortunately she's a witness in a murder case. The defendants are not going to plead guilty because that could mean going to the electric chair, or at least ending up in prison for life. Mollie knows about the gun in Anita's room and that Melwin Fanchie took it out moments before the shooting. I need her to testify about that. And the defense attorneys have a right to take her deposition before trial. I'm sorry about that, but that's the law."

"And what if I don't let her go to this deposition?"

"The defense attorneys will ask the Court to hold her in contempt and put her in jail."

"So now you're threatening us, a single mother and a poor little teenaged girl? Aren't you ashamed of yourself?"

"I'm not trying to threaten anyone, Ms. Sussman," I pleaded, "but this is a very serious case. Those attorneys have a right to talk to her."

"And what if she's not around? What if she goes out of state to visit her father? Are they gonna go get her?"

"Ms. Sussman, please don't make this any more difficult than it already is . . ."

"How about you? Are you gonna go get her, Mr. Bradley?"

I had had about enough of this. I tried being reasonable but it appeared that Susan Sussman did not respond to reason. I raised my voice a couple of decibels. "Ms. Sussman, your daughter is a material witness. If she leaves the state I'll send the police after her and bring her back in custody if necessary. Now, I don't want to do that, but I can . . . and I will if I have to." I was ready to slam the phone down on her when the tone of her voice changed. She was suddenly my friend again.

"Are you gonna be there personally for these depositions?" she asked quietly. It was the second time Susan Sussman pressed me to the wall and then suddenly caved in when the chips were laid down in front of her. I wondered whether it was a personality quirk or just a game she enjoyed playing. In either case it could explain the disappearance of Mister Sussman.

"Yes, I will personally be there," I sighed with relief.

"And can I come in, or do I have to sit in the waiting room again?"

"I can't answer that because it's not my deposition, Ms. Sussman. I'll ask, and I'm pretty sure the attorneys won't have any objection to you being in the room as long as you sit quietly and don't say anything."

"That's kind of hard for me to do."

I wanted to say, "Yes, I know," but I thought better of it. Instead, I figured I'd better reiterate the fact that I would not be running the deposition show. "I'll do my best to see to it that you're inside, Ms. Sussman, but I can't promise it. The decision is really up to the other side."

She exhaled, either in resignation or disgust. "Okay, I guess we'll be there, Mr. Bradley."

"Thank you. I appreciate that."

The Florida Rules of Criminal Procedure require the depositions to be taken "in a building where the trial will be held" unless the parties agree otherwise. I wanted it to be "otherwise" and I suspected the other side did too. I got on the phone to the defense attorneys and we agreed to hold the depos at the offices of Casello and Clark, Court Reporters, in a one-story building on Banyan Avenue in downtown Bonita. I didn't want my witnesses traipsing through a building filled with Deke Stoner's assistants before it became absolutely necessary, and the defense as usual was interested in neutral turf. While we were all still in an agreeable mood we agreed on one date that was convenient for all of the lawyers, no easy task when you're juggling court dockets and vacation calendars during late summer. At least we could get the whole business over in one long, tedious day.

So far it promised to be a one-sided affair. None of them had given me a list of defense witnesses, claiming that their investigations had not been completed. Naturally, I would not be able to depose the defendants themselves. The lawyers didn't even have to tell me if their clients were going to testify. In fact, the only thing they were required to disclose – in response to my written demand – was whether their clients intended to rely on an alibi defense. Based on the fact that the police found them all in the house when they responded to the scene, I didn't expect that to happen.

I learned one important fact while making the rounds by telephone: Peaches Bailey was the Assistant Public Defender who was assigned to represent Grace Stempo. "Peaches" is Peaches real name, and she keeps a copy of her birth certificate – with the year of birth discretely blotted out – framed in her office to prove it. She started with the Public Defender's Office back when black female attorneys were about as rare as snow in Miami. Those were the days when dark skin and "African-American" weren't "in," and Peaches would take great care to tell everyone that she was from Jamaica. As times changed so did Peaches. When it was cool to be part of the "black experience," Peaches discovered her long-lost roots in the slave trade. More recently, she had returned to her native Jamaican culture, probably in an effort to keep up with the Eighties "Miami Tropic" craze. In spite of all her insecurity over her heritage, Peaches is a smart, tough competitor in the courtroom. She had been offered a number of better positions in private firms over the years, but she stayed put. Some people put it down to a lack of ambition, but I knew better. Peaches was one of those unfortunate lawyers who really believed everyone is innocent, and she put her heart and soul into every case. Whenever we would run into each other at the local attorneys' watering hole after work, she would tell everyone within earshot that she stayed with the Public Defender to protect the downtrodden from closet Nazis like me. And I was the first to believe her.

"You gonna put my lady in the electric chair, huh?" she said when I got her on the line to discuss a location for the depositions. "Bet you'd like to throw that switch yourself, wouldn't you, David?"

"Soon come, Peaches," I said in my best West Indian accent.

"Soon come yourself, Mon. What the hell is that supposed to mean?"

"I don't know. It was the only thing I could think of in Jamaican."

"Yeah, yeah. So why don't you cut my lady a break? The son-of-a-bitch was no good anyway. We better off with him dead."

"What the hell is that, Peaches . . . a 'he-deserved-to-die' defense?"

"I'm thinkin' about it. He was miserable to them kids."

I waited for her to mention something about sexual abuse. She didn't, and I prodded her a little to find out what she knew.

"Most fathers are miserable to their kids, Peaches. I'd probably be miserable to mine if I was a father."

"Are you kiddin'? He was beatin' on them all the time, an' hollerin' and makin' everybody's life miserable. Makin' them more miserable than him, David. My lady deserves a break. I'm not sayin' let her off completely, but she deserves some kinda break."

"I'll give it a lot of thought, Peaches."

"Sure you will," she said, not trying to hide the sarcasm in her voice.

"I mean it. I'll think about it. But I'd be able to think a lot better if she had something to offer me."

"You want her to testify against her own daughter? Mon, you ain't got no heart at all!"

"She could testify against Fanchie; that would be nice."

"Maybe your case ain't as strong as you're lettin' us think?"

"You can never have too much evidence, Peaches."

"Well, I'll talk to her, but I don't know why. She told me you already got her statement."

As I hung up the phone, I thought for a moment that by asking about the possibility of her client testifying I had given Peaches too much information. Then, on second thought, I reminded myself that I had not said anything she didn't already know or soon would learn. The fact was, Grace Stempo's statement wasn't all that strong. She never actually said that she shot her husband. All of the most damaging language had come from Jim Harcourt with Grace crying and nodding her head. What looked like a confession in the high-voltage atmosphere of the F.D.L.E. interrogation room would not look the same in the cold light of a well-lit, air-conditioned courtroom. Even now I wasn't sure who pulled the trigger on Joe. Legally it didn't matter, but I would have to convince a jury of that, and if they began to have as many second thoughts as I was having, the upcoming trial could turn into a Donnybrook. I slammed my fist down on my desk and realized that here I was, well past the indictment stage and still looking for one good, clean witness.

The last call was to Bobby Greenburg. It was more of a courtesy than anything else. Bobby was not known for taking pre-trial depositions and I didn't think he was about to start doing so in what appeared to be a run-of-the-mill murder case. The other thing Bobby didn't do was negotiate pleas. His sole tactic was to bulldoze straight ahead and go for the opposition's juggler in front of the jury. I wasn't surprised when he didn't probe me about the possibility of a reduced plea when I got him on the telephone, and he seemed only mildly interested in the deposition date.

"You know, I don't pay much attention to that stuff; I'm always too busy," he blustered. "I already talked to my kid and I can guess what the others are going to say. So why is the Attorney General doing a crappy little murder case?" "Office of Statewide Prosecution, Bobby. There's more than one judicial circuit involved."

"There is, huh? I guess I'll have to research that."

I smiled at that one. The last time Bobby Greenburg "researched" anything must have been when he was a first-year law student. His confrontational style didn't require a whole lot of finesse.

"Listen, can you do me a favor?" he asked out of nowhere.

"Sure, Bobby."

"You know, I'm real busy around here. I probably won't be able to get to those depositions. Can you send me copies of your transcripts when you get them?"

"Be glad to, Bobby. You know, if your guy can't afford copies you can get him declared partially indigent and order them right from the court reporter. The county will pay."

"Yeah, but then I have to fill out all that paperwork. I don't have time for that stuff. Just send me copies, okay?"

"No problem, Bobby."

"Okay. Well, see you in Court."

He hung up almost before I had a chance to say "goodbye" and without bothering to thank me for what I had agreed to do. It was pure Bobby Greenburg: ask you for a favor and then cut you off in mid-sentence. Every lawyer in our part of the State had at least one Bobby Greenburg story. I guess that's why we put up with him. Lawyering wouldn't be any fun if we didn't have somebody to talk about.

The depositions went reasonably well. I was bored out of my skull most of the time while Peaches Bailey and Paul Berman took apart my witnesses in an attempt to nail down their stories. Mollie Sussman by now had her story down pat, and no one was ever going to cross up Jason Bonafide, the young man who had the guts to wear the wire.

Shawn was as much a problem as I had anticipated. Peaches kept going over his story, trying to nail it down. The problem was that no matter when I did with him, Shawn looked like what he was: a jailbird. This was as non-adversarial as the questioning would get, and he still looked like he was hiding something. He was just one of those people who looked like he was lying even if he was telling you the sky was blue. If I closed my eyes I could imagine Bobby Greenburg attacking him in front of a jury. It was not a pretty sight.

Peaches was also particularly interested in Sergeant Watkins' response to the question, "Did she have anything else to say?" when she was asking him about Anita's statement.

Sarge shifted in his chair for a minute and said, "Yes, she said her father was a pig; that he liked to beat up his daughters and make them fondle his privates."

"That's not in her statement, is it Sergeant?" Peaches demanded.

"No, it isn't."

The old rule about never asking a question unless you know the answer doesn't apply in discovery proceedings. That's why we're here: to find out "why."

"She didn't give it as part of a statement," Sarge explained. "She had already asked for counsel, and she just mentioned it to me and Mr. Bradley as we were going out the door."

Peaches looked at me coldly. "I wonder if I should depose Mr. Bradley? Maybe there's something else he's not telling us," she said to no one in particular when she finished her questioning.

The new player in our drama was Ian Highsmith. Paul Berman spent a lot of time questioning Ian, and the young man repaid him by unwittingly demolishing his case. If Paul was only going through the motions he didn't show it. The essence of being a good trial lawyer is also the essence of a good poker player. Never let them see you sweat, and never act surprised. Paul had to be especially upset about the gloves. If Ian was right; if Anita made him wear gloves when he handled the murder weapon, a jury could infer that she planned to use it in the crime. It was a logical argument, and one that I would certainly use at trial. Paul's problem would lie in cross-examining Ian. He came off like such a darn nice kid the jury was bound to like him. Any lawyer who attempted to twist him around would appear to be a bully and when juries react negatively to lawyers, their clients often go to jail. It's an old but true maxim in criminal law that the lawyer goes out the same door he comes in. The client may not. Paul was getting nowhere with Ian and I could see that things would only get worse with a jury watching.

To no one's surprise Bobby Greenburg never showed up. "Did he ask you for copies of the depos?" Paul asked when we were finally finished and off the record.

"Yes, and I said that I'd send them to him," I admitted a little sheepishly.

"Son-of-a-bitch, he tried the same thing with me," Paul complained. "I told him to get his client declared partially indigent and just order them from the court reporter. Why is he worried about saving money?"

"Maybe he's figurin' on billin' the county anyway," Peaches interjected.

We both looked at her in astonishment. "Not even Bobby Greenburg would do that," I protested.

"Watch and see if he don't," she replied, closing her briefcase. "Well, I got to hit the road."

"You got a witness list for me, Peaches?"

"Witness list? Whatchoo talkin' 'bout, Mon?" she replied in a heavily put-on Jamaican accent. "After what you tried to pull on me, not tellin' me about the old man playin' diddly with them girls? I'm surprised I'm still talkin' to you!"

"Come on, Peaches. If Watkins hadn't told you about it, you know I would have. I have a duty to under Brady v. Maryland, for God's sake. Here." I handed her a supplemental witness list on which contained the names and addresses of Anita's sisters. "It took us a while to locate one of them. I'm sure you're going to try to get this stuff in at trial."

"You know it, David. I'm gonna be standin' on my head, kickin' and screamin'." She shot a look at Paul Berman. "What's the matter with you not tellin' me about this?"

"I thought you knew, Peaches," he replied. "I'll set up a time for you to talk to my girl with me there any time you want."

"We'll have to fly one of the women in, Peaches," I added. "I'm going to file a motion *in limine* to keep her testimony out of the trial. Maybe we can do that and depose her in the same trip. No use putting her through too much."

"Maybe you got some kinda heart after all." She smiled, but not much. "Well, I guess we all know where we stand."

"That's what Discovery is for, Peaches," I said, extending my hand. She took it and then left quickly.

The truth was, I had held back for a reason: I wanted to find out whether Grace knew about the sexual abuse of her daughters. If she didn't, she would be hard pressed to claim it as a reason for killing her husband. The fact that she hadn't mentioned it to Peaches was a pretty good indication that she didn't know about it. I looked at Paul and said, "Now you can tell Anita that the dirty little secret is out and there's nothing to prevent her from testifying. If she doesn't tell all, Mama will."

He shook his head. "I doubt that will change her mind."

"Well, at least all of the cards are on the table, I responded as the two of us left the room together.

I didn't expect to see any of the attorneys again until somebody scheduled a suppression hearing. I was wrong. Not long after that first round of depositions, I opened the mail and found a notice from the Circuit Court advising all of us that our case had been moved out of Judge Westbroke's division and reassigned to Judge Sarah Wolfe Ives. A status conference was scheduled for Judge Ives' court the following week, and all counsel were ordered to be present with their clients.

"What's this shit?" Peaches Bailey demanded when she got me on the telephone.

"Damned if I know," I replied, knowing what she was talking about before she said another word.

"You figure you got a better shot at gettin' the death penalty with a hard-ass like Sarah Ives?"

"I thought you set this up, Peaches: going for the female factor."

"'Female factor' my ass! Judge Sarah got bigger balls than most of the men on that court. She'll be happy to introduce my lady to Ol' Sparky."

Peaches must have known that I had no intention of sending her client to the electric chair, and that even if I did, with no "aggravating factors" a death sentence would never be upheld on appeal. She was baiting me, looking for an official announcement. At this point, even an unofficial one would do. Taking out the ultimate penalty would make it easier for her to plea bargain the case. I wasn't ready to discuss penalties yet. I kept thinking I could use the threat of the death penalty as a bargaining chip, promising to give it up in exchange for Grace's testimony against Melwin, or, for that matter, his testimony against her. I changed the subject.

"So if you didn't ask for the change, and I didn't, who did? Berman?"

"Stop playin' cat-an'-mouse with me, David. You know 's well 's I do that Berman's girl is gonna plead. An' ol' Bobby Greenburg ain't made a pre-trial motion in his life. So now, who done it?"

"I swear to you it wasn't me, Peaches. And I'm not playing anything. I'm as much in the dark as you are."

"Well, I guess we'll just have to wait and see about that," she said with the disbelief apparent in her voice.

Actually, I did have a theory of what happened, but it wasn't one I was willing to share with anybody. Sarah Ives was one of Deke Stoner's former Assistant State Attorneys as was Chief Circuit Judge George Lippcot. If Deke wanted to put the blocks to a case, it was at least theoretically possible for him to ask George to reassign it to a judge who might be less than favorably inclined toward the Attorney General. The problem with that theory was that George Lippcot was one of those men who was beyond the reach of anyone. His reputation was as solid as Sheriff Bear Harper. This reassignment might have been caused by nothing more than a scheduling conflict – which is exactly what Judge Ives said when we appeared in her courtroom.

"Now, then, let's get down to business, shall we?" she said, slipping on her half glasses and peering over the top of them at me and the three defense attorneys.

"Judge, I still want to know what's behind this change," Bobby Greenburg fumed.

"I told you, Mr. Greenburg, Judge Westbroke requested that this case be reassigned, and Chief Judge Lippcot accommodated him by reassigning it to me."

"Well, I, for one, am not satisfied with that explanation and on behalf of my client, I object strongly, very strongly, to this change."

"What is the basis of your objection, Mr. Greenburg?"

"It's in violation of the Due Process Clause of the Florida Constitution and the United States Constitution."

"Fine. Your objection is noted and overruled."

"I'd like to take an exception to that."

"Your objection has been noted. There's no need for you to take an exception if you wish to appeal."

"I would just like to put the Court on notice that I intend to appeal. I intend to take this question up to the District Court."

"Mr. Greenburg, this Court assumes that any time it makes a ruling somebody will probably appeal. There's no need to put the Court on notice. Now let's get down to business. Has Discovery been completed?"

"The State has two witnesses who have not been deposed, Your Honor. One is local, but the other is from California. I anticipate filing a motion *in limine* on both of them, and counsel and I have agreed . . . at least for the moment . . . to hold off on depositions until a hearing is set." Judge Ives looked at me like I had just announced we agreed to try this case on the moon.

"Is that correct, counsel? You're agreed to hold off deposing these witnesses?" she said, looking back and forth between Paul Berman and Peaches Bailey. Paul came to my rescue.

"Your Honor, we expect their testimony to be very . . . traumatic . . . for both of them, and we all would prefer not to put them through it twice. Whether it is relevant and admissible will be up to you. If it's not admissible, that will end the matter. If it is admissible, Ms. Bailey and I are satisfied the hearing on Mr. Bradley's motion will give us all the information we will need." More than ever I realized Paul – and I guess Peaches, too – was a lawyer with a heart; one of a dying breed.

"I'm not sure I understand it, but as long as you and Ms. Bailey are satisfied," Judge Ives observed. "How about you, Mr. Greenburg? Have you completed Discovery?"

"No, Your Honor. And I have no idea what they're talking about. This is all a surprise, and it's a complete violation of my client's rights. Now, I demand a hearing, and I demand it forthwith . . ."

"Your Honor, the two witnesses in question do not have any information that is relevant to Mr. Greenburg's client. It's a family situation that . . ."

"I object!" Bobby shouted. "I object to him deciding what is relevant to my client's case! I'm going to take this up . . . all the way to the Supreme Court . . ."

"All right, all right," Judge Ives said, banging her gavel. "That's enough histrionics for the moment. Mr. Berman and Ms. Bailey are you satisfied that . . . other than these two . . . whoever they are, that you have deposed all of the State's witnesses?"

"We have, Your Honor," Peaches replied, speaking for both.

"I have not, Your Honor. I have not deposed anyone, and my client objects strongly . . ."

Judge Sarah Wolfe Ives banged her gavel again. "Enough! Were you aware of the time and place of the depositions agreed to by the other defendants?"

"Well, the Rules require depositions to be held in the courthouse, Your Honor, and I understand that these were held somewhere else."

"Mr. Greenburg, were you aware of the date, time and place wherever it was?"

"I received a telephone call from Mr. Bradley, Your Honor, but right offhand, I can't recall the information."

"Did you know the 'information' at the time," Judge Sarah demanded.

"Right offhand, I can't say, Judge."

The judge turned to me. "Mr. Bradley, did you advise Mr. Greenburg of the date, time and place of the depositions of the State's witnesses?"

"I did, Your Honor. And I confirmed our conversation with a letter to all three defense counsel. I have a copy of that letter right here."

"I don't know for sure if I ever saw that. My secretary files all my correspondence," Bobby interjected.

Judge Sarah Ives screwed up her face as if a manure truck had suddenly pulled into the courthouse parking lot and parked next to her BMW. "Fine. Mr. Greenburg, I'm going to rule that all Discovery . . . except for these two mysterious witnesses . . . has been completed."

"You can't do that!" Bobby shouted.

"I just did it."

"I strongly, strenuously object, Your Honor. I have a right under State v. Richardson to have a hearing on this matter."

Bobby was really rolling now. He didn't often cite cases; in fact he never did. Maybe he really had been doing some research.

"That's Richardson v. State," Judge Ives replied. "And you just had your hearing."

"I plan to appeal, Your Honor."

"Yes, I know. Your objection is noted." She turned away from Bobby and looked at me. "Mr. Bradley, I think Mr. Greenburg is right about one thing: we can't have you deciding what evidence is relevant to his client's case. I think you better include him on any notices for this hearing the rest of you have agreed to."

"Certainly, Your Honor."

"One other thing, Mr. Bradley. Will the State be seeking the death penalty in this case?"

I wasn't ready for that question, and I hesitated. I was still hoping to trade my answer for some information, so I tried to sidestep.

"I'm not prepared to say at this time, Judge."

"Why not? Are you trying this case or aren't you?"

"I am."

"Then you must have some idea of whether you'll be seeking the death penalty."

"I would have to confer with the Attorney General before making any final decision, Your Honor." I wasn't sure if that was completely true, but I thought it would at least be nice to tell the boys in Tally what was going on before making statements that were sure to wind up in the press.

Judge Ives looked at me with that same manure-truck-in-the-parking-lot expression. "If you have to get your marching orders from Tallahassee, that's your problem. I need to move this case on the calendar. Death cases require twelve jurors rather than the usual six. I have to know how many jurors we will need and possibly make arrangements for a bigger courtroom. I'll expect an answer from you by the time you make your pre-trial motions."

"Is Your Honor thinking about holding a joint trial?" Peaches Bailey asked incredulously.

"Unless you can convince me otherwise."

"But there are a number of confessions which might not be admissible against co-defendants." Peaches was talking about the problem I had outlined to Watkins and Harcourt back when this whole thing began. Anita Stempo's statement was clearly admissible against herself but, depending on whether or not I could prove it was made "in furtherance of a conspiracy," it would not be admissible against her mother and Melwin. The same thing was true for the statements of the other defendants. Apparently, Judge Ives had been thinking about the problem.

"We'll use separate juries, of course. But I have no intention of sitting through the same trial three times unless you can convince me I can't do it any other way."

"But, Your Honor," Peaches protested, "that means we could have thirty-six jurors plus alternates. We'll have to hold the trial at the Calkins Auditorium."

"That's why Mr. Bradley will have to speak with his boss right away," Judge Ives smirked. "I'll give everyone two weeks to file pre-trial motions. We'll set a full day for hearings and then go right to trial after I make my rulings. Is there anything else?"

We had just been ordered to get a murder case ready for trial in a matter of weeks, with no idea if the molestation evidence was going to be let in. Nobody spoke. I had been beaten up enough, and Bobby Greenburg, Peaches and Paul all looked like they were in shock.

"Seeing how there is nothing else today, the Court stands in recess." Judge Sarah got up and walked off the bench. Bobby Greenburg gathered up his papers and shot out the door almost as fast. Peaches, Paul and I were left standing in the courtroom.

"Well, at least we know she doesn't play favorites," Paul said after the judge was safely gone.

"Yeah, she treats everybody like shit," Peaches added.

CHAPTER 15

Because so much of the prosecution case rested on the defendants' own incriminating statements, I expected the first line of defense would be an attempt to suppress that evidence. I wasn't surprised when the suppression motion arrived, but I was shocked by the return address: "Law Offices of Robert J. (Bobby) Greenburg." It was far out of character for Bobby to take the lead in this sort of thing. He usually handled something of this nature by letting the co-defendant's lawyer make the legal arguments and adding a hearty, "that goes for me, too" when he or she had finished.

I was even more shocked by the second set of papers in the envelope. It was a motion to dismiss the indictment based on a rather intricate legal argument to the effect that since there was no legitimate question of multi-circuit jurisdiction, the Attorney General had no business prosecuting the case. I had heard somewhere that Bobby had a daughter in law school, and I wondered if she might be the source of all this new-found legal scholarship. If she was, she also must have convinced him to buy a word processor; even the typing was better than anything I ever saw coming out of Bobby's shop. I was staring at the papers and musing about the sudden improvement in the opposition's talent when the intercom interrupted me. Sylvia Mendez from the *Bonita Journal* was here and wanted to see me for a minute. Before I could respond, the leggy redhead was in my office.

"What's the matter, Bradley? You look like you lost your best friend."

"Just thinking about how things have changed, Sylvia. Everybody's an expert these days. What can I do for you?"

"The question is what I can do for you. I want to take you to lunch. How does Dupré's sound?"

"That fancy new place over on the Key? What's going on, Sylvia; what do you want?"

"What do I want? David, I'm shocked! Can't I do something nice for you out of the goodness of my heart? I *have* been kind of a pain in your ass sometimes. Now you're refusing my peace offering?"

I felt like a jerk. "I'm sorry, Sylvia. It's just that I don't get many luncheon invitations from attractive, intelligent women many years my junior."

"Don't flatter yourself. The place isn't officially open yet, and they're taping a television show. Something about following Chef Dupré into his kitchen. I'm covering it for the paper.

"No more true crime reporting?" I asked with a smile.

"The Journal's a small-town paper, David. We do what we have to do. Anyway, I'm on the lookout for a bigger assignment."

She drove. It was a short hop over the familiar bridge and on to Gulf Drive. We were a little early for the program, but a nice young fellow told us to take a seat anywhere and brought a bottle of wine and two glasses to a table near a window.

"So how goes the war? Anything you can tell me?" she asked after the guy poured our wine and left.

"The usual: pre-trial motions right now. I was just going over them when you came in."

"The Public Defender's Office can really crank that shit out, can't they?" Sylvia was nothing if not earthy in her assessment of the criminal justice system.

"That's what's strange about it," I admitted. "I expected the P.D. to jump right on it; maybe even get a motion from Paul Berman. But the first one came from Bobby Greenburg."

"So?"

"Greenburg's not that kind of lawyer; at least he doesn't have that kind of reputation. You generally don't get a lot of legal finesse from a guy who bulldozes his way through every trial. Maybe the fear of malpractice has finally caught up with Bobby. Anyway, I heard someplace that he has a daughter going to law school; I wouldn't be surprised if she's teaching her old man some new tricks."

"No more bulldozing for Bobby?"

"The profession is being taken over by intellectuals, Sylvia," I sighed. "All the fun is disappearing."

The wine was plentiful, and the 'taping' was about as crazy as I expected it to be: some guy telling us when to applaud, while others moved around with cameras, lights and cables. When the food finally came out of the kitchen I had to admit it was superb. If this was any indication of what to expect once Dupré's actually opened for business, I predicted it would be an instant success. I wasn't in any hurry to get back to the office, and when Chef Dupré saw us lingering at the table he sent over coffee laced with cognac, along with a little extra something he called a 'laginappe', all of which are rare for me at lunchtime. Sylvia casually stirred her coffee while I wondered what was really on her mind. "So how do you think I'd make out in Tallahassee?" she finally asked.

"Are you running for office?"

She smiled and her green eyes came alive with excitement. "Your boss is looking for a new press secretary. What do you think my chances would be?"

It was a relief to finally get to the reason for the free lunch. Obviously, Sylvia thought I had some insight into the complex world of Tallahassee politics.

"What happened to Rick Weaver . . . the current press secretary?"

"Richard is on his way out I'm afraid, but he doesn't know it yet."

"Sylvia, I don't even know what *my* chances are for anything. But I can put you in touch with my friend Tom Julian . . ."

"I've already met with Tom," she interrupted.

"You know Tom?"

"Sure. Well, probably not as well as you do, but I know him. Anyway, I've spoken with him and with John Stange, the Deputy A.G., but nobody can make the final decision other than the General himself."

"Sylvia, if you've spoke to Stange you've gotten a lot further up the ladder than I have in the past couple of years. Why don't *you* put in a good word for *me*?"

"Hey, don't worry. If I get the job, I will."

This was a young lady who had a lot on the ball. She was going places; I wouldn't be surprised to wake up one morning and hear she was in Tally – or Washington, for that matter. And wherever she went, she would be a survivor. I smiled at her. "Well, since you may soon be sitting at the left hand of my boss, I'd better get back to work. I wouldn't want you to get the wrong impression."

There was no check, of course. We were not customers,

we were an audience. Chef Dupré thanked us for coming, shook out hands and invited us to return—anytime. "But better when we are open, then you can pay for *diner, nes pais?*" he added with a chuckle.

Sylvia drove me back to my office. "Thanks for the date, Sylvia," as I was about to get out of her car.

"Anytime, Bradley." For a moment I thought her eyes were saying something they should not be saying as she added, "Anytime you want to return the favor, give me a call."

I hurried into the office. Whatever that last comment was supposed to mean, I didn't want to think about it at the moment.

It was another week before we were all back in Judge Ives' courtroom, Sylvia included. She sat in the front row, her legs demurely crossed, and took notes while we went through our dog-and-pony show. With an eye on judicial economy, Judge Ives had scheduled all of the pre-trial suppression motions for the same day. That's normally a good idea, but with three defendants making statements that implicate each other, the hearsay issues were bound to get complex. Add Bobby Greenburg's usual bombastic performance into that mixture and we were looking at a long day in the courtroom.

"Mr. Greenburg, your motion was the first one filed, so I guess you should go first," Judge Ives began.

"Your Honor, with all due respect, I'd like to give way to the lady. Let Ms. Bailey go first."

Peaches looked at Bobby like he had just called her a dirty name. "Judge, there aren't any 'ladies' here; we're all lawyers. I'll be happy to wait in line and watch Mr. Greenburg for a while."

"But I insist, Your Honor," Bobby protested.

"Well, I don't care who goes first as long as someone

does. Mr. Berman, how about you?" Judge Ives asked.

I'm sure Paul was thinking what I was thinking: we both wanted to see Bobby actually argue the law. "I'd be happy to, Judge, but I signed on late to Mr. Greenburg's motions. I think since he prepared them and did the necessary research, he should be heard first."

"Mr. Greenburg, it looks like your colleagues have placed the ball in your court. Let's get started. We'll take your motion to dismiss for lack of jurisdiction first." Judge Ives sounded like she didn't want to hear any more nonsense. It was time to get down to business.

Bobby looked a little flustered as he fumbled with a rather disorganized looking file folder. "Well, it's all right here in my papers, Your Honor. The Statewide Grand Jury is supposed to hear cases that have a statewide significance. Not, this crime . . . this *alleged* crime . . . I say alleged because they haven't proven anything yet . . . this *alleged* crime doesn't have any statewide significance. It's nothing but an ordinary murder case . . . they've just charged an ordinary murder. There aren't any statewide implications at all." Bobby got into his old groove and began to sound like he was summing up to a jury. His only problem was that this was a pre-trial hearing; there was no jury to impress. "These people . . . the Attorney General," he said, shaking his hand at me, "and all these high officials have come all the way down here from Tallahassee, and for what? This is nothing but an ordinary murder case. And they're trying to make it into something that it isn't, Judge, and . . ."

"I understand all that, Mr. Greenburg, and I imagine the murder wasn't very ordinary for the victim. Now, do you have a legal basis for your motion?"

"It's all right there in my papers, Your Honor."

"Thank you. Mr. Bradley?"

I explained that eminent counsel for the defense might

have been misled by the use of the word "statewide" in the indictment. In fact the Office of Statewide Prosecution was created to prosecute any case that arose in more than one jurisdiction. I told Judge Ives that the evidence at trial would show the gun that had been used in the murder had been stolen in another jurisdiction, namely Cypress County which is in the Twenty-fourth Judicial Circuit. And, I said, the proof will show the defendants traveled to that county to buy the illegal weapon.

"Is that all?" the Judge asked. I didn't like the sound of that question. I thought I had said enough, even using the words "illegal weapon" for emphasis. If I said anything else, I might be going too far out on a limb. I didn't want to start saying things that I couldn't prove later. Judge Ives remained silent; I couldn't tell if she was just being polite or actually thinking about granting the defense motion. I took a deep breath and decided to add just a little more fuel to the fire.

"And I believe the evidence will show the defendants carried on certain conversations in that jurisdiction which will prove they intentionally purchased the gun for the purpose of committing this murder. In other words, Your Honor, the conspiracy took place in more than one jurisdiction.

Even Bobby could see the weakness in that argument. I would have a hard time proving a conspiracy without testimony from at least one of the conspirators. Fortunately, we weren't there to argue the facts. He would have been more comfortable in front of a jury, blasting me for being one of the big, powerful State officials who were out to crucify his innocent client. "Judge, that's the whole point, he began. "He can't . . . they can't prove anything of the kind. They have to prove a conspiracy and they can't do it. They don't have any evidence of a conspiracy. There is no conspiracy. This is all trumped up by the Attorney General, and that's all there is to it."

"We're not here to try the case today, Mr. Greenburg," the judge replied. "I'm only listening to pre-trial motions. You keep arguing the facts. Do you have any arguments on the law?"

"I . . . it . . . it's all right there in my papers, Your Honor."

"All right. Anything else from the other defendants? Ms. Bailey?"

"My client Grace Stempo joins in Mr. Greenburg's motion, Your Honor."

Judge Ives turned to Paul Berman who also joined in the motion. She did not hesitate for a moment before saying, "Motion denied." I thought she was right, but it could have been a classic case of "cover your ass." Few if any criminal court judges would throw out a murder case before the trial even started. It was easier to deny the motion, and if the defendants were convicted let an appellate court handle the complex legal issues like jurisdiction.

"I strongly object to the Court's ruling, Your Honor. My client intends to take this matter up on appeal. This very issue, about the Attorney General . . ."

"Fine." Sarah Ives stood her ground. Bobby wasn't about to bully her with his histrionics. "There is no need to put your plans on the record, Mr. Greenburg. My decision stands; you have an exception and you can raise the issue on appeal. Next we'll take your suppression motion."

"I'll . . . I'll call my client Melwin Fanchie to the stand," Bobby blurted out.

Melwin had been slouched in the jury box with a court deputy behind him. When he heard his name mentioned he stirred into life and looked at Bobby with an expression of surprise mixed with fear. He only got to his feet after

Bobby hissed "stand up" a couple of times.

Defendants are not supposed to go first in suppression hearings. Either Bobby didn't realize he was taking things out of order or he thought going first was some kind of tactical advantage. I wondered if I should say something. If I kept quiet, I might be giving an appellate court a reason to overturn a conviction later. Before I could decide what to do, Peaches was on her feet.

"Your Honor, if I may. The State is supposed to present its evidence first in a suppression hearing."

"But it's my motion," Bobby said.

"Mr. Greenburg, even though it's your motion," Judge Ives explained, "the State still goes first because they have the burden of proof. They have to show that the statement the defendant gave was voluntary. You don't have to show that it was involuntary."

"Of course, I knew that, Judge," Bobby protested a little too pompously. "But you said you wanted me to go first, and I'm only trying to cooperate with the Court."

Judge Ives ignored that last remark. "As long as we're still discussing the ground rules, can we agree to hold a joint hearing?" she asked. "It appears the State witnesses are the same for each defendant. If we hold three separate hearings we'll be here all night."

The "all night" got everyone's attention. I'm sure she didn't mean it as a threat, but Sarah Ives was known for running a tight ship and was known for working very late if necessary. We quickly agreed to her suggestion. It made a lot of sense to have our side go through the entire story once, rather than holding three separate hearings and trying to confine each witness to what he did with respect to a particular defendant. We could just sort it all out at the end. Bobby, of course, had different ideas.

"Judge, I want to make it quite clear . . . absolutely clear

. . . that if we hold a joint hearing . . . if we agree to the procedure suggested by the Court . . . I am not giving up any of my client's rights to object individually and specifically . . . very specifically . . . to any of the evidence. I want to make sure my client isn't mixed up with all of these others in this thing because . . . as I said previously . . . there is absolutely no evidence of any kind of a conspiracy."

"I'll note your objection for the record, Mr. Greenburg."

"Judge, I'm not exactly . . . necessarily . . . objecting. I mean, I want to cooperate just as much as these fine attorneys here. I just want to make my position clear."

"Thank you. You've done that," Judge Ives said with a tight-lipped smile. "Mr. Bradley, call your first witness."

A defendant can only move to "suppress" confessions that are made to the State – that is, to police officers or people who are acting on their behalf. There was no way Bobby could move against the admissions Melwin had made to Shawn back when the whole thing started. Thankfully, I wouldn't have to sit through the spectacle of our teenage burglar being eaten alive on the witness stand just yet. That would come later, in front of the jury, when I called him as a witness at trial. Today Jim Harcourt and Clive Watkins were the stars of the show.

Harcourt was the consummate professional, testifying in a cool, detached manner. I led him though the preliminaries and then got down to his questioning of Melwin Fanchie and Grace Stempo. As he testified, I could see Bobby Greenburg writing furiously. He looked like a steam boiler with a stuck relief valve that might explode at any moment. He finally got his chance at cross examination:

"Agent Harcourt, you people were playing good cop/bad cop with my client, weren't you?"

"Yes, we were."

Bobby looked flustered; he was not prepared for a straight-out, truthful answer. He hesitated and repeated himself.

"So you admit you were playing good cop/bad cop?"

"Yes."

"And is that something you normally do?"

"Sometimes."

"So you admit that you sometimes play good cop/bad cop?"

"Yes."

Bobby hesitated again, and Judge Ives jumped in. " 'Good cop/bad cop' is when one questioner plays the 'good cop' who befriends the defendant and promises to protect him from the other one, the 'bad cop'. Is that right?"

"Exactly right, Your Honor," Harcourt said, turning toward her.

"I just wanted to be sure we were all reading from the same page," the Judge said before she turned the questioning back to Bobby.

"So you lied when you said you would protect Melwin from the local police?"

"Yes, of course."

Bobby looked dumbfounded. Harcourt was answering his questions like a true professional: no beating around the bush, just flat-out, straight answers. A less experienced guy might have waffled, but Jim was a pro who had testified all over the State. He knew the rules better than Bobby Greenburg did, and his answers left Bobby nowhere to go.

"So you admit . . . right here in this courtroom . . . you admit that you lied to my client to get him to make a statement?"

"Yes."

It might be time to remind Judge Ives of what the law

was. "Your Honor, I object," I said, getting to my feet. "The question before this Court is whether the defendant was advised of his right to remain silent, not whether the police officers lived up to Mr. Greenburg's expectation of fair play."

"The Court is well aware of the law, Mr. Bradley. As I understand it, the issue is actually one of voluntariness. Your question is irrelevant, Mr. Greenburg. Please confine yourself to the law."

Bobby was livid. "Your Honor, this police officer . . . this officer from the State capital . . . admits to tricking my client . . ."

"Trickery is not the issue, Mr. Greenburg," the Judge shot back. The issue is whether your client was advised of his right to remain silent and voluntarily gave up that right."

"It's not voluntary when he's tricked and deceived by the State . . . these people from the capital . . . these police officers who are pretending to be his friends."

"I'm afraid the law says otherwise, Mr. Greenburg." The Judge obviously knew the law, but Bobby was like a bulldog that had her robe clamped in his teeth and would not let go.

"This is a classic case of the State . . . these people from the Attorney General's Office . . . the State . . . trumping up a case, Your Honor, and I will not stand . . . this Court should not stand for it."

"Do you have any other questions of this witness?" the Judge demanded, her voice rising slightly.

Bobby looked at Harcourt who was still on the witness stand, cool as a fresh slice of Key Lime pie. He hesitated again and then said, "No. No, I don't have any other questions, Judge. But I want to object, and I want to reiterate my argument that this statement . . . this alleged statement by my client was given under the most deceitful circumstances, and these police officers . . . this police officer should be . . ."

"We'll get to your summation at the end, Mr. Greenburg. Ms. Bailey, do you have any questions of this witness?"

Peaches was a lot smoother, and she had a lot more to work with. She led Harcourt through his testimony and carefully pointed out that many of the most damaging statements attributed to Grace were not made by her at all.

"Now, Mister Harcourt, it's a fact that my client was greatly upset, wasn't she?"

"Yes."

"And she cried a lot?"

"Yes."

"In fact, she cried a whole lot, didn't she?"

"She did."

"In fact, most of what she was doin' in that room was cryin', wasn't it?"

"I wouldn't say most, no."

"But you did most of the talkin'?"

"I did a lot of the talking." Jim's answers began to get longer and I watched him shift in his chair. We both knew where Peaches was going, and there was no way to avoid it.

"And a lot of that talkin' was in the form of questions, right?"

"I asked her a lot of questions, yes."

"But she didn't give you as many answers, did she?"

"She answered all of my questions, Ms. Bailey."

Peaches put on the glasses that were dangling from the chain around her neck and said, "Well, now, let's look at that for a minute, okay?"

I got to my feet to interpose an objection. It would probably be overruled, but it would give Jim a breather and allow him to gather his thoughts. Peaches was getting ready for the big push.

"Your Honor, I object to this line of questioning," I pleaded. "The question before this Court is whether the defendant was advised of her rights. This is completely irrelevant."

Peaches corrected me. "The question before this Court, Your Honor, is whether my client made a knowing and voluntary waiver of her rights. And all of this goes to the question of whether her statement was voluntary."

If I read Judge Ives correctly, she knew I was stalling. She looked at me with an expression that said although we worked together a long time ago, she wasn't about to put up with any nonsense. She abruptly overruled my objection and told Peaches to continue. Peaches was ready.

"Mister Harcourt, to get right down to the meat of the cocoanut, most of this statement is you talkin', isn't it?"

"Much of it is me, yes."

"And this here, where you're tellin' her, 'You had a pair of gloves on, and you shot him. And afterwards Anita took the gloves and got rid of them. She got rid of them to protect you,' my client didn't answer that, did she?"

"Not in so many words, no, she didn't."

"Well, just in how many words did she answer it," Peaches smiled, toying with him.

"If you'll turn to the next page . . ."

"We'll get to the next page in a minute. What I want to know now is, did she answer you on this page?"

"No, not exactly. No."

Peaches looked like she wanted to follow up on that, but she paused. Maybe she figured that was as much of an admission as she would ever get out of Jim Harcourt, and, anyway, there was no jury here to impress. She could save her argument for later when it might do some good.

"And farther down this page, 'Were things that bad? Were they?' My client didn't answer that, exactly, did she?"

"Not exactly, no."

"In fact, she did do much of anythin' until here on the next page, isn't that right?" Peaches asked, indicating a line on the paper in her hand.

"When I asked her if everything I had said was accurate, yes. She nodded," Jim confirmed.

"She nodded. Did she say anythin'?"

"Not right then, no. But she nodded."

"So this whole confession you took from my client, it really boils down to you askin' questions an' her noddin', right?"

"No, that's not all. She nodded twice. And then she did make a statement."

I wished Jim had left out that "twice" business. He probably thought it helped, but to me it only pointed up the fact that he had been putting words in her mouth the whole time. Sure enough, Peaches picked up on it.

"You mean you said things twice and she nodded, don't you?"

"That's right. She nodded both times."

"Once when you asked her if everything you said was accurate, and when was the other time?"

"When I asked her if it was her idea."

"Those are pretty important questions, aren't they?"

I intervened again. "I object to that, Your Honor. It calls for a conclusion of the witness."

"Overruled. Answer the question." Judge Sarah Ives was in no mood for games now.

"Yes, those are important questions," Jim admitted.

"An' she only answered them by noddin' isn't that right?"

"That's right."

"Was she doing anythin' else at the time?"

"She was crying."

"In fact, she was sobbin', wasn't she Mister Harcourt?"

"She was crying."

"She was sobbin' and weepin' into her hands, wasn't she?"

"Your Honor, I object to the melodrama that Ms. Bailey is injecting here. The witness has answered the question."

"Mr. Bradley, the Court would appreciate it if you would refrain from making speaking objections. It's sufficient to object and state a one or two word reason for that objection."

"Very well, Your Honor," I responded. "I object. Asked and answered."

"Overruled."

"Was her head down in her hands, Mister Harcourt?" Peaches continued.

"Not always, no."

"So it was some of the time?"

"Yes."

"Was her head in her hands when she was doin' the noddin'?"

"Yes, sometimes."

Peaches turned to the paper in her hand again. "Okay, now this statement of hers, she made it after the noddin' part, didn't she?"

"Yes, she did."

"An' in it she says she'll never say she's sorry, right?"

"That's right."

"But she don't say what she ain't sorry for, does she?"

"What do you mean?" Jim asked.

"She don't say she's sorry for killin' him, does she?"

"No, not exactly."

"In fact, she might be sayin' she's not sorry that he's

dead, right?"

"No, that's not right," Harcourt protested. "Right here, she says, 'You can put me in jail, you can kill me. I don't care,' and then she says, 'I'll never say I'm sorry.'"

"But that's not like her sayin' she killed him, is it?"

"I think it is."

"You think it is? Could she be sayin', 'I don't care if you think I'm a bad wife, or a bad person, I'm still not sayin' I'm sorry'?"

"Objection, Your Honor." I was on my feet again.

"Reason, Counselor?"

"Relevance, Your Honor."

"Please explain."

That was novel. First she bashed me for making speaking objections, and now she wanted me to explain why I was objecting. I took a deep breath. "I believe the meaning of the words is for the jury to decide, Your Honor. The question before this Court is whether they were voluntarily spoken."

"Yes. I'll sustain the objection. Do you have any other questions, Ms. Bailey?"

"No, Your Honor."

Peaches sat down and I tried not to let my sigh of relief echo though the courtroom. She had done a good job of beating up on Jim; the trial – if we got that far – would be even worse. There, Peaches would be able to make her "what-did-she-mean-by-that?" argument directly to the jury. I could see a whole lot of reasonable doubt seeping into the case.

"Mr. Berman, anything from you?" the Judge asked.

"Your Honor, my client did not make a statement, so I did not join in the suppression motion. For the moment, I'm just here taking notes."

"Expanded Discovery, huh?" the Judge offered.

"In a manner of speaking, yes, Your Honor."

My second and last witness was Sergeant Clive Watkins. Sarge's testimony went a whole lot better for a couple of reasons. First of all, he had only been involved in Melwin's statement, and, in spite of Bobby's cries of foul play at the good cop/bad cop ruse, there was plenty of case law that said the tactic were acceptable. The second reason things went better was because Sarge's primary adversary was Bobby Greenburg and not Peaches Bailey.

Bobby was his usual self, berating the witness and stumbling over some of his words until everybody got sick of hearing his voice. Bobby has the not-so-unique talent of never knowing when to shut up. Add that to his inability to recognize when he's pissing off people, and you have a deadly combination for a trial lawyer. I knew Judge Ives was fed up when she started sustaining my objections before I made them. Finally, even Bobby got the hint and sat down. The Judge flipped to the first page of the yellow legal pad on which she had been talking notes.

"I'm not too concerned about the tactic that Mr. Greenburg refers to as good cop/bad cop. In spite of his protests of unfairness, I believe the technique is a standard tool of law enforcement which has been upheld by the courts." She paused and looked at me. "Mr. Bradley, you'll present the Court with a memorandum of law on that, won't you?"

Just what I needed: more work. She was asking me to do her research for her so that she could just cut-and-paste an order that her secretary would type up. I promised her that I would have the memo on her desk within a week.

"Of course, if any of you other lawyers have anything you wish to submit to the contrary, I'll be happy to look at that, too." She hesitated a moment, and then continued. "Now, I must admit that I'm much more troubled by the so-called confession of Grace Stempo. The issue that I have to decide is whether she was advised of her rights and knowingly and voluntarily waived them. The first part of that is easy: she was clearly advised of her rights. The second part is what troubles me. I don't know whether nodding while one is weeping into one's hands can be considered a 'voluntary statement.' I'm going to have to think about that. I'll give both sides two weeks to submit their research on the issue of voluntariness, and I'll issue a written decision. Court is adjourned.

Judge Sarah Ives was off the bench before the bailiff had a chance to tell us to rise. It had been a long day for everyone; she apparently wanted to get out as much as we did. As always, Bobby was out the door a moment later, heading either for the men's room or the local pub – or both. As for me, I didn't care much for the judge's use of the word "weeping." She had obviously picked up that word from Peaches' questioning, and it told me those questions had made quite an impact. Peaches came over to my table for one last tweak while I was packing up.

"Well, David," she said quietly, "maybe you ain't gonna be able to throw that switch on my lady after all."

CHAPTER 16

Four weeks later we were still waiting for a decision. The insurance company had paid off on my car, but I was under orders from Jim Harcourt not to replace it until the trial was over. Until then I had twenty-four-hour-a-day protection and I would be driven everywhere. It didn't matter, because I had nowhere to go. My life had settled into a dull routine of work at the office during the day and television at home with Clive Watkins at night. Calls to and from Barbara had tapered off. I guess I use the telephone too much in my profession; I'm always uncomfortable with it when I'm trying to say something personal. Anyway, we didn't have much to say. She was getting tired of living in Alan and Monique's spare room and wanted to look for her own place. I knew once she did that, it would be official; if I wanted to stay married to her, I would have to give up what I was doing and move back to Palm Beach – even if that meant giving up the practice of law entirely.

I was contemplating the most recent downturn in my life when Sylvia Mendez called from the *Bonita Journal.*

"So, what's Sarah Ives doing? How long can it take to flip a coin?"

"It isn't the flipping that's so hard, Sylvia," I responded, "it's finding the right coin to flip."

"Listen, Bradley, I need to talk to you." Her voice had a sultry quality to it, and I wondered if I might be wrong about the telephone being such an impersonal means of communication.

"Sylvia, I'm in my office every day. You know me: 'Overworked, Underpaid Public Servant'."

"Yeah, right. How about you taking me to the Yacht Club for dinner tonight? You're a member, aren't you? I've got something that'll make it worth your while."

As a matter of fact, social membership in the Bonita Key Yacht Club was one of the few luxuries Barbara and I permitted ourselves. I wondered if Sylvia knew that or it was just a lucky guess. As for what she had for me, I wondered if she was offering information or a part of her anatomy. Since I didn't need any temptation at the moment, I wasn't sure I wanted to find out. I almost turned her down but – Sylvia was a reporter first, and everything else second. She sounded like she had something important on her mind. I assured myself that regardless of my feelings, I could handle anything else. "Okay, Sylvia, but I'm temporarily without wheels. You'll have to pick me up."

"That's an interesting idea. I'll bet I could have fun picking you up" she teased. "I'll be at your place at six; we'll talk more about it then."

"How do you know where I live?" I demanded.

"I told you, Bradley, we investigative reporters have our ways."

Sarge had an absolute fit when he heard about my plans for the evening. "Isn't she a little young for you, Counselor?" he fumed as he unwrapped the evening's offering from the Publix deli.

"Come on, Sarge. She's a reporter; it's a professional thing. Besides, you know how I feel about reporters."

"Even the ones with long legs who wear miniskirts?"

"Sarge, she's young enough to be my daughter!"

"But she isn't, Dave. And you're a married man."

"Well maybe I won't be for too much longer," I replied.

He shot me a murderous look. For a second I thought he was going to launch into a lecture on the sanctity of the marriage bed. "Anyway you're not supposed to be going out without an escort."

"Sarge, I need a little time with someone more exciting than you to look at. I promise I'll behave, and I'll come home early. What kind of trouble can I get into at the Yacht Club?"

Watkins slammed his meatloaf into the microwave and I went into the bedroom to shower and get dressed for my dinner date. Even if the evening was going to be totally innocent, at least I would be out surrounded by real people instead of home with Sarge and the TV set.

Sylvia was right on time. I invited her to have a drink out on the patio while Sarge groused in the living room. She was wearing a deep-plunging green blouse that complemented her eyes and a short, black skirt that might have been molded to her perfectly-rounded rear end.

"Somebody smells good tonight," she said as I handed her the Scotch she had requested. "Good enough to eat, huh, Bradley?"

"Watch it, Sylvia. You're getting close to 'sexual harassment'," I warned.

"Sexual harassment, my ass. You love every minute of it. Besides, this isn't your workplace; you can't be sexually harassed here."

Before I could comment on the perfection of the aforesaid ass, she slid it onto the lounge, and I took the chair across from her. "Anyway, you and me, we'd probably kill each other after the first week," she said.

I looked at her, startled. If that was an invitation to try I might not mind dying.

"And I don't mean that way, either," she said, reading my mind. "I just meant we're two strong personalities and . . . never mind, forget it."

"You had something you wanted to talk to me about," I said, taking a sip of my drink and trying to change the subject to something not so fraught with danger – for both of us.

"Yeah, right. Bobby Greenburg," she said, demurely sipping her Scotch. "He doesn't make all those complicated legal motions, right? Want to know who's doing his research?"

"I already know. I told you, his daughter's a law student."

"His daughter's a law student at the State University of New York at Buffalo. That's a long way from South Florida."

"So she was home visiting him."

"Bobby Greenburg is divorced," she replied. "His daughter lives with her mother out on Long Island."

"How do you know all this? I asked.

"I'm a reporter. It's my job to know things."

"So?"

"So what?"

"So who's supplying Bobby's legal research? I asked. Sylvia's green eyes sparked and a smile crept across her face.

"Who's the one person in the county who most wants to derail your case? I had a hard time concentrating on her question with her looking deep into my eyes, but her sly smiled gave me the answer she wanted.

"Deke Stoner? You're nuts! That's impossible!"

"Okay, I guess I'd better be going" she said as she put down her drink and started for the door. I stopped her and apologized. It was a difficult proposition to swallow.

"How do you know this?" I asked.

"I need a cigarette," she complained. "I can't talk about this kind of stuff without a cigarette. Besides, how do I know this place isn't bugged?"

"It isn't bugged, Sylvia."

"Yeah, right. That's what Melwin Fanchie thought when he was spilling his guts to that other kid. Let's go to the Club. I'll tell you all about it there.

"How do you know I'm not wearing a bug? That's what happened to Melwin."

She moved up close to me and ran the tip of her tongue over her teeth. "We could go to a secluded little beach I know of. Then I could be sure you weren't wearing a bug."

The suggestion combined with the tone of her voice almost made me take her up on the idea, but I needed to hear what she had to say. If she was right, we could be sitting on top of a major political scandal. A state attorney using the office to assist the defense in a criminal case – a murder case no less – was the kind of thing that made headlines and got people thrown out of office. It also got them disbarred and maybe prosecuted themselves. I declined her offer of a sunset skinny-dip and we drove across the bridge to the yacht club.

The sun was still over the Gulf of Mexico as we headed north along the beach. Sylvia's skirt showed off a stunning pair of legs. She opened the window and we were immediately wrapped in a blanket of hot, humid air.

"You don't mind, do you?" she asked. "I'm kind of a fresh air freak."

"It's a little hot for that, isn't it?"

"It's never too hot for me" she replied. "I'll turn the air on if you don't like it."

"Air-conditioning with the windows open? That's burning the candle at both ends."

She reached across and squeezed my arm. "Burning the candle at both ends is the only way to live, Bradley."

I probably shouldn't have asked the next question, but it was still driving me nuts. "Just tell me one thing," I said. "How did you know about the raid before we got there?"

She turned to me and her face lit up. "Bradley! I'm shocked! I can't tell you that. That's a confidential source!"

A wicked little smile played across her lips. I would be willing to bet there weren't too many things that shocked Sylvia.

"Can you at least tell me what department it came from?"

"No," she replied, darting her eyes toward me and then back to the road. "Besides, are you taking me to dinner just to pump me for information?"

"No, I just thought I'd take a shot."

"Well shoot at something else, for chrissake," she said, leaving open all sorts of other possibilities that were getting more difficult to ignore. What's that old joke about the dog that chases the car and doesn't know what to do when he catches it? I didn't exactly decline her invitation to shoot at something else. I just wanted to think about it for a minute.

"All right," I said, "you ask the questions."

"Are you going to get the death penalty on these scumbags?"

"Never happen."

"Why not?"

I was almost grateful for the chance to revert to my lawyer role. "The Florida Supreme Court reviews every death penalty in this State. They say the presumptive penalty for murder is life without parole for twenty-five years. They'll only approve death if the murder was 'heinous, atrocious or cruel', and this one wasn't."

Her eyes widened. I was never crazy about green eyes, but hers were different. They said things. Sylvia could carry on an entire conversation with her eyes, and it didn't need to have anything to do with what she was talking about. "Not 'heinous, atrocious or cruel'?" she exclaimed. "The blew his brains out while he was asleep!"

"That's right, and the Supremes are going to say that means he didn't suffer. Believe me, going after the death penalty in this case is a waste of time."

"Can I quote you?" she said as the wicked smile returned to her lips.

"Of course not."

"So why are you telling me these things?"

"Sylvia, something tells me I could tell you a whole lot of things that I wouldn't want quoted."

She didn't respond to that, and I wondered if she was having as many second thoughts as I was having. Fortunately our arrival at the Club ended the need for further conversation – at least for the time being.

"So, what do you have for me?" I asked when we were safely seated in the dining room.

"Wow, that's a loaded question, isn't it?" she replied with that same wicked smile.

"Come on, Syl, stop fooling around."

"We haven't started fooling around . . . yet."

"Sylvia, are you going to get serious?"

"This could get real serious, David."

It appeared the lady had considered her second thoughts and trashed them. We were back to playing cat-and-mouse, and I wasn't sure which role I had. Part of me wanted to follow her down the unknown and exciting path of her illicit fantasy — a path she kept taking while always staying teasingly out of reach. The problem was I already knew where that path ended; and I still cared very much about my absent wife, even though her absence was making my life miserable at the moment.

"Sylvia, why don't you pick on someone your own age?" I pleaded.

She looked at me for a long moment with the same dangerous smile playing across her lips. "Okay, let's order a drink and I'll spill my guts. That's the phrase you guys use, isn't it?"

"Only in cheap novels. Now tell me about . . . D.S.," I said as the server appeared to take our order.

After he left she lowered her voice and said, "I got a call yesterday from one of his Assis . . . from one of the people in his office. God, this makes me feel like a spy," she giggled as her eyes darted around the room. "Anyway, she . . . my contact . . . said that her boss . . . him . . . had assigned her to a special project. She was to do all the research and prepare some motions in a certain case. And get this: she was not to tell anyone or let anyone see the papers."

"No one?"

"No one but him. Not even his secretary," she replied. "He made her do all the typing herself; and this was on top of her regular caseload! I guess that's the first thing that pissed her off!"

"And these orders came directly from Stoner?" I whispered.

"Directly."

The conversation died as the server arrived with our drinks and took our dinner order. Sylvia's eyes sparkled as she licked the salt off the rim of her margarita with a very sexy tongue. "How's that for a bombshell?" she asked after the server left.

This was heady stuff. "Can you prove any of this? Why did this gal . . . this contact . . . call you?" A hundred other questions raced through my mind.

"The power of the press, Bradley. Besides, who else was she going to call, the Florida Bar? They'd probably start and big investigation and end up disbarring her!"

"I don't suppose you'd care to share the name of your . . . contact?"

She looked at me with an expression of indignation that was a little too self-righteous. "Bradley! That's another confidential source! You can put me in jail . . . beat me with a rubber hose . . . I'll never tell." She looked at me with that same wicked expression and purred, "Besides, I might even like the rubber hose."

"All right, calm down. You made your point."

"Did I?"

Dinner arrived and I didn't have to think about her suggestion for a little while. Besides, I was supposed to be on at least quasi-official business. "What are you going to do about proof?" I asked, trying to get back on the subject.

"She won't go public, if that's what you mean," Sylvia replied.

"So I say again, 'Why did she come to you?'"

"How do I know? Maybe because she knows me. What am I supposed to do, figure out the motive for everybody who wants to give me a story?"

I couldn't shake the feeling that there was something she wasn't telling me. "Sylvia, his is a very, very serious allegation. You don't have any real proof," I warned.

"I've got proof." She slouched back in her chair and her eyes sparkled again.

"You have? What?"

"First, what's in it for me?"

"Come on, Syl, I don't have anything to give you."

There was another long silence while she licked the rest of the salt from the rim of her drink. "Okay," she said, leaning forward and lowering her voice again, "I've got copies of all of Bobby Greenburg's motions, including a few he hasn't made yet. They're in a State Attorney's Office envelope, sealed and postmarked today. And I did something else," she said, barely able to contain her excitement. "I interviewed Melwin Fanchie."

"You what? Sylvia, you can't do that without getting permission from Bobby Greenburg!"

"Who says? Besides, I got Bobby's permission."

"You got Bobby's permission? How did you manage that?"

"I told him I was doing an exposé on the Attorney General's Office. I said this whole prosecution stunk. It sounded politically motivated, and I wanted to interview his client to get his side of the story. Bobby even promised to meet me at the jail, but of course he never showed up. Now get this: Melwin didn't hire Bobby. He says Bobby just showed up at the jail one day and said he was Melwin's lawyer. Melwin thinks his family is paying Bobby."

"Maybe they are," I suggested.

"No way. They're a bunch of slimeballs without a pot to pee in or a window to throw it out of," she replied, finishing her dinner.

"How about the Jolly Boys?"

"Probably. And if they have enough money to pay Bobby to represent a loser like Melwin, my guess is they have enough money to fund a certain political campaign as well."

"Come on, Sylvia . . . you can't possibly think . . ."

"He's raised a hell of a lot of money, David. Even the A.G. is worried about next year."

"Yes, but money from a drug gang?"

"Money is money, David. It pays for a lot of signs and a lot of air time. With what I have in that envelope, somebody high up in state government might want to open an investigation. You never know what might turn up."

She was right about that. She had uncovered enough dirt for someone, somewhere to want to turn over a few rocks. I ordered coffee and after-dinner drinks and asked her what she was going to do with the information. She smiled that cat-and-canary smile again.

"I don't know yet. I might write that big story after all, or I might have a new employer very soon who might have a better use for this stuff."

"Come on, Syl. You can't do that?"

"Why not?" she demanded.

"Your 'source' gave you this information for the paper, not to boost your own career."

"My 'source' expects to see Deke Stoner thrown out of office," she replied. "I said I'd do my best to have that happen. I didn't say how I would do it."

It was an interesting approach to life. As far as Sylvia was concerned, the information that could blow the lid off the political scene had been given to her and was hers to do with as she saw fit. Her only commitment to her "source" was to use it to bring down Deke Stoner. If bringing him down happened to result in a boost up the ladder for Sylvia Mendez, so much the better. And if Bobby Greenburg got caught in the middle, well, that was his problem.

"You play rough, Syl."

"You've got to know what you want and go after it, David," she replied, not doing anything to hide the possible double meaning.

We sipped our coffee and drinks while I contemplated the latest turn of events. Even if Jolly Boy Melwin had not pulled the trigger on Joe Stempo, it looked more and more like he and his friends were the real villains in Calusa County. They just happened to get caught up in this crappy little family murder. Joe was collateral damage that occurred because Melwin had hot pants for Joe's daughter. I thought about the old saying that began, "For want of a nail, the shoe was lost; for want of a shoe, the horse was lost . . ." Melwin Fanchie appeared to be that one little nail that could bring down a statewide political campaign. What the hell had I stumbled into?

It was a beautiful night. We got the keys from the valet and walked to Sylvia's car. I was being a perfect gentleman and holding the driver's door open for her when temptation again reared its red mane. She slid into the seat, then grabbed my necktie and pulled me down closer to her. "You don't take hints very well, do you, David?"

"I'm a married man, Sylvia. I've been genetically altered to be oblivious to hints."

She didn't let go. She was wearing the same perfume she had on that first day in my office, and she was making it very difficult for me to say, "No, thanks."

"But are you happily married?" she asked. Her lips were much too close for comfort.

I thought about the question for a very long minute while neither of us moved. Finally I said, "As far as I know, I still am. And I wouldn't want to do anything to jeopardize that right now."

"That's too bad." She let go of my tie and smoothed it with her hand. "If you ever change your mind, I'll be in Tallahassee," she whispered.

What happened in the next few seconds will be forever embedded in my memory in slow motion, even though it took far less time to happen than it takes to tell. Somebody slammed into my back and shoved me forward into Sylvia's lap. I heard her scream and the screech of tires at just about the same instant, followed by a thud and the sound of breaking glass as Sylvia's door was ripped off its hinges. As I came up off her lap I looked through the windshield just in time to see the door flying end over end along the roadway and the back end of a dark-colored car with its tires burning rubber. And I saw something else, something that still haunts me whenever I think about it. A body was flying straight up through the air. It was Clive Watkins. He came down on top of the screaming car with the kind of sickening dull sound a sack of flour makes when it falls off the supermarket shelf. The impact shattered the rear window and he rolled off the trunk onto the street.

An instant later I was distracted by the sound of gunfire. I looked back over my shoulder and saw Jim Harcourt in an approved F.D.L.E. stance, two hands on the gun in front of him, squeezing off shot after shot at the quickly retreating car. In another moment it began to veer crazily and then it spun out of control and crashed into a tree at the side of the road. I never saw any brake lights.

I picked myself up off Sylvia and ran down the dark road to where Watkins was sprawled, laying on his back. One of his legs was skewed out at an angle that was painful to see, and blood was oozing from the corner of his mouth. He moaned when I knelt over him. At least he was alive. I rolled up my jacket and stuck it under his head.

"Take it easy, Sarge. Help is on the way," I said, hoping that Sylvia had enough sense to make a call from her car phone.

He looked up at me, the pain overwhelming his gray eyes. "I told you that dick of yours was going to get somebody killed," he gasped. He coughed a couple of times and more blood came out of his mouth.

Suddenly Sylvia was next to us. "They'll be here any

second," she said as she knelt down and held Sarge's head. I told her to stay with him while I ran up the road to the car that was piled up against the tree. Its front end was a mass of tangled metal and acrid steam and smoke rose high above the wreck in the humid night sky.

Jim Harcourt was already there, holding up the kid in the passenger seat, trying, I suppose, to keep him from choking to death on his own blood and vomit. Whoever he was, he was in worse shape than Watkins. His head had slammed forward into the dash and his face was a bloody pulp. But the guy in the driver's seat was beyond anyone's help. One of Harcourt's bullets had caught him in the back of his head, and there was nothing where his forehead should have been. The inside of what was left of the windshield was sprayed with a mess of blood and tissue that had once been the guy's brain. I turned away from the gruesome scene and looked at Harcourt over the top of the car. His eyes met mine and he said just two words – "Jolly Boys" – while the approaching sirens screamed in the distance.

I insisted on riding in the ambulance with Sarge, leaving Sylvia behind to retrieve what was left of her door and figure out how she was going to get home without it. The paramedics began working on Sarge immediately. I was probably more in the way than anything else as we careened down the road and over the bridge to the mainland, but I wanted him to know that I was there with him. I squeezed his hand, and he acknowledged me with eyes clouded with pain.

The hospital is the kind of nightmare experience hospitals always are when you enter them late at night through emergency room doors. Sarge moaned heavily as they unloaded him. They rushed him into one of the rooms where I was both unneeded and unwanted, so I went outside just in time to see the second ambulance pull up with the kid from the passenger seat and what was left of his face. He wasn't responding, but the way they hurried him through the doors and the fevered activity inside the room led me to believe he was still alive. The doors closed again, and I was alone. I went to the waiting room and found a pay phone; someone would have to call Sarge's daughter in New Jersey.

It was well over an hour later when an emergency room physician came out and told me that Sarge had been taken to surgery. He said there was nothing I could do there and suggested that I leave a number with the receptionist and go home. I nodded my understanding and was about to call a cab when Jim Harcourt showed up.

"They were Jolly Boys, all right," he said quietly. "The fools even had a couple of kilos in the car. Looks like they might have been on their way to make a deal later tonight." He offered me a stick of chewing gum that I declined. "I'm going to need you to make a statement."

"I know how the system works, Jim," I reminded him.

"I'd like to do it now, if you don't mind."

I really wanted to go home and pull the covers over my head, but I knew it was important to commit as much of this to paper as soon as we could. I nodded. "At your office?" I asked.

"If that's all right," Jim suggested.

I nodded again and followed him to his car.

The report took another couple of hours, and it was long after midnight when we finished. Jim said he would drive me home, but I told him I'd take a cab. I told him I didn't want any more babysitters.

He shook his head. "Sorry, Dave. This thing has gotten a lot bigger than it was. My orders are you get twenty-four hour protection. Looks like I'm your new roommate until I can make other arrangements."

I wanted to shout it was a little damn late for round-the-clock protection now, but I was too tired, and it wouldn't have done any good. None of us could have anticipated the twists and turns the Stempo case was taking. We took his car to my condo and I showed him to the room Sarge had been occupying. I was exhausted, but I knew I would not be able to sleep, so I slid into a chair in front of the TV and started flipping through the channels. I found the rebroadcast of a ball game between two teams I didn't care about and who both played like they had a desperate desire to lose. Perfect. I poured a glass of brandy, put my feet up and prepared to "chill out" as the young people say.

It might have been my imagination, but I suddenly felt like I couldn't breathe. I felt like someone had tied a straightjacket around my chest and I had a lump the size of a baseball in the back of my throat. I couldn't be happening again, I told myself—as I tried my best to deny the symptoms that I recognized all too well. I didn't have time for this nonsense right now; I had a lot of work to do. But my body was telling me it had other ideas. I was checking my pulse when Jim came into the room. The only light came from the television screen, but it must have been enough for him to see that I was, as my cousin the doctor might say, "having some distress."

"David, are you all right?" he demanded.

"Yes, I'm fine," I whispered, hoping to convince both of us.

He came closer. "Well you don't look 'all right.' In fact, you look pretty bad. What's the matter?"

"A little heart thing, Jim. I'll be okay in a minute."

"I'm going to call for an ambulance."

"No, please don't do that. It isn't necessary."

"The hell it isn't."

"Not yet, Jim. Just get me . . . there's a small bottle of

nitroglycerin pills in my bedside table. Just get them for me. Please?"

He hesitated for a moment and then hurried away. We heart patients always get our way. After all, nobody wants to cause us any more stress and maybe bring on the big one. Jim was back in an instant, helping me shake one of the tiny pills out of the bottle. I did the under-the-tongue routine again and the headache appeared right on cue. Jim sat on a nearby footstool and didn't take his eyes off me. After the first five minutes the symptoms seemed to ease up a little, but by then it was hard to tell if it was real or just a product of my imagination. I shook out another pill and did an instant replay. My head was pounding, and by taking that second pill I had just guaranteed it would do so for a long time. I tried to relax and concentrate on my breathing. The sweating eased and I could feel the color return to my lips. The baseball at the back of my throat was down to a manageable golf ball size. It looked like I was going to live after all.

"David, how long have you had this problem?" I heard Jim ask through the headache haze that occupied my brain.

"A few years." I tried to smile. "They carried me out of a courtroom on a stretcher in Palm Beach."

"You shouldn't be in this kind of game anymore," Jim observed. "Maybe you should give this one up."

"We didn't know it was going to be this kind of game when we started," I said as I squeezed my eyes shut. "I'll be fine." I looked at him and I was surprised by the concern on his face. "Honest, Jim, I'll be fine," I repeated. "Just let me stay here for a while."

He wouldn't leave my side. The only thing I wanted was to be left alone, so with his help I stood up and tried to walk to my bedroom. I pasted on a fake smile and kept saying everything was fine in spite of the fact that every footstep registered like a pile-driver in my head. We have a small two-bedroom condo, but that night it felt like my room was located somewhere in the outfield. I finally made it and was never so happy to feel a cool pillowcase under my head. There would be no reading in bed tonight. I slipped between the sheets and drifted off to Grandpa's house in Sandusky. It was summertime and I was sitting under the big pear tree in the backyard. Sunlight dappled the pages of the model railroad magazine in my hand and the hint of a cool summer breeze ruffled the pages. Soon my cousin would join me and we would begin some great adventure in the basement or invent some dazzling new gadget in Grandpa's garage. I fell off to sleep before I could decide which of those wonderful things we had done that day. And that night I dreamed of Sandusky.

CHAPTER 17

I shouldn't have gone to the office the next morning; if I had any sense I wouldn't have. But I had some very important business to take care of: plugging any possible hole in my case against Melwin Fanchie. If I couldn't get all of the Jolly Boys at least I could nail the one I had. Besides, my new babysitter Jim Harcourt had work of his own to do and, frankly, the way I was feeling I didn't want to sit around the house alone. If anything happened to me at the office, at least someone would be around to call an ambulance.

I telephoned Paul Berman as soon as soon as I arrived and told him I would be willing to accept a plea to third degree murder from Anita. I wanted to do it right away.

"Why the sudden change? Did your conscience get to you?" His boyish smile came through the telephone line loud and clear, but I wasn't in the mood for lighthearted banter.

"The case against Grace is solid, Paul, but I want Melwin, too. Once your client pleads guilty she won't be able to hide behind self-incrimination. You can tell her that I plan to subpoena her as a witness. I won't ask her a damn thing about her mother, or what her father did to her. But I want her to confirm that Melwin took that gun into the bedroom, and I want to know what he said to her before he did."

"I don't know, Dave. She's pretty scared of him. I don't think she'll testify."

"Show her the sentencing guidelines," I said. "A plea to second-degree murder requires a sentence to a state prison; third-degree lets the judge go only as high as seven years and as low as community control. If you present her as an abused kid whose only crime was helping to buy the gun that killed her abuser, Sarah Ives might let her off without jail time. And Paul . . . I won't oppose probation. How's that?"

He whistled softly into the phone. "Does your boss know about this?" Paul was a lot more serious now. We both knew this might not go down well in Tally, and once it was done there would be no way of undoing it.

"No, as a matter of fact he doesn't," I replied. "If I get fired tonight, I'll be at your door tomorrow morning looking for work."

"Dave, maybe you want to check this out first," he suggested.

"No, I don't want to check anything out," I almost shouted. "This is my case, and it's the right thing to do. My mind is made up, Paul."

"Well, if you're sure . . ."

"I've never been surer of anything, Paul," I answered apologetically.

"I'll go over to the jail right now and talk to her. What time would you like to do it?" Asking me to set up the time meant Paul knew damn well the plea was too good to pass up; he'd do whatever had to be done to make Anita take it.

"I'll schedule it with the Judge for one-fifteen," I replied.

"We can be out of there before she starts her afternoon calendar."

I hung up more convinced than ever that I was doing the right thing by focusing on Melwin and giving Anita the break I thought she deserved. I hoped the media wouldn't use my decision to blast the Attorney General for being "soft on crime." The Office had always been decent to me; I didn't want to repay it by biting the hand that had been feeding me for the past couple of years. Besides, if there was too much backlash, the best way for the General to cover his ass might be by canning mine. I telephoned Judge Ives' secretary and told her we might be coming in with a plea at one-fifteen, and then tried to put the whole thing out of my mind. I couldn't. Instead I paced around the office for a couple of hours until Paul called back at eleven o'clock.

"Okay, she'll do it," he reported. "But she wants to be released on bail until the time of sentencing."

"Fine," I agreed quickly.

"David, are you really sure about this?" Paul sounded like he was more concerned about my career than his client.

"I'll see you at one-fifteen, Paul," I replied as I hung up the phone.

Don't ask me how it happens but word always gets out when a defendant is going to plead guilty in a first-degree murder case, so I wasn't surprised to find a couple of reporters waiting for me in the courtroom. What did surprise me was that the delectable Sylvia Mendez was not among them.

Paul came in a few minutes early and two burly deputies brought Anita in from the lockup. She was wearing handcuffs and looked even more vulnerable than she had at the last court appearance.

"All rise." The bailiff gave the standing opening spiel

about the Circuit Court of the Twenty-first Judicial Circuit of Florida, and Sarah Ives came out looking very impressive in her black robe. I figured she could at least smile, but her expression was strictly business.

"Gentlemen, I understand we have a plea this afternoon," she began.

"That's right, Your Honor," Paul replied. "The Attorney General and I have agreed to a reduced plea to third-degree murder."

"Third-degree?" Sarah looked back and forth between us. "I was under the impression that the standard plea in this kind of case was to second-degree."

I didn't turn around to look at the gallery. I didn't have to; I knew the reporters were scribbling furiously. I stood up; it was time to lay things on the line and take my medicine if that's what I had to do. If Sarah wanted to blast me, I would give her full opportunity.

"After considering all of the facts, Your Honor, and after re-examining the sentencing guidelines, I believe a plea to third-degree murder will give the Court sufficient sentencing latitude to deal with this defendant."

"I see." Judge Sarah Ives twisted her lips into a knot. She didn't like the idea of me dropping this mess in her lap. "For the record, Mr. Bradley, what do the sentencing guidelines provide for third-degree murder?" Her question had to be for the benefit of the press. It would save them from looking it up for themselves, and it *could* give her a reason to launch into a "soft on crime" speech.

"Anything from community control to seven years incarceration is the permitted range, Your Honor." This was it. 'Community control' was just a fancy form of probation; if Sarah said something about the 'Attorney General agreeing to let murderers out on probation,' it would make the evening news for sure.

She didn't. Instead Sarah screwed up her mouth again, paused for an eternity, then looked at Paul and said, Mr. Berman, have you given your client any indication of what this Court's sentence might be?"

"Absolutely not, Your Honor."

"Miss Stempo, I'll ask the same question of you. Did Mr. Berman give you any idea of what the sentence of this Court would be?"

"No. I mean, well, that's what he said. Anything from probation to seven years."

"But did he tell you what I would *probably* do?"

"No."

"So you understand that if I accept this plea today, you might get placed on a very strict form of probation called community control, or you might go to a state prison for seven years, or you might get sentenced to anything in between. Do you understand that?"

"Yes," the girl said meekly.

"Mr. Bradley, will the State be making a recommendation?"

"Your Honor, after this Court receives a pre-sentence investigation report, I'm sure it will be able to mete out a just sentence without any recommendation from the State." That was the deal with Paul. The State would stand mute.

Sarah Ives twisted her mouth up again. "So you will *not* be making any recommendation at sentencing?" she emphasized.

"That's correct, Your Honor," I confirmed.

The Judge drummed her fingers on the bench. This might be her last chance to open up on me. The question was whether she would do it. She hesitated, appeared to think about it for a minute and then launched into what's known in the trade as a "plea colloquy" with Anita:

"Ms. Stempo, are you doing this of your own free will?"

"Yes."

"And are you doing it with the advice of your lawyer?"

"Yes, I am."

"Have you had enough time to talk to him?"

"Yes."

"And are you satisfied with his representation?"

Anita nodded her head, and the judge told her she would have to answer out loud for the record.

"Yes."

"Do you understand that by pleading guilty you're giving up your right to a trial? I need to make sure you understand that."

"I understand it." Anita's voice was getting weaker. She must have thought that pleading guilty meant just saying the word. In real life there's a lot more to it.

"Do you understand that you're giving up your right to have the State, represented by Mr. Bradley here, prove your guilt beyond a reasonable doubt to a jury?"

"Yes."

"That you're giving up your right to call witnesses and to testify in your own defense?"

"I don't want to testify."

"I understand that," the judge said. "But do you understand that you're giving up your constitutional right to testify if you wanted to testify?"

"Yes, I guess so."

"You can't guess, Ms. Stempo. These are very important rights; you have to understand what you're giving up."

"Yes, I understand." Anita's voice got stronger, as though she was afraid if she didn't answer correctly the judge might turn down her plea.

"At the same time, you have a right to remain silent. By pleading guilty you are giving up that right. Do you understand that?"

"Do you mean you can make me testify?"

"No, I mean by pleading guilty you're admitting guilt. In effect you're testifying against yourself. Do you understand that?"

"Yes."

"Has anyone, either me, your attorney, or anyone else, made any promises to you in connection with this plea as to what will happen to you or what the sentence of this Court will be?"

"Just what you said: anything from probation to seven years in jail."

"All right, those are the minimum and maximum possible sentences under our sentencing guidelines, but has anyone said anything else?"

"No."

The judge asked me to state a "factual basis" for the plea and I did so, telling the story of Joe Stempo's murder by his family and trying to go as light as possible on his daughter's involvement in it. Judge Ives had other ideas.

"So this defendant knew that the victim was going to be murdered before it actually happened?"

"The evidence could lead a jury to reach that conclusion, Your Honor," I replied. My back was starting to ache; I remembered that it always did during a plea colloquy, especially when things didn't seem to be going the way I wanted them to go.

"And she did nothing to stop it?" Anita was looking at the floor and trembling a little as Judge Ives spoke.

Paul jumped in. "Your Honor, I would just like to remind this Court that my client was not personally in the room when her father was shot, and I'm not sure there would have been anything she could do to prevent it if she were," he interjected.

"She might have at least awakened him and given him a

fighting chance," the judge said dryly.

All that talk about Anita "not testifying" was making me nervous. I didn't mind giving this kid a break, but I wanted to be sure I got what I wanted out of it.

"Your Honor, there's just one thing," I interjected. "I've told Mr. Berman that I intend to subpoena his client to testify in the trial. I've also given him my word that I will not ask her about her mother or father, but I do intend to use her as a witness against Melwin Fanchie."

Sarah turned back to Anita. "Ms. Stempo, do you understand that? Mr. Bradley intends to have you testify against your boyfriend. Are you willing to do that?"

Anita looked up at Paul and shook her head. He leaned down and had a hurried whispered conference with her. Finally, Paul looked at the judge and said, "Your Honor, part of the reason for this plea is that Mr. Bradley indicated he would not oppose my client being released on bail after the plea is entered."

"That's right, Your Honor," I confirmed.

Judge Sarah Ives leaned back in her chair, looked at the ceiling and let out a very audible sigh. "Let me get this straight," she demanded. "I'm going to accept a plea to third-degree murder from this young lady and then I'm supposed to release her on bail?"

"Her sisters are ready to post a bond, Your Honor," Paul said quickly. "that was part of the reason for this plea."

Sarah looked back and forth between Paul and me. Then she turned to Anita. "I'm not sure I agree with Mr. Bradley on this, Ms. Stempo. Perhaps he has some reasons I don't know about, but from what I've heard so far, I'm not sure I agree that up to seven years in prison is sufficient sentencing latitude. In other words, after I get the pre-sentence report and think about this, I might decide that seven years isn't a long enough sentence for this crime? Do you understand me?"

Anita shuddered. "Yes, I understand, I guess," she said quietly.

"I'll tell you what I'll do," the judge continued, "I'll accept your plea conditionally and order a pre-sentence investigation. If that convinces me that Mr. Bradley is right, you can come back here in a month and I'll sentence you in accordance with this agreement. But if I don't agree . . . if I think that seven years isn't a long enough sentence . . . I'll allow you to withdraw your plea and go to trial in front of another judge, someone who knows nothing about you or this case. How's that?"

"Okay," Anita replied weakly.

"Mr. Berman, is that acceptable to you?"

"Yes, it is, Your Honor," Paul replied.

"Very well then. I'll accept the plea on that basis, order a P.S.I. and schedule sentencing for four weeks from today." She turned to Paul. "Mr. Berman, do you have any particular number in mind for bail. You seem to be running the show around here."

"My client's sisters can post twenty-five hundred dollars cash, Your Honor. Anything over that, and they'll have to get a bondsman . . . which, of course, means more expense to them."

"Very well, twenty-five hundred dollars cash bond in a murder case following a guilty plea," Sarah said almost apologetically to the reporters. She turned and looked at me. "Mr. Bradley, have you gotten your marching orders from Tallahassee yet on whether the State will seek the death penalty on the other two defendants?"

Okay, so if the editorial comment on bail and "marching orders" was as bad as I was going to have to take, I could handle them. I might as well lay it all on the line and get it over with.

"Your Honor, after reviewing all of the evidence in my office as well as much of the case law, I am convinced that even if I could persuade this Court to impose the death penalty on the remaining two defendants, the sentences would not be upheld on appeal. In light of that, the State will not seek the death penalty in this case. I'm not here to waste the Court's time."

Sarah looked down at me without expression. She hesitated for a long time, and I was afraid she might be re-thinking her earlier decision to lay off blasting me or my office. I suddenly regretted the remark about wasting the Court's time. If she had a mind to do so, she could pick up on that and say something like, "Well if you don't want to waste time, why don't you mind your own business and let the State Attorney do his job?"

The pause must have seemed longer than it really was because Paul told me later that he didn't notice it. From my perspective it felt like I could have gone home for dinner, come back, and still have had Judge Ives looking down at me, drumming her fingers. My back was really killing me now. Finally, she spoke.

"The Court appreciates your candor, Mr. Bradley. I have enough to do around here without engaging in an exercise in futility."

"For the record, Your Honor, I want it clear that the idea for this plea . . . and the decision on the death penalty . . . those decisions were mine and mine alone. The Attorney General took no part in them." Hell, the guy had always been good to me. If the news people wanted to blow this thing up, the least I could do was take responsibility for my own actions.

"For the record, Mr. Bradley, the Court was speaking to you and you alone," Sarah said with the hint of a smile.

"But the Court does appreciate your candor. Now that it's decided we can move ahead with this case. I'll schedule a pre-trial conference for the end of the week and see if I can switch courtrooms with Judge Westbroke. I think he has a bigger jury box. Sentencing for Anita Stempo will be in four weeks. If there's nothing else, Court will be in recess."

She was off the bench quickly, and I headed for the door. Her reference to a larger courtroom left no doubt that she intended to hold a joint trial with separate juries for Grace and Melwin. With Peaches doing her "soon come" Jamaican routine and Bobby playing his usual bull-in-the-china-shop, it promised to be one for the books. A young reporter from the Journal caught up with me at the elevator.

"Mr. Bradley, can I ask you a few questions?"

"Sure. What happened to Sylvia Mendez? I thought she had the courthouse beat." I wouldn't have minded having a drink with Sylvia right about then. I might even have re-thought my reluctance of the previous evening.

"Ms. Mendez took off for a few days. She had to go out of town on a family matter."

'Family matter.' Right. My guess was Syl was in Tally right about now, trading Deke Stoner's head for her new career. "What do you want to know?" I asked the reporter.

"I understand about the death penalty stuff, but when you said that it was your decision alone, was there some reason for saying that?"

This kid was going to need a lot of work if he was going to replace someone with Sylvia's insight. "No, there really wasn't any reason," I replied.

"I mean, you made it sound like you and the Attorney General had some disagreement about how to handle this case."

Where the hell did they find this kid? Did he really

expect me to respond to a comment like that? The elevator arrived and he got in with me. "There is absolutely no disagreement between the Attorney General and me about this case, mostly because we haven't discussed it," I told him. In fact, that happened to be true. The General didn't talk to people at my level. He talked to people who talked to me.

"So he agrees with you about not seeking the death penalty?"

"I don't know; you'll have to ask him." This guy was fishing for a headline.

"Then why . . ."

The elevator doors opened and I cut him off as we stepped out. "Look, the reason I said what I said is because I've heard some rumors to the effect that the Attorney General has some devious reason for prosecuting this case. That is false. Anybody who has such an idea can just forget it. I wanted it known that our office is simply doing its job. And since I'm in charge of the local office . . . and this case . . . I make the decisions. This is my case, and win, lose or draw, nobody is responsible but me. Okay?"

"Can I quote you on that?"

"That's why I said it."

I really didn't mean to sound so abrupt, but I had pretty much used up my store of available patience. Besides, the kid wasn't my type: no long legs and no mini skirt for one thing. I hurried across the courtyard to a little place called Mama's where I promised to meet Jim Harcourt. We planned to visit Clive Watkins in the hospital on our way home. I ordered a glass of orange juice, stirred the ice with a plastic straw and thought dark thoughts about the criminal justice system. Last night must have worn me out more than I was willing to admit. I was tired; not just physically tired but mentally fatigued. Everybody involved in this mess had some personal agenda. Even that new reporter sounded like he had something to prove. I was tired of figuring all the angles. Then I looked deeper into the glass and reminded myself that I had a personal agenda too. I had gotten into this because I wanted to prove I could still make it as a trial lawyer. Who was I to criticize anyone when my big fat ego was the thing that had gotten me involved in the first place?

"You look like hell." It was Harcourt, standing over me.

"Thanks. Same to you," I replied.

He sat down across from me. "I'm not kidding, Dave. You really look tired. Maybe we should skip the hospital."

"Forget it, Jim. We owe the guy." I looked down into the glass. "Today I laid it all on the line in court, Jim. Gave Paul Berman the reduced plea he wanted from the beginning; announced we weren't going for the death penalty. I even said . . .in so many words . . . that I wouldn't oppose probation for Anita. Everything."

"I see," he said solemnly. There was a long pause. Well, was it the right thing to do?"

"The right thing? How the hell should I know?" I snapped. "I'm not the Oracle." He looked at me quietly while I stirred my orange juice. Finally, I said, "Yes, I think it was the right thing to do."

Jim reached across the table and slapped my arm. "If it was the right thing to do, I wouldn't worry about it. Things have a way of working out."

I looked up and smiled. Maybe he was right; maybe I was trying too hard, reading too much into everything.

"Come on, let's look in on Sarge and then we'll go out to eat," he said. "I don't think I can take another night of hanging around with you at your place."

Sarge wasn't doing too well. Both of his legs had been broken -- one of them in multiple places. He also had fractured ribs, a punctured lung and other assorted internal injuries, and he was going to be in Intensive Care for a long time. Jim and I spent quite a bit of time with his daughter and son-in-law in the hospital waiting room. Sarge's daughter understandably did not want to join us for dinner, and we bagged Jim's idea of a nice quiet place in favor of joining her and her husband in the hospital cafeteria.

It was after ten o'clock when we got to my place, and the telephone was ringing as I opened the front door. I didn't want to pick it up. The way things had been going lately, it could not be good news. Jim answered it and handed me the receiver. "It's Tom Julian calling from Tallahassee," he said with a worried look.

"Okay, Tom, give it to me straight," I began.

"How's things going in Bonita, Bubba?" he asked. "Any gators come out of the swamps yet?"

"Tom, I know why you're calling," I replied. "I did the right thing in court today and you know it. If the General wants me out, that's fine. I covered his ass the best I could. I'll submit by resignation for health reasons or whatever way he wants it."

"Whoa! Whoa there, Bubba! Nobody's resigning from this office. I just called to ask you how you were, Boy!"

"The General didn't tell you?"

"As a matter of fact, the Man did hear about your little speech this afternoon, and he was quite pleased by the way you handled things."

"So I'm not getting canned?"

"Now why would he want to can a guy who stands up and is willing to take some heat for him?"

"I hadn't thought about it in that light."

"As I recall it, David, the deal was if there's a victory it's his; if there's a defeat it's yours. So far nobody's been defeated."

"You're right as usual, Tom."

"You know, Bubba, people seem to forget that our boss was a damn good trial lawyer before he started playing around in politics. He knows what'll fly and what won't in a case like this. Maybe you went a little light on the girl for my taste, but, hell, we can show some mercy once in a while. It won't kill us."

"Thanks, Tom."

"Now there's something you can do for me."

I sat up straight and listened. This had to be the real reason for the call. "Name it, Tom. Anything."

"What do you know about this Mendez gal who's looking to become the General's press agent?"

I wondered if I should tell him about Sylvia's proposal of the previous evening. She was a savvy woman with the right instincts for the job, and I didn't want to hurt her chances by saying anything that might be taken the wrong way. On the other hand, my first loyalty had to be to the office and to Tom who seemed to be making a career out of protecting me.

"She's a sharp lady, Tom. I think she'd do a really good job for the office. But I'm glad it's you who'll be working near her every day instead of me. She can provide the kind of temptation that's sometimes hard to resist." I looked at Jim who raised his eyebrows.

"I know what you mean, my friend," Tom laughed. "But I'm not worried about that at the moment. I'm more interested in the scuttlebutt around town. Has she got any problems — drinking too much; sniffing a dab of white stuff every once in a while, that sort of thing."

"Might she do something to embarrass the office?"

"You got the idea, Bubba."

"Nothing like that, Tom. I've never heard a word. But to tell you the truth, I don't spend much time listening. Most people around here seem to like her. She might be a little too aggressive sometimes, but that's about all."

"Well, do me a favor and sniff around for a few days, okay? If you hear anything at all, I'd appreciate knowing about it asap."

"I'll sniff around for you, Tom."

We signed off with the usual pleasantries. I knew what he wanted. It sounded like Sylvia was pretty close to becoming the General's new press secretary. The F.D.L.E. was probably doing an official background check even as we spoke, but Tom was asking me for things that might never turn up in an official record, and I wondered for a moment if he was asking on behalf of the Attorney General or himself. If I learned anything, would the General see it, or would it stay in a file in Tom's office against the day when he might need to use it as leverage to get himself out of a jam? I put down the telephone and looked at Jim. "God, I hate politics," I said wearily.

CHAPTER 18

Anita's plea broke the logjam. A few days later we got Judge Ives' ruling on the suppression motions. It consisted of a one-word order: DENIED. So much for thinking out her written decision. The following week we started our final pre-trial hearing, technically called a "Motion *in Limine*". In plain English, it's a lawyer's way of trying to prevent the other side from offering evidence that's irrelevant and prejudicial. I was making the motion, and the stuff I wanted to keep out was the business about Joe Stempo diddling his daughters.

I had every reason to believe Peaches was going to pursue her "he deserved to die" defense, trying to paint Joe as the foulest thing to wash up on Florida's shores since Bluebeard. It wasn't a legal defense, of course. You can't kill somebody just because he happens to be a pervert. But when your client has confessed or almost confessed, you have to do the best you can. In this case, the best Peaches could do was take a shot at a jury pardon.

Although we had stuck to our agreement not to depose the Stempo daughters prior to this hearing, I heard enough from Anita the night she was arrested to have a pretty good idea of what they were going to say. Nevertheless, I told myself that I was upholding the law by keeping their testimony out; even a slime like the dearly departed was entitled to due process of law. Right. Let's face it, I was doing it for the same reason all trial lawyers do things: I wanted to win. Not that I thought Grace and Melwin were innocent; they weren't. But I wasn't about to get all teary-eyed about Joe, either. If he really did what Anita said he did, a jury might very well say, "So the Old Lady killed him? So what?" The more I thought about it, the more inclined I was to agree. If I were going to win this case, I would have to keep out any mention of abuse. Today's testimony could range from abuse that was just bad to incredibly terrible, and the worse it was, the more important it would be to keep it away from the jury. We would soon know just how bad it could get.

Anita was present, seated in the last row of the courtroom and looking very much alone when Peaches called her first witness, Grace's oldest child, Delores Visconti.

"Delores, do they call you that, or something else?"

"Most people call me 'Didi,'" the woman replied. She was tall, blonde and painfully thin, with a face prematurely aged by creases around her mouth and eyes.

"Okay, Didi," Peaches continued, "you are the child of Joseph and Grace Stempo, is that right?"

Three questions into the hearing, we all got our first surprise. "No, not exactly," the woman replied.

"Okay, tell us about that," Peaches responded.

"Grace Stempo is my mother. I don't know who my real father was. Joseph Stempo adopted me after he married my mother." She looked directly at Grace and said, "She refused to tell me the whole story."

"In any event, you lived with Joseph and Grace Stempo

when you were growin' up, is that right?" Peaches sounded flustered. I didn't expect to know the family secrets, but it sounded like Grace hadn't bothered to reveal this one to her own lawyer. Chalk up another error to Grace. She had violated the Rule Number One: Never, ever, keep anything from your lawyer.

"Yes, I lived with them," Didi responded.

"Do you live at home? With them, I mean?" Didi had already answered that question, but I didn't object. Peaches was definitely off her stride.

"I haven't lived with them since I got married," the woman said.

"When was that, Didi?"

"When I was seventeen."

"While you were living with your parents, did you ever see your father abuse your mother?"

"Yes, Joe abused her often."

"What did he do?"

"A lot of violent, hurtful things: twisting her arm behind her back, throwing her against the wall, pulling her hair and throwing her down the steps."

"Do you recall any incident in particular?" Peaches asked.

"One time, while we were still living up North, before we moved down her, my sister Cathy and I were in the bedroom just off the kitchen, and they were fighting. And I saw him grab her and she cried out and he grabbed her arm and I heard her arm go . . . it made a sound . . ." The woman hesitated. Peaches asked her if she wanted a drink of water, but she shook her head and continued.

"I could see him holding her against the wall with her arm behind her back, and I heard a popping sound. And the next day she had to go to the hospital . . . because he had dislocated something in her arm."

"Are you all right, Didi?" Peaches asked again. "Do you want to take a recess?" Once again the woman shook her head. Didi looked as if she only had the strength to go through this once, and if we took a break she might not make it back into the courtroom.

"Now, after that incident, did you notice any change in your mother?" Peaches asked.

"She became very quiet and withdrawn. She spent a lot of time avoiding him. Then when we moved down here, she moved into a separate room for a while and that's when things got really bad with . . . about the sexual abuse."

"We'll get to that in a minute, okay?" Peaches said. "But now, were there any times when he struck you?"

"All the time."

"How?"

"He used to just beat me. He would . . . if I did something that he didn't like, he would grab clumps of my hair and pull my hair out and just punch me and kick me."

"Was this once in a while?"

"It could be a couple of times a week, or it could be . . . it could go for months in between."

"How about the sexual abuse, Didi? How did that start?" Peaches asked softly.

The woman took a deep breath. "After we moved to Florida, my parents . . . well, Joe and my mother . . . slept in separate rooms, and my sister Cathy and I shared the other bedroom. Well one night my sister had the flu and my mother told me to sleep on the couch in the living room. When Joe came home from working the night shift I guess he saw me there and . . . I don't know what happened . . . but I remember him waking me up and placing my hand on his penis."

"When you say 'him', you're referring to Joseph Stempo,

is that correct?"

The woman nodded and then said "yes" when Judge Ives told her she would have to answer out loud for the court reporter.

"What happened after that first time?" Peaches asked.

"It's hard for me to remember a lot of things because I've blocked a lot of it out. But once when I was about thirteen, he was in the bathtub and he called me in and made me masturbate him until he ejaculated."

Didi reached for the water glass the bailiff had put in front of her. Her hand was shaking visibly and some of the water spilled as she raised it to her lips. After a moment she continued even though Peaches had not asked another question.

"After that, he would tell me that I was to go with him to the store or to go on some errand, and what he'd do, basically, is pull off on some side road and force me to masturbate him. And sometimes when my mother was in her room, he would tell me to come watch television with him late at night, and . . . the same thing."

"How long did this continue, Didi?" Peaches asked.

"Until I moved out when I was seventeen."

"Now, before you moved out, did you have any violent thoughts about your father?"

"When I was . . . I don't know . . . fifteen, maybe . . . used to wake up in the middle of the night and stand in front of his bedroom door . . ."

She put her head down and began to cry. Even though we had agreed that today's hearing would take the place of the usual Discovery depositions and it would be pretty wide open, I wanted to object. There was no reason for this question. We were forcing her to re-live a time of her life that no one should have to go through even once. Worse yet, if Peaches couldn't somehow connect all this up with this particular murder, it would be completely inadmissible.

"Do you want to take a break, Didi? We're almost finished," Peaches said softly.

The woman shook her head, wiped her face with a tissue the judge handed her and continued. "When I was fifteen, I used to wake up in the middle of the night and stand in front of his bedroom door with a butcher knife and pray that I could go in and kill him."

Peaches looked at me. "I have no further questions, Your Honor. Your witness, Mr. Bradley."

Thankfully, there was no jury present. Still, I would have to be very careful with the way I handled cross-examination. Didi's testimony had affected all of us deeply. A judge is supposed to be immune from sympathy and favor, but I wouldn't want to bet heavily on Sarah Ives' impartiality right about now. Besides, Didi had been though a lot thanks to our criminal justice system; I didn't want to add to her anguish if I could avoid it. All the same, I was sure what she had told us was completely irrelevant. I tried to steer my questions in that direction.

"Ms. Visconti, this is a very personal question, but I'm afraid I have to ask it," I began. "How old are you?"

Didi smiled with relief. "Thirty-four. No, thirty-five, I'm sorry," she said.

"That's okay. So you've been out of the house for what, eighteen years?"

"That's right."

"And you live out on the West Coast now, is that correct?"

"Yes. My husband and I live in San Diego," she replied.

"Do you get back here to Florida very much?"

"No, not really."

"How often would you say you've been back here since you moved out?"

"I don't know . . . maybe four or five times over the years."

"Do you stay at your parents' house when you do?"

"Absolutely not. No. Never."

"Now, if you moved out eighteen years ago, that must have been just about the time Anita was born, wasn't it?"

I had to be careful here. Florida law allows a person to use deadly force to prevent an attacker from inflicting death or great bodily harm on oneself or another person. I didn't want to give either Grace or Melwin an opportunity to claim they killed Joe because they were defending Anita.

"My younger sister was still there. She's eight years younger than I am," she replied not answering my question.

"That's Cathy?" I asked.

"That's right."

"She was ten when you moved out?"

"Something like that; nine, ten, eleven."

"Did you ever see your father abuse Cathy when you were living there?"

"I don't remember Joe ever abusing Cathy." It was clear from her answers that although Joe Stempo adopted Didi, she did not consider him her father.

"Did you ever tell your mother about the abuse you were suffering?"

"Not in so many words, no."

"What words did you use, to the best of your recollection?"

"I tried to tell her once, that he was forcing me . . . that I was being abused by him without actually coming out and saying it. I was afraid if she didn't believe me, I would get . . . things might get a whole lot worse. So I never . . . I never said exactly what he was doing."

"You never told her about the masturbation, for example?"

"No."

"How about the beatings?"

"She knew that; she saw those."

"But you really don't know what's been going on in that house for the past eighteen years, do you?"

"People don't change, Mr. Bradley," she said bitterly.

"Ms. Visconti, you really . . . of your own personal knowledge . . . you don't know, do you?" I repeated quietly.

"No, I don't."

I had gotten as far as I could and I sat down. I had preserved my argument that all of this testimony, sordid as it was, had no bearing on Grace or Melwin. I was both surprised and a little relieved when Bobby Greenburg announced he had no questions. Didi was free to go. She got up and left the witness stand without so much as a glance at her mother. On her way out of the courtroom, she stopped and said something to Anita who shook her head in the negative and remained seated in the back row. I had a hard time believing Grace didn't know about all this crap when it was happening; Florida houses are pretty small and incidents like the ones Didi described are difficult to ignore. I wondered if Grace might have moved into her own room and turned a blind eye to her daughter's plight in order to save herself from her husband.

Peaches' next witness was Cathy Delaney, "nee Stempo" as the society editor of the *Journal* would say. Except that the Stempo family wasn't likely to wind up on the Society Page of anybody's newspaper.

"Cathy, you are the second child of Grace and Joe Stempo, is that correct?" Peaches began.

"That's right." With her dark hair and slightly plump figure, the younger woman looked something like her mother. Didi must have taken after her biological father.

"And you lived with them until you were how old?"

"Eighteen. One year longer than my sister."

"How much older is your sister Delores . . . Didi?"

"Eight years. Right now I'm twenty-seven; Didi's thirty-five," she said without hesitation.

"During the time you lived with your parents, did you ever see Didi sexually abused?"

"Yes, I did. When I was . . . let's see . . . I must have been around five or six because we were still living up North. I was in the closet trying on my mother's clothes. I was in a place I shouldn't have been and when I heard somebody come into the bedroom, I hid there and waited for them to leave. And when I peeked out of the door, I saw my father and Didi . . ."

The young woman hesitated; Peaches encouraged her to continue.

"He started taking off my sister's clothes and she wanted to know what he was going . . . what he was doing, and he kept saying, 'You're not my daughter; you're not mine. It's all right.'"

"So he got her undressed and put her on the bed and then he took off his clothes, and it was the first time I had seen any male naked . . . and he got onto the bed and my sister was laying on the bed and he kept pinching her on the breast area . . . only . . ."

There was another long pause. The bailiff poured a glass of water and Cathy thanked him for it.

"Go on, Cathy," Peaches encouraged.

"Only . . . she didn't . . . have anything. I mean, she wasn't developed or anything. And at that point, his penis started to go up and it shocked me because I had . . . I had never seen a man like that and I didn't . . . well, I didn't know that it moved like that."

She took another sip of water and continued. "So he started to take his penis and go to her vaginal area, and I just stayed in the closet because I was terrified. And my sister started screaming and she kept saying, it didn't fit, you know . . . like, 'It don't fit; it don't fit.' And he kept trying to do it . . . you know . . . to get it in there, and she kept screaming and crying."

Cathy was a lot more composed on the witness stand than Didi had been. Maybe she hadn't been as badly traumatized because she was an observer rather than the physical victim of the attack. I wondered if she had ever talked to her older sister about it, or if she had done what many children do and tried her best to forget it. Now we were forcing her to remember. Why? What for? I turned around for a moment. Anita was still in the back row, staring straight ahead, unmoving.

"And then Didi screamed," Cathy continued. "She screamed and her legs, like she tried to get her legs up, to get out from underneath him, and he slapped her face and told her she better lay there and I . . . I don't . . . And then, you know, he kept trying to do it, and she kept telling him that, you know, she didn't understand what he was trying to do. And then the phone rang, and it kept ringing and ringing and ringing."

Cathy took another sip of water; her hand did not tremble. "And he said something about, 'It must be your mother,' and he left the room. And then he came back in and told her to get dressed and they left and I waited in the closet until I heard the front door shut.

"Were there any other times?" Peaches asked quietly.

"Just one other time that I remember," Cathy replied.

"Tell the judge about that, please."

This was, I would say it was . . . I was about eleven. I remember because I had just started having my monthly cycle. We were living down here, in Florida, and I came home from a friend's house. And I came into the house and I heard my sister Didi gagging, so I thought she was getting sick and I went to try . . . you know . . . to help her. And I couldn't find her anywhere."

Cathy stopped again and hesitated as if the incident was too intense for her to talk about. "Anyway, I went into my father's room . . . he and my mother were sleeping in separate rooms at the time . . . and . . . well, that's where the sound was coming from, and . . . he was laid out on the bed, on his side, and my sister . . . my sister had her head down at the area of his penis . . ." She broke off the story and looked away, her lips drawn tight and her expression a wooden mask.

"Go on, Cathy," Peaches said quietly.

"And it was in her mouth and that's what the gagging was," she said hurriedly as if she wanted to get the memory out of her mind as quickly as possible. "And, anyway, he saw me," she continued. "He told me to get out, so I went outside. And then he came out and told me if I ever told anybody what I had seen, he would make sure that I was off this earth for good." She hung her head for a moment and added, "I never told anyone before today."

I looked back at Anita again; this time her face was buried in her hands. Once again Peaches left me with a witness who had the sympathy of everybody in the courtroom – including me. Now I had the thankless task of honing her story, finding out exactly what did and did not take place over the years in the Stempo household. As I stood up to take over the questioning, I remembered Peaches comment that we were better off with Joe Stempo dead. She was right.

"Cathy, my name is David Bradley. I'm from the Attorney General's Office," I began.

"I know."

"Now, this second incident, the one that took place in

Florida, did you ever talk to Didi about it?" I guessed the answer had to be "no" because the older sister hadn't mentioned it. Either she had suppressed the memory or was too humiliated by the incident to tell us about it.

Cathy shook her head. "Like I said, I never talked about it before today: not to Didi . . . not to anyone."

"So I guess you never told your mother?"

"Are you kidding?"

That was a strange answer. "Is that a 'no'?" I asked, wondering why she was suddenly so defensive. My instincts told me to explore that relationship, but I would have to do so very carefully.

"That was a 'no'," she replied. I didn't say anything and she added, "If I wanted to live, that is."

"Were you, yourself, ever the victim of any abuse?" I intentionally left the question open-ended, not limiting it to "sexual" and not mentioning anything about abuse from her father. I wanted to see where the answer would take us.

"Yes, I was," she answered, looking directly at Grace Stempo for the first time since she entered the courtroom.

"Can you tell us about that?"

"I had physical abuse from both parents. My mother, mostly hers was a slap in the face." Grace stared straight ahead, unmoving.

"Anything else?"

"That was kind of basic," she replied. "When I was younger it was the belt; she would hit me with my father's belt. But growing up later, in my teenage years, it was a slap in the face."

"Would that be from both parents?

"No, my father . . . I was about sixteen and he got upset with me because I wasn't cleaning . . . we lived out east of town, closer to the 'Glades . . . and we had a barn, and I wasn't cleaning the barn fast enough. And I told him, I says, 'I'm going as fast as I can,' and he just got real upset. So he picked up a two by three . . . I know because I measured the darn thing afterwards . . . and he started beating me over the head with it. So I put my hands up to protect my head, and . . . you know, my fingers got all swelled up . . . and he wouldn't take me to the doctor's."

"Did you tell your mother about that beating?" I asked.

"Why? So she could give me another one?" Cathy said bitterly. Grace slumped in her chair at the counsel table and put her hands to her face. "I mean, I tried to tell her what happened," Cathy continued, "but she didn't want to hear it. She just told me to put ice on my hands and then she walked away."

"Ms. Delaney, going back to the sexual abuse of your sister Didi, do you know anything about an incident in a bathtub?"

"A bathtub?" she asked quizzically, as if I was giving her new information. "No, all I know about is what I just said." Apparently, the sisters did not discuss the episodes of sexual abuse with anyone – even with each other.

"Did he ever sexually abuse you?"

"No," she replied. Given her previous answer I didn't know whether to believe her or not.

"How about your younger sister, Anita?"

"I never saw him do anything to Anita," she said flatly, looking at her younger sister sitting in the back of the courtroom.

I had no further questions, and I was once again surprised when Bobby stayed out of the fray. This kind of thing was the stuff of life to him, but he was strangely subdued. I figured he was saving everything for the trial.

Peaches stood up. "I'd like to ask one or two questions on re-direct, Your Honor."

"I think I've heard everything I need to hear, Ms.

Bailey," Judge Ives replied.

"This will be very brief," Peaches assured her.

It's not at all unusual to ask a witness questions on re-direct examination. The reason for it is supposed to be to clear up something that the other side developed on cross; the real reason often is to get your points in last, so they have a greater effect on the judge and jury. Cathy's testimony ripped her mother as much as it did her father. Peaches was going to have to try to repair that.

"Cathy, you told us about an incident where your father beat you with a two- by-four . . ."

"Two-by-three," the witness corrected her.

"All right, two-by-three. Was that the only incident of physical abuse . . . was it the only time he beat you?"

"No, we were getting beaten all the time."

"Can you tell us about any particular incident?"

"No, just a lot of general stuff. One time he hit me on the side of my head with one of my schoolbooks, and I had a ringing in my ear for a couple of days. Stuff like that."

"When you say 'we', do you mean you and Anita?"

"Me and Didi, mostly," the woman replied. "Things calmed down a little after she moved out."

"Did you see any acts of abuse directed toward Anita?"

Peaches was pressing. That was a bad question and she must have realized it too late. She had to somehow connect all of this up to Grace pulling the trigger on Joe. It wasn't coming together that way. Now if Cathy said something, 'Oh, no, my father treated her like a princess,' Peaches argument might go down the tubes.

"Not anything special," Cathy answered. "Just the general kind of stuff that was going on in our house all the time: beatings, slaps, that kind of thing."

"And did you have any feelings of hatred or violence toward your father because of that abuse?

"Not really. I hated her more," she said, nodding in Grace's direction.

"What do you mean by that?"

Peaches was really off her game. She had just violated another big rule of trial lawyers: 'Never ask 'Why'? because the witness may tell you something you don't want to hear.' It was a small mistake and one that we all make from time to time, especially when we get an answer that catches us off guard. Even I wanted to know how Cathy could have grown up in that household without hating her father.

Cathy composed herself and looked directly at her mother. "She should have done something," she said coldly. "She could have gotten us out of there; she could have stopped it. But she just let it happen. And she did a lot of it herself."

Peaches sat down quietly. The judge excused the witness, and Cathy left the courtroom with Anita right behind her. Peaches should have argued first because she was proffering the evidence, trying to get it into the trial, but she appeared to be in shock from that last answer. I picked up the ball.

"Your Honor, we've heard some disgusting, terrible, awful testimony here today, and I would be the first one to argue that no one should have to live in a house . . . or anywhere for that matter . . . under those conditions. But the fact is, all of this testimony relates back to many years ago. No one testified about anything that was going on at the time of the murder. No one testified to any abuse of Anita. Whatever the defendants Grace Stempo and Melwin Fanchie are claiming, it can't be self-defense or even defense of another person. This testimony is designed purely and simply to show what a rotten, evil person the victim was; and that's not a defense in a murder case."

"Your Honor, if I may," Peaches had recovered and was

on her feet. "It was never my intention to argue self-defense. But there are two other issues here. The first is the battered wife syndrome. This is 1985. We have begun to recognize that a woman can be pushed to the point where she cannot be held responsible for killing an abusive spouse. Second, there is ample case law to support the proposition that I should be allowed to present evidence that a person other than my client had a motive to kill the victim. I submit that the evidence tends to show that all of the children in the household were abused, and that Anita Stempo had as much of a motive to kill Joseph Stempo as my client did."

"Your Honor, on rebuttal . . ."

"Thank you, I've heard enough, Mr. Bradley. First of all, with respect to the battered wife syndrome, there just isn't enough here. Delores Visconti testified to an incident . . . the dislocated arm . . . that happened twenty-five or thirty years ago. There was no testimony of any recent spousal abuse. I can't see this testimony coming in for that purpose."

"Now, as to your second argument, Ms. Bailey, "the judge continued. "This morning you gave me some cases, and I read them over at lunchtime. You want to show that the other daughter, Anita, who is not on trial here, also had a motive to kill her father. And I suppose you'd like the jury to infer that she and not the mother fired the fatal shot. There is case law to support the proposition that you should be allowed to show that Anita had a motive, but I'm afraid the testimony here today just doesn't do that. Delores Visconti moved out of the house when Anita was born, and Cathy Delaney said she never saw any particular abuse directed toward Anita. I'm afraid you'd need a lot more to show that she had a motive for murder."

"But, Your Honor," Peaches wasn't ready to throw in

the towel just yet. "We have evidence of a violent, abusive father who sexually molested and terrorized his own children. We can surely infer that he continued that with the youngest child."

"We have evidence of an abusive mother as well," Judge Ives reminded her. "And the sexual abuse seems to have been confined to the oldest girl, the child who was not his. Unless you can get Anita to testify otherwise at the trial, or have something that shows this kind of behavior taking place with her, the only purpose I can see for this kind of testimony is to assassinate the character of the deceased. No matter what my personal feelings are for Mr. Stempo . . . and I can assure you they are not good . . . I can't permit that. The State's motion *in limine* is granted. I'll prepare a written order from my notes. Court stands in recess."

The judge left the bench and Bobby Greenburg was out the door without a word. "What's the matter with him?" I asked Peaches after the deputies had taken Grace and Melwin out. "I've never seen Bobby so quiet. Especially when there was so much mud he could have wallowed around in."

"You're gonna win this case, David," she said as she stuffed her file back into her briefcase. "I can see it comin'. But I still say the son-of-a-bitch deserved it."

"Come on, Peaches, I'll buy you a drink," I said. "I don't like this case any more than you do."

It was still early and I didn't have anyone except Jim Harcourt to spend time with. Peaches and I walked to Chef's Bistro, a little place two blocks from the courthouse where the jazz pianist starts at five. If we tried hard enough we would be able to knock down two or three before he got there. I didn't have to worry about driving: I had my own personal bodyguard who would probably raise hell with me for me leaving the courthouse without him.

Chef's had become the unofficial hangout of the State Attorney's Office in recent years, and we were surprised to find a number of well-dressed young people huddled around the tables whispering and looking glum a few hours before quitting time.

"What's going on, Ernie?" I asked the bartender as I paid for our first round.

"Going on? Haven't you heard? Deke Stoner just resigned," he replied.

It was the kind of information you had to hear twice, and I asked him for details. There was no mistake. State Attorney Deke Stoner officially resigned his post at 3:00 p.m. that afternoon. His chief assistant, Rusty Zylka, was in charge of the office until the Governor could appoint a new State Attorney. Stoner's press conference had been brief: he said he had been offered a "very prestigious" position as house counsel to a well-known billionaire. It was, Deke said, a "life-changing" decision for him, and, since he was confident the State Attorney's Office was in good hands, he left with no regrets.

The glum-looking people at the tables apparently were assistant state attorneys wondering what happened to their boss, and if—whatever it was—might soon be happening to them as well.

"Well I'll be a jerked chicken," Peaches muttered beside me at the bar. "What happened?"

"Who knows?" Ernie replied with a shrug. "You know Deke: 'keep 'em guessing'. Personally, I think he was telling the truth. He must have got offered a gazillion dollars to represent some big shot, and he jumped at it."

Peaches looked at me and chuckled. "A gazillion dollars, huh? I never knew Deke was such a good lawyer."

"Neither did anybody else," I said with a smile.

"You really want to know what I think?" Ernie added. "I

think he just got fed up with politics."

"Yeah," I agreed, looking into my glass while I thought about Sylvia Mendez and what had most likely gone on in Tallahassee during the past few days. "I guess it's a tough way to make a living, Ernie."

CHAPTER 19

There is a saying among trial lawyers: "If you have the facts on your side, pound on the facts; if you have the law on your side, pound on the law; if you have neither on your side, pound on the table."

My pre-trial maneuvering had pretty well removed the facts from the field of play. As long as Peaches and Bobby couldn't stink up the courtroom with a lot of testimony about Joe's abuse of his daughters, I didn't worry too much about a jury pardon. But there was still the legal issue of *corpus delicti*. And Peaches and Bobby were both experienced trial lawyers; they were bound to find the weakest spot in my case. At the moment it looked like that weak spot was the medical examiner.

Dr. Carter Mitchell was the guy in question. He had become the county medical examiner soon after Deke Stoner took office. Some people said the job was a payoff for his heavy financial support of Deke's campaign. I had heard the rumors along with the rest of the legal community. Lawyers are nothing if not excellent gossips. I didn't know if the rumors were true, but I did know this: Carter was the one who originally ruled Joe Stempo's death a suicide, and he spent far too much time during his pre-trial deposition refusing to accept blame for the screw-up.

The medical examiner is the county official who investigates deaths, especially sudden, unexpected deaths due to violence. Although part of the job involves performing autopsies, the medical examiner is more than a county pathologist. A good M.E. is also a detective, and he has investigators as well as medical people on his staff. Ideally, the medical examiner or one of his investigators is called to the scene of a crime to make observations about the placement of the body and its relationship to other items of physical evidence – items like guns and patterns of blood splatter, for example.

During his pre-trial deposition, Carter told us that he was alone on the night of Joe Stempo's death; both of his investigators were off on vacation. He did not bother to show up at the crime scene because the paramedics who responded to Melwin's call already had moved the body. According to Carter, once both the body and the gun were moved, there was no longer a crime scene in the technical sense, and it would have been a waste of time for him to respond. He also told us that when he performed the autopsy the next morning, he did not bother to swab the hands of the deceased for gunpowder residue. He explained there was no county-wide policy on such matters and each police department decided on its own whether to perform such a test. He could have done it, he said, but he had not been asked to; and without a specific request from the police department he did not feel he had the authority to act on his own.

Traditional trial strategy calls for a prosecutor to present his second-strongest witness first, save the best one for last, and sandwich everything else somewhere in the middle. Doctor Carter Mitchell was definitely a middle-witness kind of guy. I needed his testimony for only one purpose: to prove that a human being named Joseph Stempo was in fact dead. I was certain that my last witness would be Anita Stempo. Her testimony was sure to finish off Jolly Boy Melwin who might then, I hoped, have a last-minute change of heart, take the stand in his own defense, and try to pin everything on Grace. If that happened, if the two of them began pointing at each other, the jury would be more likely to buy my "principal" argument and convict both of them of first-degree murder.

The big question of the moment should have been simple: who to use for the opening? Mollie was good; she was believable and could put the gun in Melwin's hand shortly before the fatal shot was fired. The down side of that approach was that it might put too much of the spotlight on Melwin. Although I no longer gave a damn about Grace, neither did I want to see Peaches slip her out from under the net. Shawn the teenage burglar linked Grace to the gun, but he left a lot to be desired in the believability department. Still, using him first would allow me to present the case in logical sequence, which is always important in a complicated, multi-defendant case. And as the believability of my witnesses increased, the jury might forget about Shawn's shifty eyes and remember only that the other witnesses bolstered his testimony. I made the final decision riding home in silence with Jim Harcourt hearing the news at Chef's. When the trial started, I would candidly admit in my opening statement that the crime had come to light because of a young burglar and then I would call Shawn Planer as my first witness.

"I'll save Anita for the end," I said to Jim when we got inside. "That'll put the blocks to Melwin. How are you coming on the rest of the Jolly Boy investigation?"

Jim didn't answer. He got himself a glass full of ice, a

splash of water and went to the liquor cart in the living room where he filled the rest of the glass with Bourbon.

"Jim, I asked you how the Jolly Boy investigation was going."

Again he did not look at me, preferring instead to inspect the mixture in his glass and stir the ice around with his finger.

"Jim, do you mind talking to me?"

He looked up at me, tight-lipped. "There is no investigation, David. The F.D.L.E. has been pulled off the Jolly Boy case. It's being turned over to the locals."

The news hit me like a sledgehammer. "You can't be serious," I demanded.

"I'm dead serious. I got the word today."

"You work for my department," I reminded him. "The only one who could pull you off that case is the Attorney General."

Jim did not respond.

"That's it, isn't it?" I demanded. "The General got Deke Stoner's resignation. He's out of the political picture . . . maybe forever . . . and now, everything else . . . Deanna Tracy's death, Watkins, my wife, me . . . everything is going to be swept under the rug. Is that it?"

Once again Harcourt did not answer but took a sip of his "Bourbon and Branch" instead.

"I won't stand for it, Jim. I'm calling Tom Julian right now. I'll go to the press if I have to," I said, picking up the telephone receiver.

"I wouldn't do that, David." Jim's voice was mellow and cool but there was something vaguely ominous in his tone.

"Are you threatening me, Jim?"

"I'm simply giving you a lesson in political reality, Counselor," he replied, taking the telephone out of my hand and hanging up. "People way above our levels have made a decision, and if we want to keep our checks coming in, we have to respect that decision. And most of all, we have to keep our mouths firmly shut." Jim was pouring another tall Bourbon while he talked and handed it to me. "Here, get your own ice and water," he said quietly.

"God damn it, this really stinks," I said bitterly.

"Not as much as you think, David," he assured me as he followed me to the icemaker. "I have been assured that the new State Attorney is quite capable of cleaning up whatever is left of the Jolly Boys – with the help of the F.D.L.E., of course."

"And who might that new State Attorney be?" I asked.

"We'll know when the Governor makes the appointment – with input from the Attorney General, of course. Now drink up, you have a long day in court tomorrow."

The courthouse rumor mill was churning out of control the next morning. Everyone from the Chief Judge to the lowest bailiff had an explanation for the sudden retirement of Deke Stoner, and a prediction of what would happen next. The story pushed our little murder off the front page, and not a single reporter sat in the audience as Peaches, Bobby and I selected the juries.

Every trial lawyer has a theory about jury selection. Defense lawyers want teachers, mothers, ministers and anyone who believes "there is no such thing as a bad boy." Prosecutors look for nice, stable, middle-class people who are likely to be hard on crime and not care too much about things like civil rights. We also want unanimity. The prosecution needs a unanimous verdict for conviction; anything less results in a "hung jury" – a mistrial – and we have to do the whole thing over. A prosecutor's nightmare is one free-thinker holding out and deadlocking the jury. I wanted these defendants tried by people who looked alike, dressed alike and thought alike. A guy with a bow tie was not likely to remain on either jury if I had a peremptory challenge left.

Technically, a group of prospective jurors is called "a venire." The lawyers question the veniremen and decided whether to allow them to serve on the jury. A lawyer can ask to have a prospective juror excused "for cause" if that person admits in open court that he or she has a fixed opinion about the case and cannot be fair. Good luck with that. Most people will come back with something that sounds like, "Of course I can be fair to the guilty bastard."

The other kind of challenge is peremptory. Each side gets a certain number of "peremptories" depending on the nature of the crime charged; the more severe the crime the greater the number of peremptory challenges for each side. Lawyers need not give a reason for using these challenges, and they apply them based on a combination of amateur psychology and intuition.

Peremptories fell from grace in the early 1980's thanks to an old practice of a few knuckleheaded prosecutors who used them to keep minorities off their juries. I wasn't one of those people. It always struck me as pretty stupid, not to mention downright embarrassing, and I was sure anything that blatant was bound to piss off the rest of the jurors. Besides, I grew up in an integrated city, and I knew hardworking, God-fearing people of every race and creed. I never had a problem with racial minorities on a jury, but a guy with a bow tie, or, worse, an earring, had to go.

I've played the game for a lot of years now, and I know all the percentages and rules about who to keep on and who to throw off. And lately I've begun to think it's all a lot of hokum invented by lawyers who really don't know what they're talking about. An example of conventional wisdom would be for me to keep women off the jury in this case. Women know what it's like to be married to a "couch potato;" they might sympathize too much with the defendant. But conventional wisdom doesn't account for the fact that women aren't killing their husbands all over the place. If you think about it from that angle, I could make a case for having a jury of six women and arguing, "Heck, lady, you didn't kill yours. Why should she get away with killing hers?" Maybe I have too much faith in the jury system, but I've found that if you get six ordinary, decent human beings together, they generally do the right thing.

Lawyers use the jury selection process for more than just selecting a jury. This is when you start persuading, arguing, getting your case across. Defense lawyers ask jurors if they agree with the idea that no one should be convicted of a crime unless they are convinced beyond a *reasonable* doubt – making "reasonable" sound like a standard nobody could ever meet in any case – while prosecutors try to shade the same argument the other way, emphasizing that "reasonable" means a doubt for which you can give a "reason." The judge keeps one eye on the clock and tries to move the whole process along while ruling on objections which one side makes whenever the other side begins injecting too much "argument" into what are supposed to be questions. In the end, it all comes down to the strike-out process: I strike out the people who I think will be favorable to the defense, and they strike out the people who they think will be favorable to me. And whatever is left is our jury.

Judge Ives didn't stand for much nonsense during jury selection, and, with her constant prodding, we picked sixteen people by the end of the first day. Six plus two alternates would hear the case against Melwin Fanchie, and an equal number would decide the fate of Grace Stempo.

The second day of the trial began with opening statements. I followed my game plan and frankly admitted that my first witness was a burglar. I told the jurors that, although he had come forward only to try to help himself out of his own trouble with the police, their subsequent investigation confirmed his information at every turn. I told them about Sergeant Clive Watkins who, unfortunately, had been in an automobile accident and might have to testify by deposition. I told them about Mollie Sussman and what she had seen. I told them about Boy Scout Ian Highsmith; how he got a bullet from the murder weapon and how that bullet matched the bullet that was found inside Joe Stempo's brain. And, finally, I told them about Jim Harcourt and the role that Jason Bonafidie played in getting a confession from Melwin.

Good Old Bobby didn't disappoint me. He stayed true to form, bashing the Attorney General and me personally for sticking our noses in where they didn't belong. We were the cause of all this trouble, he explained. We – the General and I – should be ashamed of ourselves for inflicting more pain and suffering on a grieving family that had already lost a husband and father through suicide. That's what it was, he assured the jurors: a suicide, pure and simple. The State's own Medical Examiner had said so. This whole case had been cooked up by a burglar who could not make a deal with the State Attorney and went running off to the Attorney General instead. Then, Bobby said, once the ball got rolling, a bunch of overactive teenage imaginations took over. Mollie never saw a gun; she never even mentioned it to the police until long after the rumor spread that Joe had been murdered. Anita let Ian shoot the gun that her father kept in the house – that's right, Joe's gun, the same gun he used to kill himself. Bobby was really smoking. I could have objected any number of times, especially when he got into the personal attacks, but I figured if I let him run on long enough he would eventually open his big mouth wide enough to attract his foot. He did. "Look for the evidence," he shouted to the jury. "There isn't any evidence against my client: no evidence at all." I made a note to use that statement in my summation. Bobby had painted himself into a corner.

Peaches took a different approach, one that took me by surprise. She used my gambit of admitting the worst up front. Joe and Grace did not have a happy marriage, she said, and although Grace was upset by his death, in truth it was a relief. She bought the gun, all right, but that was not illegal. And the State could not prove she did anything else. Peaches reminded the jury that the fact that Joe died from a gun that Grace bought did not mean Grace was responsible for his death. Peaches, too, invited the jury to "look at the evidence," but she did it without the shouting and arm-waving of Bobby Greenburg. It was a well-reasoned, rational opening argument and it worried me.

With the histrionics over, it was time to call my first witness. Two deputies who mercifully – for me – agreed not to keep him in handcuffs brought in Shawn from a side room. I hoped he would not repay the favor by heisting the judge's gavel if she happened to turn her back. All things considered, it didn't start off too badly. Shawn admitted right up front that he mentioned the gun incident to Sergeant Watkins because he wanted to make a deal with the State. He also said he had been promised nothing, but expected that I would go to bat for him when the time came.

With his motive out of the way, it was time to get down to the meat of his testimony. I specifically avoided asking him about the phone call from Anita that started things in motion because I didn't want to draw a "hearsay" objection. Instead I began with him being picked up at his house by Melwin, Anita and Grace. Things went along pretty well until, in response to a question, Shawn said, "And Anita said . . ." It was as far as he got. Bobby Greenburg and Peaches Bailey were both on their feet objecting to hearsay and I asked for a "sidebar conference" so we could go up to the bench and discuss the problem outside the presence of the jury. Sarah Ives went me one better: she sent the jury out of the room.

"Well, Mr. Bradley, is Anita Stempo going to testify or not?" she asked when the last juror was gone.

"I have her under subpoena, Your Honor, and I plan on calling her later in my case. However, certain statements were made in that car in furtherance of a conspiracy. The law provides that the statement of one conspirator is attributable to all of them. I've tried to be careful about hearsay, but at this point when they're all in the car together, this testimony should come in as an exception to the hearsay rule."

"Let me get this straight: you want me to allow him to testify about what another person said, even though that person has not testified at the trial?"

"Exactly, Your Honor."

"Defense?"

Bobby pounded on the table for a while, and when he finished Peaches made a very cogent legal argument that made a lot of sense. It amounted to the old chicken-and-the-egg argument: I shouldn't be allowed to get Anita's statement in front of the jury unless she herself testified or unless I first proved a conspiracy existed.

"But, Your Honor, I pleaded, "that's completely unreasonable. How can I prove a conspiracy unless I can use the statements of the conspirators?"

"That's your problem, Mr. Bradley," Judge Ives responded. "Perhaps you need to call Anita out of your planned order. I can't tell you how to try your case, but if I allow this witness to testify to an out-of-court statement that was made by someone else, and you don't prove a conspiracy somewhere down the line, I'm going to have to declare a mistrial. I don't want that and neither do you. You'll have to instruct your witnesses to refrain from testifying about anything Anita Stempo said until such time as she testifies or the Court is satisfied that you've made out a *prima facie* case of conspiracy."

I didn't want to use Anita for what was said in the car; I planned to save her for the sole purpose of burying Melwin at the end. The judge was telling me that without Anita I had to use other evidence to show "at first blush" that a conspiracy existed. Until that time I would have to confine Shawn's testimony strictly to what Grace said and what Melwin said – and what Shawn did in response. Anita's statements were out – at least for the moment.

The jury came back looking confused and I attempted to continue, but my questions were necessarily stilted. Instead of, "Okay, what happened?" I had to get very specific: "What, exactly, did Grace Stempo say at that time? What did Melwin Fanchie say? What did you do in response to that?" In spite of the awkwardness of the situation, I got Shawn's story out in a reasonably understandable manner. By the time I sat down, I was feeling pretty good. Maybe I was just getting used to Shawn, but by now he seemed almost likeable. It looked like my strategy of bringing out all the worst right up front was going to work.

Bobby pounced on him like a junkyard dog. "Melwin never said anything about killing anyone when he was checking out the gun, did he?" Bobby demanded. Shawn admitted he hadn't.

"In fact, no one in the car that day said anything about killing anyone, isn't that true?" Bobby shouted.

Shawn admitted that for all he knew the family was

merely buying a gun for self-protection.

"All my client did in that car was check out the gun as say, 'This is all you'll need,' isn't that right?"

Shawn nodded. "Yeah, I guess so."

"You guess so?" Bobby exploded. "This is a court of law, young man. My client is on trial for murder. Is that all you can do? Guess?"

I objected to the form of the question as being argumentative, and my objection was sustained.

"I'm sure of it," Shawn said belatedly.

Next Bobby attacked the schoolyard incident where Shawn claimed Melwin had threatened him. By the time he was finished, Bobby was passing off Melwin's statement – "You better just forget about that, man, 'cause you'll be next" – as nothing more than righteous indignation in response to Shawn's suggestion of murder.

Peaches came next, but did no additional damage. I began to breathe a little easier when Shawn got off the stand. The weakest part of my case had been exposed early and the other side hadn't done too much damage. I was starting to get into the rhythm of the trial, and the old question-and-answer routine had fallen into place. Although I could feel the tension in the small of my back, it didn't bother me. I had come to associate backaches with trials – and frequently with winning. I've heard some famous actors have to fight off terrible bouts of stage fright before they go on stage, but they still do it because they're hooked on whatever it is they get from performing before an audience. The same thing is true for trial lawyers; at least it was for me. At the moment I was so pumped up that nothing short of another heart attack was going to get me out of that courtroom.

With three opening statements and two defense lawyers doing separate cross-examinations, it was time for lunch when Shawn was excused. My second witness should have been Clive Watkins, but Sarge had only recently been moved to a private room. I would have to do without him and explain his absence through one of the other witnesses. In all honesty, he wasn't that important as a witness. He couldn't testify to anything that Jim Harcourt didn't know, and leaving him out gave the defense one less opportunity to squawk about the good cop/bad cop routine. We had already established it was a legal interrogation technique; there was no use dragging it out in front of the jury more than necessary. All the same, it wasn't any fun leaving Sarge out of the trial. He had done so much for the case that he deserved a few minutes in the spotlight at the end.

Mollie Sussman and her mother were waiting in the hall when we broke. I would have liked to take them to lunch, but I always made it a practice to eat light and at the counsel table when on trial. Big lunches make me sluggish. I'd rather go home hungry than be daydreaming and miss an important point on cross-examination. I slipped Mollie twenty bucks and told her to treat her mother to lunch on me. It was the least I could do for them; I expected the afternoon would be a grueling one.

It was. Bobby latched on to the fact that Mollie was the only one at the scene who connected his client to the gun, and he cross-examined her brutally about the amount of light in Anita's bedroom when Melwin came in, and the exact distance she was from Anita's dresser where he got the gun. Mollie began to get flustered, and Bobby, sensing that, hit her with the oldest line in the defense lawyers' bag, "Would you swear to that?" Asked with the right amount of incredulity, it can shake up a witness. Few witnesses stop and think that it's a silly question. They're under oath from the moment they step into the witness box: they're 'swearing' to everything they say! Sure enough, Bobby finally badgered Mollie into saying the thing in Melwin's hand "looked like a gun" which was something of a retreat from her original testimony that it "was a gun."

"It looked like a gun," Bobby crowed as he turned to the jury. "So you wouldn't swear it was a gun!"

"I would swear . . . it looked like a gun," Mollie repeated, now afraid of being too sure of anything.

And still Bobby wasn't finished. After he got her softened up, he started in on asking what she and Anita were doing in the bedroom with Melwin and probing into "what kind" of videos they were watching. Judge Ives shot me a look that said I was supposed to object. I didn't. I already knew the answer: "Edward Scissorhands." I also knew Bobby didn't know the answer; no one had asked it during Discovery. If I objected – the question was clearly irrelevant – Mollie would not be allowed to answer, and Bobby would be able to leave the jury with the sleazy impression he obviously intended. Mollie answered, and Bobby went right on, as if that was exactly the answer he expected all along.

As expected, Peaches did a much smoother job. She picked up on the fact that Mollie had said Anita Stempo was crying *after* Melwin left the room and *before* she heard the shot, which, of course, implied that Anita knew what was going to happen before it happened. Peaches pinned the sequence down nicely and spent the rest of her cross-examination going over exactly what Melwin and Anita did when he came back into the room, and where Grace was at the time. I could see where Peaches was going with her line of questioning: with Anita safely out of the way as a defendant, if Peaches could minimize Grace's participation in the gun purchase, she could argue the whole thing was a murder plot cooked up by Anita and Melwin that took Grace completely by surprise. It was a shitty thing to do to

Anita, of course, but it was a defense – and this was a murder case. I mentally starting reviewing the testimony I expected from my other witnesses. Peaches might just pull Grace out of this.

It was late in the afternoon by the time Mollie was excused – just enough time for me to get Ian Highsmith on the stand. Judge Ives sent the jury to the jury room again telling them it was time for a "bathroom break," while we went through the process known as "determining the competency of a witness," otherwise known as figuring out if he knew the difference between the truth and a lie, and knowing he could be in big trouble for telling one instead of the other. Ian was pretty nervous and didn't want to be there, but there was no doubt that he understood right from wrong. He was a competent witness. The jury was called back into the courtroom and I took Ian through the day he got the bullet from Anita Stempo. She took the gun out of her dresser drawer, he said, and told him he could only hold it if he put on rubber gloves – he called them "dishwashing gloves." He had asked her a whole lot of times, a whole lot of times, he repeated, and she finally gave in and let him shoot it once into a pillow on her bed. Then they put the gun back in the drawer, he took off the gloves and felt around for the bullet until he found it. He kept it in a secret place at home, in fact he kept the whole thing a secret until I showed up at his house and started asking him questions.

People like Ian don't understand the subtleties of language, and because of that they can destroy a lawyer who tries to cross-examine them. Ian could never be conned into saying something "looked like a gun" because he didn't understand the difference between something "looking like' something and actually being that thing. If Bobby had tried that kind of tactic on Ian rather than

Mollie, Ian would have just kept repeating, "It was a gun!" with increasing frustration and increasing volume. Besides which, any attempt at bullying him would alienate every juror. Even Bobby must have recognized the danger he faced and uncharacteristically told the judge he had no questions.

Peaches announced she had "just one or two" questions and started in slowly and carefully, keeping her voice low and smiling the whole time. She told Ian that she was sure he was telling the truth, but she just wanted to clear up a couple of things. Mrs. Stempo wasn't at home when he shot the gun, was she? Ian agreed that she wasn't. No one was home; it was just him and Anita, right? And the pillow was on Anita's bed. It was Anita's pillow, right? Ian agreed that it was. And whose idea was it to wear gloves when he fired the gun? Anita's. By that time, I was getting really concerned that Peaches had indeed found a new angle. She was leaving her options open: if Bobby's suicide defense didn't fly, she could shift gears and claim that her client Grace knew nothing about the murder plot. Now I understood why she had maneuvered Bobby into taking the defense lead in opening statements and cross-examination. It was close to five o'clock when Peaches finished her cross, and Judge Ives wanted me to call another witness. I begged off, telling her no one else was available at the moment, and assuring her that the case was going much faster than I had anticipated. At this rate, my part of the case would be concluded no later than the day after next, I assured her. She made her manure-truck-in-the-parking lot face again and reluctantly adjourned court for the day. I walked out with Ian to meet his parents in the hallway.

"Ian did a fine job, Mrs. Highsmith," I said, clapping the young man on the shoulder. "He made an excellent witness."

Ian smiled that same smile I first saw at his house when he showed me his Boy Scout uniform. "I did real good, Mom. Mr. Bradley said I didn't make a mistake or nothing."

His mother's usually rigid face softened with an expression resembling pride. "I'm sure you did a wonderful job, Ian," she told him.

I reached into my pocket and took out the medal that I fished out of my jewelry box that morning: a silver eagle hanging from a red, white and blue ribbon. "Ian, I'd like you to have this," I said as I handed it to him.

His eyes widened more than I would have thought possible. "That's your Eagle Badge, Mr. Bradley!" he said. His voice carried a note of awe that embarrassed me.

"That's right," I replied. "I don't have a son, Ian, but if I did, I would want him to be a Good Scout, just like you. I can't think of anyone better than you to hold onto this for me. Will you do it?"

"I'll never let this go, Mr. Bradley," he said, cradling it in his hands. "I'll keep this forever."

I extended my hand and he shook it. "Take care of yourself, Ian. I know you'll always be a Good Scout."

CHAPTER 20

I was back in the courtroom early the next day when Paul Berman arrived, noticeably shaken and without his client.

"Where's Anita?" I demanded. "Don't tell me she took off!"

"Let's talk in the conference room, Dave," he said without a trace of his usual good humor.

"Paul, she better not have taken off," I warned after we closed the door. "I'll go after her with every resource I have."

Paul's eyes were sadder than I had ever seen them. "Anita Stempo is dead, David," he said quietly. "She took an overdose of sleeping pills last night."

His words hit me in the gut and I turned away from him. Maybe it was the stress of the trial, but I suddenly felt sick and tears began to well up in my eyes. Paul came up behind me and put his hand on my shoulder.

"It wasn't your fault, Dave. She and Delores were staying at Cathy's house, and she found Cathy's sleeping pills. Delores found her in bed this morning."

"Poor Didi," I whispered. "First we dragged out all that

crap about her being raped by her father, and on top of everything else, she had to be the one to find her sister." I turned and faced him. "I don't care anymore, Paul," I said bitterly. "Look at the mess I've made. My wife's partner was murdered; Clive Watkins is in the hospital, and now this poor kid is dead. All because I wanted to prosecute Joe Stempo's killer. And you know what, Paul? I think Peaches Bailey was right all along: we're all better off without him."

"David," he said quietly, "Peaches, you, me . . . even Bobby. We're sworn to uphold the law. We're doing our jobs. You can't kill a slimeball just because he's a slimeball. Justice has to take its course. Is this going to damage to your case?"

I looked at him and said, "Who knows? Let's let justice take its course."

We walked back into the courtroom just in time for the arrival of Dr. Carter Mitchell. I wondered if he finally settled on who had screwed up this case the first time around. Surely, it could not have been him!

Carter was about forty-five, and stood about five-eight with a medium build. The most distinctive thing about him was his perfectly-coiffed hair that looked like it was kept in place with a high grace of shellac. Add to that his ever-present horn rimmed glasses and you have a pretty good picture of the guy who did autopsies for our county. He came in looking flustered and asked if he could talk to me. I took him to the conference room Paul and I had just vacated.

"I've been going over my notes," he said after he carefully closed the door and checked it. "I'm absolutely sure no one asked for an atomic absorption test on the decease's hands."

"You said that in your deposition, Carter," I reminded him.

"Well, I just wanted you to know that I double-checked. You see, the thing is, I had been trying to get Deke Stoner to require an absorption test on every decedent for years, but he always left it to the discretion of the local police agency. I guess you could say, 'my hands were tied,'" he said with a sheepish smile at his own comment that I'm sure he thought passed for humor.

The second rule of politics – "What have you done for me *lately?* – appeared to be hard at work. Now that Stoner was out of office, it was okay to lay the blame for sloppy M.E. procedures on his doorstep. Maybe if the trial went on long enough, we would find out he killed Joe Stempo too. He might even be responsible for the disappearance of Jimmy Hoffa.

"If you try to change your story now, Carter, the defense will slice you up like one of your specimens," I cautioned.

"No, it's not a change," he said nervously. "I'm not changing anything. I just wanted you to know that I double-checked, that's all."

I opened the door and escorted him back into the courtroom where we waited for the defense lawyers and the judge. By nine-thirty, Carter was on the stand and we were back at it. My strategy was the same as it had been for Shawn: get the worst out of the way early and hope his later testimony would be strong enough to compensate for it. We both knew Dr. Carter Mitchell had made a very serious mistake by failing to perform a crucial test on Joe Stempo's body. There was no way around that fact, and I would have to deal with it. I got him qualified as an expert witness and threw him a nice, easy question.

"Now, Dr. Mitchell, can you tell the jury what was the first thing you did when you began the autopsy?"

"The very first thing I my lab assistant and I did was take pictures," he replied. "We do it in every case."

"What did you do next?"

"I observed the body for evidentiary materials that I knew might be lost during the cleansing process. At the same time, I inquired from the police that were present at the time of the autopsy whether they were certain things they were going to do prior to my performing the actual autopsy, such as collection of evidentiary materials, that is in the purview of the local police in this county."

I didn't ask the question, but after a momentary pause Dr. Mitchell continued, "The police agencies collect their own trace evidentiary material such as hairs that might be in the hands, fingernail scrapings, and review testing of the hands . . . that sort of thing. Then I inspect the body, such as in this case, there was a gunshot wound in the head. Looking at it prior to any cleansing to see if there were any characteristics of the wound that might provide important information that might be of a legal consequence."

Carter was trying hard to avoid the issue. I would have to force him to get to it. "You mentioned 'hands,' Doctor. Was there anything unusual about the hands on his body when you first saw it?"

"Nothing unusual, no."

No, of course not, you moron; they were only wrapped in plastic! I thought. I smiled and asked, "Were the hands encased in plastic bags?"

"Yes, the hands were bagged, but that is not unusual."

"Did you do anything with the hands?"

"Yes. I removed the bags and inspected them for evidence of anything with the naked eyes and a hand lens, that is, a magnifying glass, to see if I could see evidence of gunpowder residue, smoke, soot . . . material on the hands."

"Did you see any such residue?"

"No," he replied. That was at least a little something for

our side. If Joe had shot himself, there should have been gunpowder residue on one of his hands. I made a mental note to come back to that. The subject of "hands" appeared to be making Carter uncomfortable and he kept shifting in the witness chair. He knew what was coming next, and he didn't want to talk about it.

"Did you at any time conduct what is known as an atomic absorption test or any sort of chemical test for gunshot residue?"

"No. The atomic absorption test is a laboratory analysis for gunpowder and primer residues," he explained, doing more than just answering my question. "It consists of swabbing the hands with an acidic solution in various areas. The swabs are collected and analyzed in the laboratory."

"And can you tell the jury why you did not perform that test?"

"Because of budgetary constraints, tests such as that are within the purview of the police agencies in this county," he replied. "I have tried to have that policy changed for many years, but Mr. Stoner, the State Attorney . . . or I guess I should say the former State Attorney . . . felt the decision in each case should be left up to the local police department."

"Did anyone perform such a test in this case?"

"Not to my knowledge. It is rarely done in this county because of the cost."

"Did anyone ask you to perform such a test?

"No."

"Then if no test was going to be performed, why were the hands bagged?" That question bugged me, and I was sure the jury would have trouble with it, too.

"It is not uncommon for the local police to do that when I am not able to be at the scene to preserve whatever physical evidence is on the hands. That was the evidence I was looking for earlier and did not find," he said, relaxing a little in the witness chair.

"Is it your policy to be at every crime scene?"

"Yes. Either I or one of my investigators goes to the scene of every unnatural death in this county. Unfortunately both my investigators were on vacation, and since the medical personnel had moved both the body and the other physical evidence in an attempt to resuscitate Mr. Stempo . . . the deceased . . . there was no longer a crime scene, from my standpoint, and I did not think it was important for me to respond."

"Tell the jury what you did find, if anything, after you unbagged the hands."

"Well, principally I was looking for, as I said, gunpowder residue. Suicides hold the handle of the gun with one hand and frequently hold the barrel with the other one, to steady it, I suppose. You see different types of residue deposits in different areas of the hands. I believe one hand, the right hand, had blood on it, which, of course, can cover residue. I did not see any residue on either hand."

"Let's talk about the gunshot wound itself. What can you tell us about that?"

Carter leaned back in the witness chair and went into a more relaxed, "expert witness" mode. He was a lot more confident in this part of his testimony.

"The entrance was in the left temple of the head, here," he said, placing a finger to the side of his own head, "and the exit was on the right side above the right ear." Again he demonstrated on himself using his finger. "The differentiation between the wounds in this case was very easy. The exit wound was a simple tear in the skin. There was no evidence of gunpowder residues or what is commonly called powder burns. At the entrance wound site, I saw obvious gunpowder residue that had deposited on the surface of the skin. The configuration of the hole at the entrance wound was also larger, slightly larger, and it had an irregular configuration."

"Dr. Mitchell, could you describe for the jury how that residue is deposited on the skin? What causes that?" I was asking the kind of questions Carter liked to answer, and he assumed the professorial tone I had come to know and hate so much.

"At the time a weapon is discharged, a number of things come out of the barrel, principally the bullet, of course, but also other things like a small flame together with hot gasses, smoke, and gunpowder particles. The bullet will go in a straight line, but the other materials will spread out. So we look in a gunshot entrance wound for evidence of these materials. Around the hole caused by the bullet will be a small abraded area of the skin; it will indent the skin and scrape off the edge of the skin as it goes through. You can see where the particles struck the skin. The farther the gun is away from the body, the fainter and more spread out the marks will be. If the gun is very close, you will see the effects of the flame and the skin around the wound will be burned or scorched."

"What if the barrel is pressed right up against the skin?" I asked.

"You won't see any residues. You will see burning, just a little burning at the margin of the hole, and all of the materials will be deposited internally into the soft tissue."

With the medical lesson completed, I was going to try my best to rule out suicide. "Was the pattern of gunshot residue which you observed on Mr. Stempo consistent with tight contact?"

"No, because there was residue at the site of the wound and no residue in the soft tissue."

"Based on your examination, can you state within a

reasonable degree of medical certainty how far the muzzle of the gun was from the wound when the shot was fired?"

"Based on the effects of the flames and hot gasses on the skin and the soot residue pattern, I would estimate somewhere between half an inch to one inch."

"And did the bullet cause instant death?" It was not a relevant question, but I hoped the defense was asleep. A little gory testimony might get the jurors pissed off enough to overlook some gaps in my case.

"No, it did not cause instant death," Carter answered. "He was alive long enough to form a blood clot in his head. In addition, he aspirated a lot of blood into his lungs."

My next question, whether Joe had suffered any pain, drew an expected irrelevancy objection that the judge sustained. It appeared both Peaches and Bobby had awakened. It was time for me to wrap this thing up.

"Dr. Mitchell, what does the phrase 'cause of death' mean?"

"It's the disease or injury which produces the death of the individual."

"And what do you base a determination of 'cause of death' on?"

"Primarily on my autopsy findings as well as the circumstances of the individual's death."

"All right, what was the 'cause of death' of Joseph Stempo?"

"Gunshot wound to the head."

"Now, Dr. Mitchell, what does the phrase 'manner of death' mean?"

Carter shifted in the witness chair again, and the professorial tone began to waiver. "'Manner of death' refers to a classification on the death certificate as to whether the cause of death was due to natural disease, was accidental, a homicide, a suicide or undetermined."

"What do you base your opinion of 'manner of death' on?"

"It's based in part on the autopsy findings, but also on the circumstances of the death."

"What does the autopsy tell you about the 'manner of death'?"

"It's just one tool in the investigation," he replied. "My office also performs an investigation." He hadn't really answered my question, but it would do for now.

"All right, and would you tell the jury how you perform such an investigation?"

"We gather information on the case. What were the circumstances of the death? Is there any medically history? That sort of thing. We also gather information from the police, and finally, we gather information from the family."

"So your 'manner of death' finding is a combination of your autopsy results and this additional information?"

"All the information we gathered in this case," he repeated. "The police gave us information, and the wife also provided information."

"Is there any particular reason for making a finding as to 'manner of death'?"

Carter Mitchell shifted in his chair again. "A function of the medical examiner is to serve the people, and we try to do that to the best of our ability. If at all possible, we try to list a 'manner of death' in every case for the benefit of the family: for insurances and other such legal purposes."

"Directing your attention to this case, Doctor, did you form an opinion as to the 'manner of death'?"

Carter shifted again. "Yes, I did. I formed an opinion twice," he replied.

"Can you tell the jury about that?"

"The first time was based on the information provided by the police and the wife. The police were not going to pursue the investigation further, and because of that, there did not appear to be any reason to list the manner of death as 'pending.' They were convinced as to the manner of death, and since I had no additional information, I classified the manner of death as a suicide."

"Did anything happen later to change your opinion?"

"Yes, I was provided with additional information from the Florida Department of Law Enforcement. I received a telephone call from an Agent Harcourt, and . . ."

I cut him off in mid-sentence. He couldn't tell us what Harcourt told him; that would be hearsay. But I could ask him if, as a result of the telephone call, he formed a new opinion as to the manner of death of Joseph Stempo.

"Yes," he replied. "Based on additional information provided to me by Agent Harcourt, I changed the classification of 'manner of death' from 'suicide' to 'homicide'."

There was nothing left to say, and I turned Dr. Carter Mitchell over to the not-so-tender mercies of Bobby Greenburg and Peaches Bailey. As usual, Bobby pounced first.

"Doctor, all of the test results you had, caused you to certify the manner of death as a suicide the first time, is that correct?"

"That is correct. The manner of death was consistent with a suicide."

"And all of the physical evidence was consistent with suicide, isn't that correct?"

"That is correct."

"And all of the information you received was consistent with suicide, isn't that correct?"

"That is correct."

"For instance, you had received information, you knew that the man had financial problems at the time of his death, isn't that true?"

"Yes, that's true."

"And you knew that he had been depressed for some time prior to his death, isn't that true?"

Carter admitted that he had been told of Joe Stempo's depression. Both of Bobby's questions were objectionable since they called for answers that were clearly based on hearsay. I let it slide. I had Melwin on tape – twice – and I was planning on pounding Bobby with that. If I began objecting now the jury might think I was trying to hide something.

"All of the information provided to you by Mr. Harcourt did not include any additional evidence. It only involved him telling you certain things that other people, other civilians, said to him, isn't that right?" Bobby demanded.

Carter shifted in the witness chair again. "Yes, I guess you could say that."

"Now, Doctor," Bobby continued, "it would have been much better for you to visit the scene of the death yourself, wouldn't it? Instead of just relying on third-hand information?"

"As I explained earlier, once the body is moved, and the physical evidence is moved, there is no longer a crime scene. It has no evidentiary value."

"So in this case, you would have gone to the scene, except you were told that these items, the body and other items, had been moved, is that correct?"

"Yes, that's correct," Carter agreed.

"That's pretty poor police work, isn't it?"

I objected. Dr. Mitchell was a medical examiner, not an expert on police procedures, I said. The judge agreed and sustained my objection, but Carter answered anyway.

"I understood that the items had been moved by emergency medical technicians before the police got there," he said.

Bobby charged ahead. "At the time you performed the autopsy, you thought you had enough information to make a determination about the manner of death, isn't that true?"

"Yes, that's right."

"And you certified the manner of death as a suicide, is that correct?"

"Yes, at that time I did."

"And you also certified the 'cause of death' as a gunshot wound to the head, isn't that right?" Bobby asked, holding up a copy of the death certificate and looking at it for dramatic effect.

"That's correct."

"But that 'cause of death' doesn't mean that someone else shot him, isn't that right?"

"That's up to the jury, Mr. Greenburg," It sounded like Carter was tired of being beaten up and was going to fight back.

"That's right. That's up to this jury," Bobby almost shouted, turning to the jurors. "You cannot tell us who pulled the trigger can you?" he demanded.

"There was a gunshot wound to the head. Who pulled the trigger, I cannot tell from the autopsy findings." Well, so much for fighting back, I thought.

"So to this day," Bobby shouted, waving the copy of the death certificate in the air, "based on your own personal knowledge you don't know if this was a suicide or a homicide, do you?"

"No, I do not," Carter admitted meekly.

Bobby had gotten as far as he could. He sat down and Peaches began her cross-examination on behalf of Grace Stempo.

"Doctor, would you agree that it is absolutely essential in the circumstances of this case to perform an atomic absorption test?"

"No. It would have been helpful, perhaps, but not essential."

"Any professional investigator, yourself included, would have wanted that done, wouldn't they?"

"Well, yes. My opinion is that it always should be done, Carter replied. "But my opinion doesn't . . . didn't . . . count for much with the former State Attorney."

"Dr. Mitchell, you testified that Mr. Stempo's hands were bagged. Didn't that indicate to you that an atomic absorption test was in order?"

"I didn't know . . . let me rephrase that . . . I still don't know why they bagged the hands. It might have been for such a test; however a lot of homicide detectives will bag them so we don't lose other trace evidence such as hairs, fibers, or other materials that may have become embedded during a struggle. There is also the problem of lighting. We have much better lighting in the lab, and can often see things that might be overlooked at the scene."

"The body comes in," Peaches asked, gesturing with both hands as if it were stretched out in front of her, "the hands are bagged, you see that. You don't automatically wait for the police who are handling the case to arrive and take their swabs?"

"As I said earlier," Carter was sweating a little now, "the decision of whether or not to perform such a test is up to the local police department. Any homicide or shooting death we usually call the police and ask them if they are going to take any hand washings. If they answer yes, then we do nothing until they come and do so."

"Was that done in this case?"

"I really couldn't . . . my notes do not indicate that anyone asked for such a test."

"But do your notes show whether or not you called

anybody and asked whether they intended to perform such a test??

"No, they . . . my notes do not show that, either."

"So you can't say whether you asked and the answer was 'no,' or whether you did not ask, and the police did not have an opportunity to respond, is that what you're telling us?"

"Yes, well, no. If they . . . ordinarily, if they had wanted such a test performed they would have made their request known when the body was delivered." Carter took out a handkerchief and wiped his forehead. I wished he hadn't done that; it made his nervousness even more apparent.

"But you just said that it's your policy to call the local department and find out if they want such a test performed before you do anything, isn't that right?"

"Yes, well, that too. We sort of double-check with them before we proceed."

"But you can't say whether anyone double-checked in this case?" Peaches was not like Bobby; she never raised her voice. She didn't have to – her questions were devastating enough.

"No, I can't," Carter admitted.

"You did learn, didn't you, that an atomic absorption test had been performed on my client, Grace Stempo?"

"Yes, I have heard that."

"What was the result of that test?"

The test was negative, of course. The swabs had been taken almost as an afterthought, long after the body had been removed. I knew all about it. Peaches' question called for a hearsay answer, and I could properly object to it: Carter hadn't performed the test, and anything he knew about it was the result of what someone told him. But again, I didn't want the jury to think I was hiding anything. It was better to let Carter answer the improper question.

Ian Highsmith had already testified that he had only been allowed to handle the gun after he put on rubber gloves. It didn't take a genius to conclude that whoever shot Joe Stempo probably used the same precaution. Besides, if the negative test result didn't come out now, Peaches was sure to get it out of Jim Harcourt later in the trial. All of the arguments for and against a legitimate objection went through my mind in far less time than it takes to tell. Judge Ives looked at me; I didn't object and Carter answered the question.

"To the best of my knowledge, the test on Mrs. Stempo's hands was negative."

"So it's accurate to say that based on all of the physical evidence you have, you can't rule out suicide, can you?"

"I can't rule it out, no."

"And, obviously, you can't say that Grace Stempo shot him."

"No, I can't say that, either."

Peaches sat down. It had been an excellent cross-examination: no arm waving, no theatrics; just persistent, probing questions. It was tough for me to gauge how much damage she had done. True, she knocked hell out of us for not doing that damn test, but what did that prove? I stood up to make a final point with re-direct examination in case anyone needed to be reminded.

"Doctor, when you said the test result on Mrs. Stempo was negative, does that mean she did not fire the gun?"

"Oh, no. Certainly not. It merely means that no residue was found on her hands. There could be any number of reasons for that: if she had been wearing gloves, for example."

Good Old Carter, in there pitching to the very end. Maybe he wasn't as big a jerk as I thought he was, or maybe he figured that in light of Deke Stoner's sudden departure, he needed to be on the good side of whomever was going to be the new big gun in town. Whatever his reason, I appreciated his attempt at a final boost. Even Peaches was afraid of opening up the can of worms his gratuitous comment left behind, and Carter was excused without another question.

My second witness of the morning was the ballistics guy who testified that the bullet which went through Joe's brain was fired from the revolver that was found in the house; the revolver which, I would later argue, was the one that Shawn had sold: the one that Ian Highsmith had fired, and the one that Mollie Sussman had seen Melwin Fanchie take out of Anita Stempo's drawer. But now I no longer had Anita who could confirm that fact; it all rested on Mollie. The ballistics guy escaped without any cross-examination. Everybody was tired and hungry, and besides, the defense practically admitted that the gun in evidence was the gun that caused the death of Joe Stempo. The two questions the jury would have to decide were whose finger was on the trigger at the time, and how much the other defendant, the non-shooter, knew about the murder before it happened.

I had two witnesses left who might be able to come up with the answers: Jim Harcourt and Jason Bonafidie. As we broke for the luncheon recess, I asked for a conference in chambers where I informed Judge Ives and both defense counsel that Anita Stempo was not available to testify after all.

"It's a good thing I didn't let you get into that hearsay," Judge Ives observed. "Are you going to request a *capias* for her arrest?"

"She's beyond the jurisdiction of the Court, Your Honor. Anita Stempo committed suicide last night."

Judge Ives and Peaches were visibly shaken; Bobby merely smiled.

"I'm very sorry to hear that, Mr. Bradley," Judge Ives said. "She must have been a very troubled young woman. It's so sad." She looked at me sympathetically and added, "Will you need some time to reorganize your case?"

"No, Your Honor. I'll put on my last two witnesses this afternoon and call it a day," I said quietly. "I guess maybe there are more important things in life than this case after all."

As we filed out of chambers, I wondered which one I should call last. Jason Bonafidie made a heroic appearance: a kid who felt it was his duty to report a crime. But Jim Harcourt had taken Grace's statement and also took the statement from Melwin when Melwin dropped the dime on Grace. With two juries, Peaches could argue that Melwin's statement was pure hearsay against Grace: it was an out-of-court statement made to prove the truth of the matter asserted. And if Judge Ives wasn't satisfied with the evidence of a conspiracy, she might not let Grace's jury hear that statement.

And there was this to consider: Jim had recorded the conversation between Jason and Melwin. I could call him last for the purpose of authenticating the tape, and then play it for the jury – or not. The choice was mine. I might be able to get the most damaging parts of his statement before the jury without letting them hear the whole thing – the part where he blamed the murder on Grace. She was a broken old woman; for all practical purposes her life was over. Melwin, on the other hand, was a Jolly Boy. He was a prize worth fighting for. I no longer had Anita to lower the boom on him, but I was considering a strategy – admittedly a far-fetched one – that might force him onto the witness stand. The jurors could get an up-close and personal look at him; see him as the thug he really was rather than the misled youth Bobby was portraying him as. It was a crazy idea that might work. I decided Jim Harcourt would be batting clean-up for our team.

CHAPTER 21

Jason was as good as I expected him to be. The jurors sat in rapt attention as the confident young man talked about how he had gone to the movies with people he thought were his friends and how, after he got there, Melwin Fanchie told him that he killed Joe Stempo. Jason talked about his fear of getting involved and his reluctance to do anything. And finally, he told us how he had gone to his mother with the disturbing news.

It was almost time to play the tape. I set the stage by having Jason testify about how Jim Harcourt and Clive Watkins strapped a hidden transmitter on his body and drove to a drop-off point near the Stempo house. He described how he walked the last block alone, talking to his unseen companions and hoping they could hear him. As I questioned him, I noticed several jurors sitting on the edges of their seats. They wanted to hear that tape, but they couldn't – not yet. It still was not an exhibit in evidence, and it would not be until Jim Harcourt testified.

I was very careful to limit my questions. I wanted to protect Jason from one of Bobby Greenburg's ruthless cross-examinations, so I intentionally avoided asking about

Melwin's actual statements. Since cross-examination is limited to the subjects brought up on direct, Bobby would have to shout and carry on about the "fairness" of the Jason's actions, but he would not be able to attack what had been said. The jury would hear that at the end, and the tape would speak for itself. Not even the great Bobby Greenburg could cross-examine a tape recorder.

That didn't stop Bobby from attempting to terrorize Jason on the witness stand.

"Now, young man, you claim to be a friend of Melwin Fanchie, is that right?"

"No. I was his friend at one time. I'm not anymore."

"But you were his friend at one time?"

"That's right."

"Were you his friend when you went to the movies with him?"

"That's why I went to the movies with him . . . along with some other people."

"And at the movies . . . that's when Melwin told you . . . allegedly told you . . . whatever story you say he told you, is that right?"

"Excuse me?"

"Listen to me," Bobby said, raising his voice, "Do you know what 'allegedly' means?"

"It means I have to prove it, right?"

"That's right, you have to prove it. The State has to prove it. Now, you claim that my client told you something that night at the movies, is that right?"

"That's right," Jason replied.

"And you believed him?"

"Yes."

"And that's when you decided to go to the police and become a spy for them?"

"No, not right away I didn't."

"You didn't do it right away. How long did it take?"

"Like I said, I thought about it for a couple of days."

"And then you told your mother?" Bobby demanded.

"And then I told my mother."

"So it was your mother's idea to spy on your friend?"

"He wasn't my friend anymore," Jason replied.

"He wasn't your friend because of this story he told you?" Bobby said incredulously.

"Yes."

"A story you didn't know if it was true or not?"

"I thought it was true. It sounded true."

"You *thought* it was true," Bobby shouted, looking at the jury and smiling as if he had just solved the entire case. "You *thought* it was true. What if it was false? What if it was a joke? Would he still be your friend?"

"Yes. No . . . I don't know. I guess maybe he would." Jason's face flushed; Bobby was getting to him.

"So not knowing whether the story was true or not, not knowing whether Melwin was your friend or not, you agreed to spy on him, isn't that right?"

"He wasn't my friend anymore," Jason insisted.

"But you said that he would have been your friend if the story was not true . . . if it had been a joke."

"My friends don't joke about things like that," Jason shot back. It was a good enough answer to make Bobby change the subject.

"Now, when these men taped that transmitter to your body, what did they tell you to do?"

"Just act natural," the young man replied.

"Did they tell you want to say to Melwin?"

"Only that I should try to get him to talk about . . . you know, talk about the murder."

"So they told you more than just to act natural, isn't that right?"

"I . . . yeah, I guess so. That's right."

"You were the one who brought up the subject of the murder, weren't you?"

"Not the first time . . . not at the movies."

Bobby's face reddened. "We're not talking about the movies. You weren't wearing a transmitter then, were you?"

"No."

"Well, pay attention."

I objected to that. You can do a lot of things on cross-examination, but you can't argue with a witness. Judge Ives sustained me and told the jury to disregard Bobby's last remark. But the warning didn't slow him down.

"When you were wearing the transmitter at his house, you were the one who brought up the subject of the murder again, weren't you?"

"Kind of . . ."

"Did you or didn't you?"

"Yes."

"And Melwin went right along with it, told you the same story again, didn't he?"

"Yes."

"No different from that the first time, isn't that right?"

"That's right."

"Exactly the same?"

"I . . . I think so."

"He didn't add any fresh details, did he?"

"I . . . I'm not sure. I don't think he did."

"So it was just the same cockamamie story he told you the first time, isn't that right?"

"It was the same story," Jason answered.

"And you believed him?"

"Yes, I believed him."

"And after Melwin got arrested, you talked to other

young people about it, didn't you?"

"A few, I guess."

"You guess? You talked to Mollie Sussman, didn't you?"

"Yes."

"And you told her what Melwin told you?"

"Yes."

"And that's when Mollie suddenly remembered seeing him with the gun?"

I objected to that question. There was no way Jason could know when it was that Mollie first remembered seeing anything. The judge overruled my objection and said that Jason could answer the question "if he knew" the answer.

"I don't know when she remembered about it," Jason said, taking a hint from my spoken objection.

"Well, she didn't go to the police until after you talked to her, isn't that true?"

Again, I objected, but Jason said, "I don't know when she went to the police," before the judge could rule. I needed to slow things down a bit, and I asked Judge Ives to instruct Bobby to stop badgering the witness. Actually, I didn't care whether the judge did that or not, but I figured that by standing up and arguing for a minute or two I might break Bobby's concentration and give Jason a chance to collect his thoughts.

"Your last objection is sustained, Mr. Bradley," Judge Ives replied as she turned toward the jury. "The jury is instructed to disregard the witness' answer about what another person may have done or when she spoke to the police." The judge turned back toward me. "Other than that, the Court will not interfere with Counsel's cross-examination. You may proceed, Mr. Greenburg."

I don't know whether Sarah was trying to help me or not, but my objection and her speech threw Bobby off his stride. He looked vaguely flustered, like he had forgotten what he was going to say next. He walked over to the counsel table for a whispered conference with his client.

"Do you have any other questions, Mr. Greenburg?" Judge Ives asked.

"You still don't know, from your own knowledge, who shot Joseph Stempo, do you?"

It was the one question Bobby shouldn't have asked.

"All's I know is your client told me he did it," Jason responded.

Bobby hesitated for a moment. He had gotten the worst kind of answer: the kind jurors remember. He needed to come back from it without doing further damage to his case. His face reddened again and his voice got louder.

"Listen carefully," he shouted. "Do you know what 'of your own knowledge' means?"

"Something that I know?" Jason asked innocently.

"Something that you know . . . that you saw or heard yourself," Bobby blustered. "Now, from your own knowledge, do you know who killed Joseph Stempo?"

"Like I said, from my own knowledge, your client told me he did it. I heard that myself." Jason looked from me to the judge with an expression that asked if that was the proper answer.

"Judge, I ask that you make him respond to my question," Bobby demanded as his face grew redder. This was more like it, the classic Bobby Greenburg style: confuse the hell out of the witness and then complain about it.

"Jason, Mr. Greenburg wants to know if you know who killed Joseph Stempo without relying on what anyone else told you," Judge Ives explained patiently.

"Without relying on what he told me," Jason said, pointing to Melwin, "no, I don't know who killed him."

Bobby looked like he wanted to ask another question, hesitated, whispered something to his client and finally blurted out, "I don't have anything else, Judge," as he sat down.

Peaches announced she had no questions of this witness, and the judge excused him. It was time for Agent Jim Harcourt to wrap things up.

Jim was nattily attired in a tailored blue blazer and tan pants. He took the witness stand with an air of comfortable familiarity, and he looked directly at the jury whenever he answered one of my questions. I wondered whether the F.D.L.E. gave classes on "how to be a witness," or if his polished performance was the result of hard-won experience in courtrooms throughout the State.

First we cleared up the matter of the missing Clive Watkins. In response to my questions, Jim told the jury that Sergeant Watkins was in the hospital as the result of an automobile accident. I offered no details. If the defense attorneys wanted to touch the hot potato labeled "Jolly Boys," they were welcome to do so. I suspected neither one would go near the subject with a ten-foot pole.

Jim then told the jury about the investigation, how he and Clive Watkins wired Jason for sound and then sat in a car and listened to Jason's conversation with Melwin while they recorded it. He talked about the night of the arrest, how we executed the warrants at the Stempo house and found the murder weapon in a drawer in Anita's bedroom. Finally, he told the jury about how he took statements from Melwin and Grace the night they were arrested. At that point, I asked the judge to excuse the jury for a legal argument. I felt that I had set up a situation that would force Melwin to testify. Now it was time, as my college baseball coach used to say, to execute the play on the field.

"Let's hear your argument, Mr. Bradley," Judge Ives said

after the jurors were out of the courtroom.

"Your Honor, we are at the point where the State would ordinarily seek to play the tape recordings. However, I intend to move only two of them into evidence: the Bonafidie tape and the one of Grace Stempo's confession. I will not seek to admit the tape of Melwin Fanchie's confession."

Peaches looked at me like I was crazy, and Bobby was obviously bewildered.

"Would you care to expand on that, Mr. Bradley," the judge asked.

"Yes, of course, Your Honor," I explained. "We obviously have two separate juries in the courtroom. Fanchie's second statement, the one in which he implicates Mrs. Stempo, cannot be played for the Stempo jury because of the hearsay rule; it's an out-of-court statement which the State would be seeking to admit to prove the truth of the matter asserted. In other words," I added for Melwin's benefit, "if we play Melwin's statement, the one in which he accuses Grace of pulling the trigger, he would in effect be testifying against her without taking the witness stand."

"The Court is well aware of the rule against hearsay, Mr. Bradley," Judge Ives said through pursed lips.

"I'm sure you are, Your Honor." I really wasn't talking to her. It was a good bet that Bobby Greenburg hadn't told Melwin about this wrinkle. I was sure he hadn't even figured it out himself. It was time for me to launch into my prepared lecture on the law disguised as an argument.

"The problem is," I continued, "if the Stempo jury hears Fanchie's first statement . . . the one in which he tells Jason Bonafidie that he killed the victim . . . and it does not hear the statement in which he implicates Mrs. Stempo, her jury will not have the benefit of all of the evidence. We could end up with a situation in which Fanchie convicts himself of murder and Mrs. Stempo is acquitted, all because of a statement that Melwin made to Jason and that Melwin later said was untrue."

"What's he talkin' about, man? What's he mean, 'convicted myself?'" Melwin was on his feet; I guess I got his attention.

"Mr. Fanchie, sit down or I'll have you removed from the courtroom," the judge said sternly.

"But he's not tellin' me what's happenin', Judge . . . Your Honor," Melwin protested, pointing at Bobby.

"That's not true, Bobby shouted, jumping to his feet as well. "I've advised him of our strategy at each and every step of this trial."

"No, he hasn't, Judge," Melwin protested even louder and the courtroom deputies began to close in on him. "He didn't say nothin' about the jury not hearin' that tape. I mean . . . I didn't pull the trigger. She did it. The old lady did it. The jury should hear that!"

Sarah Ives banged her gavel. "All right, everybody sit down. Mr. Fanchie, if you say another word, the deputies will take you back to a cell. Now, Mr. Bradley, you started this ruckus, do you have a solution?"

"My suggestion is that the Stempo jury hears only the Grace Stempo tape and the Fanchie jury hears Bonafidie/Fanchie tape, Your Honor," I said "If Mr. Fanchie wants to testify . . . or if he wants to admit the tape of his own confession to Agent Harcourt, that's up to him."

I expected Peaches to be on her feet in a second. She was.

"I strongly object to that, Your Honor," Peaches said. "That first tape is where Fanchie tells Jason he's the one who killed Joseph Stempo. It's exculpatory evidence for my client, and she is entitled to have her jury hear it."

"How about that, Mr. Bradley?" Judge Ives asked. "Doesn't Mrs. Stempo have a right to present exculpatory evidence?"

"Then we're back at the beginning, Your Honor. The Stempo jury will hear Fanchie's admission, but won't hear his retraction. He convicts himself and Mrs. Stempo goes free. That's fine with me, as long as all of the parties know where we're going from this point forward." They say misery loves company; I was counting on Melwin to make sure he wasn't going down alone. It must have worked; I could see a lot of hurried whispering at Bobby Greenburg's end of the counsel table.

"Your Honor, if I may," Bobby said, brushing off Melwin and standing up again, "my client needs a little time to . . . we need a little time, Your Honor."

"It looks like Mr. Bradley has everybody bagged," Judge Ives observed. "I'll give you fifteen minutes, Mr. Greenburg. And when we reconvene, I want to know whether your client intends to testify. If he does, I'm inclined to let everybody hear everything. Court stands in recess."

The judge left the bench and Bobby took Melwin into one of the conference rooms with a deputy close behind. Peaches sat at the counsel table with Grace and shook her head a lot in response to Grace's whispers. It looked like I had just ruined everybody's day.

We were back in session without the jury promptly at three-thirty, and Bobby opened things up by announcing that his client had decided to testify after the State rested. Peaches screamed bloody murder claiming that I had sandbagged her, but there was nothing anybody could do. Melwin wasn't my witness. I wasn't calling him to testify for the State; and a defendant can't be prevented from testifying in his own defense.

"All right, in view of that development, I intend to let both juries hear all of the tapes. Is there any objection?"

"I still object, Your Honor," Peaches said. "Fanchie's second tape is still hearsay with respect to my client. And now with him going to testify, he will just be bolstering his own testimony."

"I don't think the tape will be hearsay if he testifies, Ms. Bailey, but you have a point about bolstering," the judge replied. "All right, how's this: in view of the fact that Mr. Fanchie is going to testify, I'll exclude the second tape from both juries, but I'll allow Mr. Bradley to use it for rebuttal purposes if Mr. Fanchie does not testify in a manner consistent with the tape. How's that?"

It was a good deal for our team. Melwin would tell his story in person rather than through the cold tape recorder, and I would get a chance to cross-examine him and pound him with his inconsistencies. I was sure I could break him in front of the jury. There was one thing I didn't like about the idea, and I told the judge so. Melwin could change his mind overnight and double-cross everybody by refusing to testify the next morning.

"If that happens, Mr. Bradley, I'll allow you to reopen your case and play the tape for the Fanchie jury," the judge replied. Now, unless there's another objection, I don't intend to explain any of this to the jurors. We'll just go ahead with the evidence, and at the end of the case let each jury come to a verdict on its particular defendant."

"I'd like to preserve a continuing objection for the record, Your Honor." Peaches sounded like she knew the game was over. She was getting set for the appeal.

The jurors came back in looking bewildered. We had just made a number of critical decisions that would determine what they would hear and would no doubt affect the outcome of the case, but as far as they were concerned, the judge might have been in the lavatory and the lawyers sipping coffee somewhere. No one understands what goes on in courtrooms — least of all jurors.

During the recess, Jim had set up a tape recorder on a table in front of the jury box. After we reconvened, I went through the standard questions and answers with him, confirming it was the actual tape and that it had not been altered. The judge accepted it into evidence, and Jim hit the "Play" button. The sound of Jason's voice filled the room.

"Okay, I'm getting' close to the house now, and I hope you guys can hear me," we heard him say. There was the sound of knocking and Jason's voice again, "Hey, 's Mel home?"

"He's out back, workin' on the car," a female voice replied."

"Hey, man, how's it goin'?" It was Jason's voice again.

"It'd be goin' a lot better if this car wasn't such a piece of shit," came the reply in Melwin's voice.

The banter continued for a few minutes, mostly centered on the late Mr. Stempo's car, and Melwin's low opinion of it.

"I can't believe you did it, man," Jason finally said.

"Did what?"

"You know . . . what you were tellin' me the other night at the movies."

"Yeah, well you better keep your fuckin' mouth shut, man, or the same thing could happen to you."

"Hey, Mel! C'mon, man. I just meant you really had to have a lot of balls to do something like that. That's all."

There was a snicker, and then Melwin's voice replied, "Yeah, I guess it was pretty cool."

"You popped him, right?" Jason asked, sounding awed.

"Man, I just put that gun to the old dude's head, man, and . . . Pop!"

"Did he, like, move or anything?"

"He jerked a couple of times; no big thing."

"Lots of blood, I bet."

"Not that much. Some, but not like all over the place."

"Man, that must have been cool," Jason said, again sounding awed. "Why'd you do it, anyway?"

"'Cause he was a piece of shit, just like his fuckin' car, man. Oow! Shit!" came the reply along with what sounded like a wrench being thrown to the driveway. "Now don't bug me about it, okay?"

"You okay?"

"Yeah, just a knuckle."

"You don't want to think about that other stuff, right?"

"It's not that. Like I said, the old man was a piece of shit, just like his piece of shit car. I just don't want anybody walkin' out here an' hearin' you runnin' your mouth, okay? So just fucking shut the fuck up about it!"

"Yeah, sure. Okay. Sorry." There was a long period of silence, and then a female voice called out, "Jason, your mother's on the phone an' says your old man wants you home in five minutes or our ass is grass."

The rest of the tape consisted of Jason's end of the telephone conversation with his mother, and Harcourt and Watkins picking him up. Jim shut off the recorder, and replaced the tape with the one of Grace's confession. Once again, we went through the necessary authentication process, and the judge accepted it into evidence. Jim played the tape and I saw some of the jurors leaning forward, straining to catch every word. It isn't often you hear someone confessing to a murder, and now we had two people sharing the blame for Joe Stempo's death.

Bobby's cross-examination was confused. He had started out the trial with the theory that Stempo had killed himself; that the whole murder idea was nothing more than the result of runaway teenage imaginations. But now Melwin was going to take the stand and tell the jury the exact opposite: that he had, in fact, taken the gun into the Stempo bedroom, but he gave it to Grace who then shot her husband. Bobby had to change his strategy, and that's never a good thing to do in the middle of a ball game or a trial. Knowing what was coming, there was little Bobby could do to Jim Harcourt's testimony, so he rehashed his cross-examination of Jason and basically accused Harcourt of "spying" on his poor, beleaguered client.

Peaches did a lot more damage, much as she had done at the suppression hearing. "Now, Mr. Harcourt," she began, "that second tape that we heard, what we heard was you askin' a lot of questions, didn't we?"

"That's right," Jim admitted.

"An' Grace was mostly cryin', wasn't she?"

"She was crying, yes."

"We heard her cryin' and carryin' on, didn't we?"

"I don't think she was carrying on all that much, no, Ms. Bailey," Jim replied.

"Well, she was weepin' into her hands at one point, wasn't she?"

"At one point she was, yes."

"An' you don't think that's carryin' on?"

"In my opinion, she was in complete control of her emotions."

I wished Jim hadn't said that. It was the weak spot that Peaches was looking for and she went to work.

"You think she was in control of her emotions?"

"Yes, I do."

"But you had just arrested her at her home an hour or so before that, hadn't you?"

"Yes."

"She didn't have any warnin' of that, did she?"

"I don't know."

"You didn't give her any warnin', did you?"

"No."

"This was pretty much a surprise raid, wasn't it?"

"That's right."

"So you surprised this woman in her home, in the middle of the night, an' arrested her for killin' her husband, and you think she was in control of her emotions?"

"It wasn't the middle of the night, Ms. Bailey."

"Oh? What time was it?"

"We raided the premises at 2205 hours, that's five minutes after ten p.m."

"Was it dark out?"

"Yes."

"The people in the house, they weren't expectin' you, were they?"

"Once again, I don't know what they expected."

"Now, this statement you took, Mr. Harcourt, a lot of it is you suggestin' what my client did, isn't it?"

I objected. The tape spoke for itself; there was no need for Peaches to characterize it. Judge Ives sustained me.

"You asked her a lot of leadin' questions, didn't you?" Peaches asked.

I objected again; same grounds. Once again the judge sustained me.

"All right, let's try it this way," Peaches said. "The questions you asked, the way you asked them, is that accepted police procedure when you question a suspect?"

"Yes, it is," Jim replied.

"An' part of that procedure is to make the suspect, in this case Grace Stempo, think that you know a lot more than you really know, isn't that right?"

"That's right."

"An' to do that, sometimes you feed a little information

to the suspect, an' see if she agrees with you, isn't that true?"

"Yes, that's true."

"That's pretty much what you were doin' to Grace Stempo, wasn't it?"

"Pretty much."

"You were feedin' her information an' she was agreein' with you, wasn't she?"

I objected again. "I hate to sound like a broken record, Your Honor, but the tape really must speak for itself." This was the weakest part of our case against Grace, and I wanted to keep as much of Peaches' argument as I could away from the jury.

"I'm going to overrule you this time, Mr. Bradley. I think that Ms. Bailey is attempting to characterize the question and answer process rather than the words themselves."

I wasn't sure there was a difference, but Peaches took Judge Ives' comment as a sign to swing away. "This whole process, it was you suggestin' and her agreein' with you, wasn't it?"

"Not all the time, no."

"Some of the time?"

"Some of the time," Jim agreed.

"Most of the time?" Peaches asked.

"No, just some of the time," he answered.

Peaches had gotten about as far as she was going to get with Jim, and she sat down. I didn't see any particular need for re-direct examination. I excused him and then announced the State rested its case.

"Ladies and Gentlemen," the judge said, turning toward the jury, "the State has rested, which means there will be no more evidence from the prosecution. There are several legal matters that we now have to take up outside your presence which are of no concern to you, so I'm going to excuse you at this time. Please be here bright and early tomorrow morning; I'd like to get started right at nine o'clock. In the meantime, do not discuss this case with anyone. Do not read about it or listen to any news reports about it. And do not form any opinion about it until after I give it to you, which should be sometime tomorrow."

Two things happen in a criminal trial at the end of the State's case. Defense lawyers always move for a "judgment of acquittal," claiming the State's evidence, even if true, is insufficient to convict their clients. It's a motion that is almost always summarily denied, and Judge Ives did so without batting an eye. The other thing that happens is a discussion about jury instructions. They're in a book unimaginatively titled, "Florida Standard Jury Instructions in Criminal Cases." Both sides get to suggest the instructions they think are appropriate, and the judge makes the final selection and reads them to the jurors after closing arguments. The idea is to instruct the jurors on the law, but the reality is like trying to teach somebody how to play baseball by just reading the rules of baseball. There are too many rules to try to explain them all. You can't really understand the game unless you've played it.

"You'll want instructions on all of the lesser included offenses, I suppose?" the judge asked the defense attorneys.

"That's correct, Your Honor," Peaches answered for both of them.

"First-degree murder, second-degree, third-degree, manslaughter," Judge Ives ticked them off. "And I'm required to instruct on justifiable homicide and excusable homicide, too. Boy, I'd better have a glass of water up there."

"I believe the evidence requires an instruction on 'principal in the first degree'," I added.

"You're right, Mr. Bradley. I'll give the principal instruction," she replied. Chalk one up for our side, I thought. If the jury found that Grace and Melwin were acting in concert, the principal statute said they each were liable for Joe's murder, regardless of who pulled the trigger.

"But there's no evidence of acting in concert," Bobby protested.

"That's up to the jury to decide," Judge Ives replied.

"How about an instruction on self-defense?" Bobby suggested.

The judge looked at him with that same, pursed-lips expression. "You can't be serious," she said. "Whatever this was, it wasn't self-defense."

"I disagree, Your Honor. I think an instruction on self-defense is vital in this case."

"Fine, Mr. Greenburg. If your client gets convicted tomorrow, you'll have another point to raise on appeal," the judge replied as she got up and walked out of the courtroom.

I went home feeling better than I had in a long time, and dinner out on the patio that evening with Jim Harcourt was almost as good as things used to be before all of this craziness started. The only thing missing was my wife. As soon as this case ended, I would try to put that part of my life back together.

CHAPTER 22

We were down to the last day, and Jolly Boy Melwin wasn't looking very jolly. I was sure that by now he knew he had little hope of an outright acquittal. If Bobby had explained the "principal statute" to him, he had to know that his "I didn't pull the trigger" defense wasn't much good. Ordinarily, he might hope for the jurors to vent their anger on Grace and show him a little mercy, but because of the unusual procedure we used – two juries deliberating in separate rooms – his case, and his conviction, would stand or fall on its own. Regardless of that, he had a much more basic reason to testify: to sink Grace Stempo. If he had to go to prison, he wasn't going alone. He would drag somebody down with him.

Court was called to order promptly at nine o'clock. Judge Ives had made it clear that we were going to end this case that day. That meant the remaining testimony, summations and jury instructions all had to be completed before five o'clock if we were to have any hope of getting a verdict at a decent hour. As soon as the jurors were seated, the judge asked whether the defense had anything it wished to present. This was it. Melwin was either going to keep his mouth shut and let Grace have a fighting chance, or he was going to get on the stand and sink her. Apparently, misery really does love company; Melwin hesitated for a moment, then stood up and walked to the witness stand where the clerk swore him in.

"Now, Melwin, you're one of the defendants in this case, is that right?" Bobby Greenburg asked by way of introduction.

"That's right," came Melwin's response in the same voice we heard on the previous day's tape recording.

"And you've heard all of the testimony over the last couple of days, haven't you?"

"Yeah."

"Now, I'd like you to tell us about the time when you and Grace Stempo and her daughter bought a gun from a young man by the name of Shawn Planer. Do you remember that?"

"Sure do."

"How were you involved in that? Tell the members of the jury."

"Well, it was like this: Grace had told me . . . she said that she wanted to buy a gun, because, like there was a lot of crime and stuff in the neighborhood, you know? An' Anita said . . ."

I objected. Melwin could tell us what Grace said, she was on trial. But he could not say what Anita said; that was hearsay. I really didn't care about the answer, but it felt good to stick it to Bobby for a change. My objection was sustained, and Bobby went right on as if nothing had happened.

"All right, listen to me. You can't say what somebody else said. Just tell us what happened."

"Well, I just said that I would check it out for them, you know? Just check it out an' make they weren't gettin' ripped off or nothin' like that." Bobby nodded his encouragement and Melwin continued. "So we get to this kid's house an' picked him up, and he like gets in the car with this, you know, this gun. An' I check it out, and I go, you know, 'That's all you'll need.'"

"Now, when you said that, 'That's all you'll need,' what did you mean by that?" Bobby asked.

"You know, like, 'That's all you'll need to protect yourself.'"

"Did you have any idea at that time that the gun was going to be used in a murder?

"Hell, no . . . excuse me . . . heck, no. If I'd 'a known that, I'd 'a been outta there, man."

"Did the subject of murder ever come up before?"

"Well, you know, Grace was always sayin' things like . . . Can I say what she said?" Again Bobby nodded. "She was always sayin' things like, 'I wished he was dead,' an' 'Why don't he just die?' You know, stuff like that."

"Did she ever ask you to kill her husband for her?"

"One time she, well, she sorta asked me. You know, she goes, 'If he was dead, you'd get a pretty good car.'"

"What did you do?" Bobby asked.

"Nothin'. I figured she was just blowin' off steam, you know, just lettin' it all out. I wasn't gonna kill nobody for no car."

"You were living in the Stempo house?"

"Yeah."

"With Anita Stempo, the daughter?"

"You were sleeping together, isn't that right?" Leave it to Bobby to get into the sleaze.

"Everybody knew it?"

I could have objected to that. Melwin couldn't possibly know what "everybody knew." I let it go.

"Yeah. I mean, we didn't hide it or nothin'," Melwin

answered.

"And her father didn't object?"

"I guess not. He didn't throw me out or nothin'."

"Okay, now, do you remember the night he was shot?"

"Oh, yeah, I remember that real good."

"You heard Mollie Sussman say that you carried the gun into his room, isn't that right?"

"Yeah."

"Did you do that?"

"See, like Grace didn't want Joe to know she had bought a gun, you know? Like she didn't want him to know that she had spent money. So she like . . . we kept it in our room, I mean, Anita's room. So anyways, one day she starts thinkin' about it, I guess, and she goes, 'A gun ain't much good if you don't got it next to you,' an' she asks me to give it to her. Only she says, 'Wait 'till later, when he's asleep, so's he don't know I bought it.'" Melwin hesitated, and Bobby nodded again. "So, anyways, that night, that's when I brought it in to her, an' I figured she's gonna put it in a drawer or somethin' an' I like hand it to her, an' I'm almost gonna turn around an' go out the door, an' she just puts it to Joe's head an', 'Pop!' She shoots him."

"That isn't what you told the police, is it?" Bobby asked.

"Yeah, it's pretty much what I told them."

"I mean that night. That isn't what you told the police that night, is it?"

Melwin admitted that it wasn't. He said he was in a state of shock, seeing Joe Stempo murdered like that, and then Grace started yelling that Joe killed himself, screaming that Joe committed suicide, and he wasn't sure what to do. He said after a few minutes he thought maybe he had seen it wrong; maybe Joe *had* committed suicide. It was like a bad dream – a nightmare.

"But then you told Jason Bonafidie that you killed Joe

Stempo, didn't you?" Bobby sounded like he was cross-examining even when he was doing direct examinations.

"Yeah, but I was just jerkin' him off . . . I mean, you know, I was just goofin' around."

"You were kidding?"

"Well, you know, I guess I was braggin'; makin' it sound like I was a real bad dude."

"How about when Shawn asked you outside of Anita's school and you threatened him, were you bragging then?" Bobby demanded.

"Well, yeah, same thing. An' besides, I didn't want everybody sayin' I did it, because I figured I might . . . that somethin' might . . . you know, that I could get in trouble or somethin'. Just like right now."

"Now, what you told us here today, is that the truth?"

"The whole truth, man. I swear it."

"And is that what you told the police after you were arrested for this charge?"

"Yeah . . . kinda. I mean . . . I was tryin' to cover for the old lady . . . Grace . . . a little bit, I guess. But, like I kept tellin' them, you know, I didn't pull the trigger. I didn't kill nobody. An' I didn't, man."

Bobby sat down. I was sure his client had just committed perjury, either with or without Bobby's connivance, but there wasn't anything I could do about it. Melwin's testimony was close enough to his prior statement so that the judge would probably not allow me to play the tape for the jury. I would have to break him down through regular cross-examination.

"Mr. Fanchie," I began, "how old are you?"

"Twenty-two."

"And how long have you been living at the Stempo house?"

"About a year . . . less than a year."

"Anita Stempo was a high school student when her father was shot, wasn't she?"

Bobby objected and asked for a sidebar conference at the bench. When we got up there, he accused me of trying to bring in evidence of another crime by implying Melwin was sleeping with an underage girl. He was right, of course, but I denied it. I said I was only trying to get the players straight – to figure out the time sequence involved. The judge didn't buy my explanation and told me to lay off the subject. I did, but I was sure that at least some of the jurors had gotten the point.

"All right. Mr. Fanchie, you just testified that you walked into the Stempo bedroom and handed the gun to Grace Stempo, isn't that right? I asked, changing the subject.

"That's right," Melwin replied.

"And you did that because she wanted the gun, right?"

"That's right."

"You didn't have any idea that she was going to murder her husband."

"No idea at all, man," he said, shaking his head.

"And, of course, you had no intention of murdering him yourself, did you?"

"Why would I do that, man? Like I said, the guy never did me no harm."

"Now, Melwin, do you remember talking to the police shortly after you were arrested?"

"Oh, yeah."

"You gave a statement, didn't you?"

"You should know; you were there."

"That's right, I was there. Do you remember telling me that you put the gun right up to Joe Stempo's head?"

"Yeah, but . . ."

"Do you remember telling me that you put the gun to his head, but you couldn't pull the trigger?"

"Yeah, I said that, but, see, I was really shook up, man. I didn't mean I tried to kill him."

"What did you mean, Melwin?"

"What I meant was, I *handed* her the gun, man. And his head was right there. And I *could have* done it, if I wanted to, but, like I didn't, okay? I handed her the gun, and, yeah, when I did that, it was like right next to his head. So I *could've* done it, but I didn't want to, and I couldn't pull the trigger. Okay?"

"So you never said," — I made sure the jury saw I was looking at notes written on a yellow legal pad — "you never said, 'I had the gun right up against his head, man, but I couldn't pull the trigger.'"? It was an important question. If Melwin denied saying it, I would ask the judge to let me play the tape to impeach him. On the other hand, if he admitted it, there would be no reason to impeach, and, therefore, no reason to play the tape. I wondered if Bobby had explained all the nuances to him.

"Yeah, I said that," he replied. "But I never said I *pointed* it at him. I had the gun right up against his head, you know, right near his head, when I reached over and gave it to her. That's what I went when I said I couldn't pull the trigger." It sounded like Bobby and Melwin had gone over Melwin's statement with a fine-toothed comb, and Melwin had an explanation for everything.

"How about, 'So I come in with the gun, and I put it to his head, but I couldn't do it.' Did you say that?" I asked, again reading from my notes.

"I don't know for sure . . . I'm not sure of what I said, exactly."

"Would you like to hear yourself on tape? Would that refresh your recollection?"

He looked desperately at Bobby and said, "No, that's okay. Yeah, I said that. If you say I said it, then I said it."

"'I put it to his head, but I couldn't do it.' What was it that you couldn't do?"

"I couldn't pull the trigger, man. I would never want to kill that old man."

"But you put the gun *to* his head, didn't you?"

"I put it *near to* his head. It was right *near* his head when I handed it *to* her."

"But you said '*to*': 'I put the gun *to* his head.' Didn't you say that?"

Yeah, like I said, I said that. But I meant *close to*. You know, like *near*. Melwin had settled on an explanation, and he was going to stick to it. Hell, by then he had been coached so well and said it so often, that he might even have believed it himself. I had to make sure the jurors heard what I had heard in the F.D.L.E. interrogation room.

"So when you said, 'I put the gun to his head, but I couldn't do it,' you meant that you put it close to his head but you couldn't pull the trigger, is that your testimony today?"

"That's right," he said with a self-satisfied smirk.

"Now, you also said that Grace Stempo wanted her husband dead."

"Yeah. She wanted him dead," he confirmed.

"And at one point she even suggested that you kill him?"

Peaches objected to my question as being an unfair characterization of Melwin's testimony. The judge reminded her that this was cross-examination, and that I had a lot of leeway. Her objection was overruled, but the interruption gave Melwin time to think.

"Like I said, I don't know . . . she like, she said that if Joe was dead, I would get his car."

"And you took that to mean she wanted you to kill him?"

"Like I said, I figured she was just blowin' off steam, you

know, like people do."

"Did she ever say to you, or did she ever say in your presence, 'I want him dead.'?"

"Yeah, she said that."

"Did she say it more than once?"

"Yeah, I guess . . . I don't know. I didn't count."

"Didn't you say to me," I asked – again making sure the jurors saw that I was reading from my notes – "Didn't you say, 'She was always after me, sayin' "I want him dead."' Didn't you say that?"

"Yeah, I said that. But like I said, I don't know exactly how many times she said it."

"But she was always after you, saying it, wasn't she?"

"She said that a lot, man. Okay?"

"And when you handed her the gun, late at night, in Joe Stempo's bedroom, and he was sleeping there, right next to her in the bed, you had no idea she was going to shoot him with it, is that right?"

"Man, I would never have believed it."

"You were just delivering a gun to her so that she could have it close by, right?"

"Yeah, she wanted it for protection."

"This woman who *always* was after you, saying she *wanted* him dead. She wanted that gun, late that night, for protection?"

"That's right."

"You had the gun *close to* his head, you couldn't pull the trigger yourself, so you handed the gun to her, this woman who *wanted him dead*, but you had no idea that she was going to kill her husband?"

Bobby objected to the question as being repetitious, "asked and answered" is the legal phrase, and the judge sustained him. I didn't need an answer. That question was for the jury; the point had been made.

There was one more question I wanted to ask: what the hell did he say to Anita that caused her to start crying after he left the room and before the shot was fired. "I'll be right back sweetie; I'm going to blow your father's brains out."? The problem was, with Anita gone, I didn't know the answer to that question, and I wasn't about to let Melwin surprise me. I was planning on using that gem in my summation. By holding off and arguing it after all the evidence was in, Melwin wouldn't be able to contradict the inference I planned to draw. I looked at him for a long moment and almost bit my tongue to prevent myself from asking him.

"No further questions, Your Honor," I announced as I sat down.

Peaches' cross-examination was short. She had a time bomb on her hands and she knew it. Melwin had shown no reluctance to sink Grace if he could save his own skin, so Peaches focused on what Grace had not said.

"Now, Melwin, my client never came right out and asked you to kill her husband, did she?"

"No."

"So this business about his car, she was just sayin' that if something should happen to him, you'd be driving his car, is that right?"

"Pretty much, I guess."

"You'd be sort of the family driver?"

I could have objected to that question – what Grace meant was a conclusion on Melwin's part. But I felt sorry for Peaches. I had maneuvered Melwin into taking the stand, and I owed her a little something. I kept quiet.

"I guess," Melwin answered.

"She never said, 'If you kill him for me, I'll give you his car,' did she?"

"No, she never said nothin' like that."

"And when she said she wanted him dead, those were times when she was mad at him for somethin', weren't they?"

"Yeah, I guess."

"You didn't think she really wanted to kill him, did you?"

"Like I said, I figured she was just blowin' off steam."

"In fact, she said that about a lot of people, didn't she: 'I want so-and-so dead.'?"

"Not really, no."

Peaches didn't expect that answer. She must have asked it because Grace told her something like, 'I say that all the time about everybody.' That's the problem clients have when they lie to their lawyers. It's also the problem lawyers have when they believe too strongly in their clients. Sometimes people trap themselves.

"You never heard her say that about anybody else?" Peaches asked, making a bad situation worse.

"No, not really. Just about him."

She better sit down, I thought. Any more of this and the jurors would never forget that Grace confined her death wish to her husband. Peaches must have gotten the same idea. She ended her cross-examination and announced the defense rested.

"Ladies and Gentlemen," the judge said to the jurors, "I'm going to give all of you a chance to stretch your legs. If you want a soft drink or anything, I'm sure you're familiar with the snack bar on the first floor. Please don't discuss this case or allow anyone to discuss it in your presence, and don't form any opinions until after I instruct you on the law. Be back here in about twenty minutes and the lawyers will start their closing arguments."

More motions for judgments of acquittal, and more summary denials; we were finally in the bottom half of the ninth inning. Now we ran into another peculiar wrinkle in Florida law circa 1985, the "sandwich rule:" because the defense did not call any witnesses other than a defendant, they would get the opening and closing parts of the closing argument; my argument would be "sandwiched" in between.

There's one final thing, Your Honor," Peaches said before the judge recessed. "I don't think we should have both juries in here at the same time for closing arguments. We might take different positions in our arguments," she said, probably thinking ahead to what Bobby would most likely do.

I was about to protest, to point out that both juries had heard exactly the same evidence when I realized she was right, and her argument cut two ways. With the other jury out of the room, I, too, could take "different positions" without looking like a horse's ass. I could blame each of the defendant's for Joe's murder. I could argue that Melwin was lying, that he had pulled the trigger; and then I could argue that Grace pulled the trigger. And I could also say – in both arguments – that it didn't matter because the principal statute covered both of them.

Peaches added, "I just think having both juries in here for final argument, could lead to reversible error."

Way to go, Peaches! When the going gets tough, tell the judge you're going to appeal, and if you're right, we'll have to do this all over again.

"You may have a point there, Ms. Bailey," Judge Ives replied. "In an abundance of caution, I'll hold one jury out while you argue to the other one. But to keep things moving along, I going to ask you to limit yourselves to thirty minutes per side."

"That's not much time, Judge. I need a lot more time than that," Bobby protested.

"I'm sure you can cover everything in thirty minutes, Mr. Greenburg," the judge replied. "What do you want, twenty minutes for closing and ten for rebuttal?"

"Judge, this is a murder case," Peaches protested.

"All right, forty minutes per side; twenty and twenty, or thirty and ten. Tell the clerk how you want to split it up. That's it. Mr. Bradley, you have the middle argument in each case. I'd appreciate it if you didn't use your full forty minutes."

"I'll do my best, Judge."

The jurors came in a short time later and Sarah explained how we would proceed. Since Bobby Greenburg had taken the lead for the defense throughout the case, he would go first. The Stempo jury would be sent out while the Fanchie jury heard closing arguments. Then the Fanchie jury would be sequestered while we argued to the Stempo jury. After all of the closing arguments were finished, all of the jurors would be brought back in for instructions and then they would be sent to separate jury rooms to deliberate.

Sixteen people looked at each other as if to say this procedure confirmed what they already suspected: that the court system and everyone connected with it was nuts. After the judge again told the Stempo jury not to discuss the case or form any opinions, the bailiff led eight people to a small room where they would wait for almost an hour and a half and presumably discuss the weather.

Bobby went first and he used his opening twenty minutes to blast Grace. Melwin was nothing but a dupe, he said. Grace wanted her husband dead. She inveigled Melwin into helping her buy the gun, and then she had him deliver it to her in the bedroom where she used it. "Imagine what it must be like," he shouted, "to see someone shot to death right before your eyes!" No wonder Melwin was so confused; no wonder he began to think maybe it was a suicide, Bobby argued. Of course, Melwin was stupid for trying to show off, for bragging to his friends that he was tough – that he killed a man. But that just went to prove Bobby's point: Melwin was a child-man who was easily led. He was not a murderer, Bobby argued. If anything he was stupid: a stupid, unwitting accomplice, dragged in by a woman who needed someone to blame for the murder of her husband.

I pointed out the inconsistencies of Melwin's defense. His attorney was the one who said this case was nothing more than a suicide complicated by overactive teenage imaginations. I pointed out Bobby had badgered Mollie Sussman, implying that she had not seen a gun in Melwin's hand, and then Melwin took the stand at the last minute, this very morning, and admitted Mollie was telling the truth after all. There were other inconsistencies, I argued. Melwin was the one who said, "That's all you'll need," after checking out the gun, and he was the one who threatened Shawn, telling him, "You'll be next," because, he said, he didn't want everyone repeating the story. But that incident took place long before Jason Bonafidie came into the picture. Melwin himself was the one repeating the story. He was the one who told Jason, not once but twice, that he shot Joe Stempo. "He even used the same word that he used here this morning, testifying on that stand," I argued. "He said the gun went 'pop.'" I told the jurors to remember that because a man's life had ended with that "pop." And there was something else, I said, about to use the argument I had saved during Melwin's cross-examination: Mollie testified that Melwin said something to Anita before he left their room with the gun in his hand. *And Anita began crying before, not after, the fatal "pop!"* Could there be any doubt that Melwin knew Joe Stempo was about to die? Then I pointed out the inconsistencies in his own testimony. He admitted he told the police he put the gun *to* Joe's head, but this morning, on the last day of trial, the *to* suddenly became *near*. Then I offered my own explanation and said it was the only one that fit all the facts: Melwin intended to kill Joe. I didn't know why; maybe it was for his car, or maybe just for the thrill of it. But he intended to kill him when he walked into Joe's bedroom with a loaded gun. And then, with Joe's wife watching, he put that gun to Joe's head and murdered him in cold blood. "Listen to the testimony," I told them. "Listen to the tapes. Is there any doubt, any doubt at all, that Melwin knew Grace wanted her husband dead?" Melwin pulled the trigger, I argued, and even if he didn't – even if Grace did it for him – he was still guilty of first-degree murder.

Bobby did nothing much but pound the table during his twenty-minute rebuttal. I felt the extra time worked to my advantage; he ran out of things to say after about ten minutes but, in true Bulldog Bobby fashion, he wouldn't give up any of his allotted time so he just ranted and raved and pissed everybody off instead.

There was a short recess while the Fanchie jury was warned against discussing or forming conclusions, then taken out and replaced by the Stempo jury. This time Peaches was first at bar. What happened at the Stempo house was a murder, all right, she argued. But the murderer was Melwin Fanchie. He told you so himself. He admitted that he put the gun to Joe Stempo's head. "Only now he wants you to believe he chickened out." But he didn't, Peaches argued. He shot Joe Stempo before Grace could stop him. Peaches admitted that Grace said she wanted her husband to die. Theirs was not a happy marriage. In fact, it was a lousy marriage. Grace even told the police that she would never say she was sorry. "But wantin' somebody to die, even bein' happy they're dead isn't a crime, and it doesn't mean Grace would kill her own husband right in his own bed!"

"Who saw it?" Peaches demanded. "Who is here to testify against this woman, except a man who has everythin' to gain by blamin' it on her." And, she reminded the jurors, how about the scientific tests? There was no powder on Grace's hands, and Melwin did not say she put on gloves before taking the gun from him. So Grace told everyone that Joe killed himself. So what? So she tried to shield her daughter's boyfriend. Grace admitted that she wasn't sorry to see Joe dead. Why not just close the book on it? Why drag Melwin down? But Grace was not about to take the blame for Melwin's crime. Melwin did it, Peaches repeated. He did it and now he was blaming Grace to save his own skin.

"So why did Grace buy the gun?" I began when it was my turn to argue. It was ludicrous to believe that she bought the gun from a juvenile burglar for protection. Could she really have asked Melwin to come into her bedroom at night so that she could put the gun away without her sleeping husband seeing it? Why not do that in the daytime, when Joe was out of the house? No, I argued, that gun was kept in Anita's room so there would be no possibility of Joe finding it. He would never suspect that he was about to become the victim of a murder plot. Grace was the mastermind of that plot, I argued. She wanted her husband dead, dead, dead. And she got Melwin to do the dirty work for her. But the flaw in her plan occurred when Melwin balked; he didn't have the guts to pull the trigger. So Grace grabbed the gun away from him and did the deed herself. "Look at the evidence," I argued, "What other explanation fits all the facts?" Powder? It was a long time before the police got there – plenty of time for her to wash her hands. These people knew about fingerprints. Ian

Highsmith said he wasn't allowed to handle the gun without rubber gloves. If they were talking those kinds of precautions early on, is it so far-fetched to conclude that Grace wiped off the gun and washed her hands before the police arrived? "If she didn't do it, why did she try to make Joe's death look like a suicide?" I asked rhetorically. "And why did she keep up the pretense after she was arrested? To protect Melwin?" To believe that, I argued, the jury would have to believe that Grace was willing to put her life on the line for him. And that, I said, was completely unbelievable. Grace did it, I concluded. She planned it, bought the gun, set it up, and when her plan failed, she took matters into her own hands. Even if she didn't personally pull the trigger, she was guilty of first-degree murder.

Peaches didn't come up with much on rebuttal, except to say that Melwin was almost like a son-in-law in the Stempo household. Grace loved her daughter, and it follows she would go far to shield Melwin; far enough to mislead the police, but not far enough to go to prison for him. Melwin did it, she insisted again. Melwin did it, and Grace was nothing more than in innocent bystander who should be acquitted.

And then, at last, we were finished. The Fanchie jury was brought back in, and Judge Ives began reading the jury instructions to all sixteen people. She told them about the lesser-included degrees of murder, that second-degree was an unplanned killing "by an act imminently dangerous to human life," that manslaughter was a killing caused by procurement or culpable negligence of the defendant. The judge told them about the "principal statute:" that when two people commit an act together, they are each responsible. She told them they should convict the defendant for the highest crime proven by the State, but, if they had a reasonable doubt, they should find the defendant "not guilty." And she told them a "reasonable doubt" was "not a possible doubt, a speculative, imaginary or forced doubt," but a doubt for which they could give a reason. In a criminal trial, she explained, the State always had the burden of proof, and she warned them they could not draw any inference from the fact that Grace Stempo did not testify, or hold that fact against her in any way. In was another half-hour of legal mumbo-jumbo before Sarah excused the four alternate jurors and sent the two juries to separate rooms to deliberate.

And then there was nothing for the rest of us to do but wait for their verdicts.

CHAPTER 23

Verdict: it means the jurors are supposed to "truthfully speak." Some people think it's Latin. It isn't. It's Norman French, the language William the Conqueror spoke when he invaded England a thousand years ago. Lawyers have clung to parts of that language ever since William's great-grandson, Henry II, created the Anglo-Saxon judicial system at the Clarendon Assize in 1166.

Waiting for a verdict is the most difficult part of a trial. Some lawyers claim they put everything out of their minds once the jury goes out. If they're telling the truth, they're the lucky ones. Most of us pace the courthouse and second-guess what we did or didn't do, how we should or shouldn't have asked a particular question, how we could have made things clearer. I'm one of those. I drive myself crazy thinking about what I should have done. I guess that's why my cardiologist sent a little bottle of pills to my office.

I probably should have taken one of them, but I didn't. Dr. Crandall said they would "just take the edge off." What he didn't understand was I needed that edge; it's where trial lawyers do their work. I could take the edge off later, maybe, after the verdicts were in, with three or four drinks at Chef's or the Yacht Club, but I couldn't take the edge off yet; too much could still happen.

"We heard from the Fanchie jury first. They sent out a note requesting a transcript of the *second* Fanchie tape – the one that implicated Grace. The problem was we had never played that tape for them. It was only going to be used if Melwin did not testify or as rebuttal if he changes his story. Yes, I had made a show of reading from "notes" on a legal pad, but they were my notes. My notes were not an exhibit.

"Well, Lady and Gentlemen, what do you propose I do?" Judge Ives asked after she read us the note in her chambers.

Peaches Bailey spoke first. "I think we need to bring both juries in and inform them that the recording of Melwin's statement to the police is not an exhibit in evidence and they are not to consider it."

"And re-instruct them on reasonable doubt at the same time," Bobby Greenburg added.

"Judge, that's ridiculous," I protested. "There's no reason to give a reasonable doubt instruction again."

"Ridiculous?" Bobby shouted. "It's the law. I know of at least three or four cases . . ."

"All right, everybody simmer down," the judge warned. "I'm not going to re-instruct anybody at this point. I'd like to answer the question without reconvening court and bringing them back in. Are any of you going to object if I just send in a note?"

"What do you propose, Judge?" Peaches asked.

"I propose to write, 'There is no transcript of Mr. Fanchie's statement to the police,' and leave it at that."

"I think you should also tell them his statement is not an exhibit and should not be considered," Peaches replied.

"All right, how about, 'There is no transcript of Mr. Fanchie's statement; his statement is not an exhibit in evidence and should not be considered by you.' Can everybody live with that?"

I couldn't. It would make it sound like they shouldn't consider any of Melwin's prior statement, even the parts I read to him and that he admitted making. Those words were now part of this testimony. They were evidence, and the jury should consider them.

"All right, the judge said with a scowl, "I guess we can't agree on this. We'll have to bring them back in."

We went back into the courtroom and waited for the deputies to bring the defendants in from the lockup. After everybody was assembled the judge told one of the bailiffs to bring in the Fanchie jury.

"Ladies and Gentlemen," she began, "you've asked for a transcript of Melwin Fanchie's statement to the police. That statement was not put in evidence and should not be considered by you in your deliberations. However, any parts of that statement that he admitted to making, or anything he said on the witness stand, is part of the evidence and you may consider it. Do you have any other questions?"

A couple of people glanced back and forth, but nobody spoke. "All right then, if you have no other questions, you may now retire to continue your deliberations."

The jurors left the courtroom and Bobby Greenburg objected to the judge's failure to re-instruct them on reasonable doubt. I wasn't paying attention to his histrionics any more. I had a sick feeling in the pit of my stomach. It sounded like the jurors were hung up on Melwin's change from "gun to his head" to "gun close to his head," and without hearing the statement in his own voice they might buy this morning's explanation. I should have taken the other approach at trial: excuse the Stempo jury and let Melwin's jury hear both of his tapes during my direct case. That way I might not have been able to force him to testify against Grace, but at least I'd have a rock-solid first-degree murder case against him.

It seemed like only a few minutes before the jurors sent out another note. They wanted to hear a read-back of my cross-examination of Melwin Fanchie.

I'm going to object to that, Judge," Bobby said when he heard the news. "You should either have all of his testimony read back or none of it. Reading back only the cross-examination violates my client's right to due process."

"I didn't make the request, Mr. Greenburg; the jury did," Judge Ives responded. "As long as they're not asking for reinstruction, as far as I'm concerned they can ask for as much or as little testimony as they want."

We reconvened in the courtroom again, and the judge had one of the bailiffs bring them back in.

"Ladies and Gentlemen, I understand that you would like to have some of the testimony read back by the court reporter," the judge said.

An older man stood up. He must have been the foreman. I wondered why he didn't just speak up earlier and save all this waltzing in and out. "That's right, Your Honor," he replied.

"All right, you just tell Mr. Jennings here what you want, and he'll find it for you."

"Just Mr. Bradley's cross-examination of Mr. Fanchie is all we want, Your Honor."

"All right," the judge responded. "Mr. Jennings, you're on."

The court reporter began reading from his notes: "By Mr. Bradley: Question, 'Mr. Fanchie, how old are you?'

Answer, 'Twenty-two,' Question, 'And how long have you been living at the Stempo house?' Answer, 'About a year . . . less than a year.'"

And on it went, my entire cross-examination of Melwin Fanchie in that rapid monotone that is the trademark of court reporters. No emotion, no emphasis on any particular word or phrase; just the words directly from the notes, read as quickly as possible, as accurate and unimaginative as the stenotype machine itself. I wanted to stand up and shout, "Listen! Listen carefully! Can't you tell he's making this up? Can't you see he's changing his story from 'to' to 'close to'?" But, of course, that was out of the question. It was too late now, and if anybody screwed up, it was me. I was the one who kept Melwin's second tape out of evidence in order to – I thought – force his hand against Grace. I was sure I could break him on cross-examination. I didn't expect Bobby Greenburg to do such a good job preparing him: explaining away "to" by substituting "close to" may well have been perjury, but it was masterful perjury. Because of my maneuvering, the jury would never hear the statement that Melwin made after being subjected to the good cop/bad cop routine.

The drone of Jennings' voice finally ended. I saw two of the jurors exchange glances and nod at each other before they all got up to return to the jury room. Those glances and nods meant something; I wondered what it was.

"All right, any objections?" Judge Ives asked after the jury left the courtroom.

"I object, Your Honor," Bobby replied. "I think they should have had the benefit of all of my client's testimony."

"Thank you, Mr. Greenburg," she replied. "I'll note your objection for the record. The Court stands in recess pending the call of one of the juries." Sarah left the bench, the defendants went back to the holding cells, and I went back to pacing the hallways and second-guessing myself.

It had been stupid of me to argue that Melwin pulled the trigger. I should have gone with the flow of the evidence, accused him of not having the guts to go through with the murder, and then hammered him with the principal statute. Then I reminded myself that Melwin's jury hadn't be in the courtroom when I argued to Grace's jury. They didn't know that I took inconsistent positions, just like everybody else in this case. So what went wrong? Why were they so confused?

I don't know how many trips I made around those long, empty hallways before the bailiff stopped me and said the judge wanted to see all of the lawyers in her chambers.

"It's almost six o'clock," Sarah said after we assembled. "I'd like to send both juries out to dinner. Are there any objections?"

Everyone nodded in assent.

"We'll send them out separately, then let them come back and deliberate until, what, ten o'clock?" No one objected. "If they don't have verdicts by then, I'll sequester them overnight, and we'll start again at nine tomorrow morning."

Sarah was interrupted by a knock at her door. One of the bailiffs came in and handed her a slip of paper. "Well," she said after reading it, "I guess I was premature. It looks like the Stempo jury has reached a verdict."

My heart sank. It had to be bad news for the prosecution. Conventional wisdom held that juries acquit quickly; they take longer to convict people, especially when they've been asked to convict them of murder. It looked like Peaches had pulled this one out.

We took our seats in the courtroom and watched as the somber-looking jurors came in. I noticed that none of them glanced at Grace. That was a good sign; normally, it would have meant they had found her guilty, but I couldn't believe they had done it in less than three hours.

"Ladies and Gentlemen, have you reached a verdict?" the judge asked when they were all seated.

A rather plump woman stood up with a paper in her hand. "Yes, we have, Your Honor," she said.

"All right, please hand your verdict to the bailiff."

The bailiff who had been assigned to the Stempo jury accepted the folded slip of paper from the woman and took it to the judge. Back in the days when I was an Assistant State Attorney, our regular bailiff, John, would give me a clue at this point. If it had gone my way, he would turn in my direction and look at me; if not, he would turn away. That was a long time ago. But now I was a stranger in this courtroom, and this time there was no friendly bailiff to give me a clue. The tips of my fingers were icy cold as Sarah silently read the verdict. Her expression gave no hint of the outcome. "All right," she finally said, looking at the jury, "the verdict appears to be in proper form. I need to tell you that the other jury is still deliberating. We're going to announce both verdicts at the same time. So at this time I'm going to send all of you out to dinner at the county's expense. I'd going to do the same thing with the other jury. Except you can have a drink . . . just one," she said with a smile, "because your work is completed. After dinner, you'll all come back here and wait in the jury room until the other jury reaches a verdict."

A man whispered something to the plump woman who asked, "What if they don't reach a verdict tonight?"

"We hope that won't happen," Sarah replied, "but if they don't, we may have to sequester all of you in a very nice hotel until they do. But let's not worry about that now. Let's have a nice dinner on the county, and then we'll come back and see what happens. Okay?"

Two bailiffs escorted the jurors from the courtroom. "Are there any objections, Mr. Greenburg?" the judge asked after they left.

"No, I don't have any objections, Your Honor," Bobby replied.

"Ms. Bailey?"

"Well, I don't see why we can't read the verdict now, but I can't think of any legal objection, Your Honor."

"Fine. I'll send the Fanchie jury out to dinner now, and Court will be in recess pending their call."

Nothing was going to happen for at least an hour, and with nothing better to do I walked to Chef's Bistro, the place near the courthouse where Peaches and I first heard the news of Deke Stoner's sudden retirement. It could have been romantic with the right person, but my right person was somewhere in Palm Beach, and I was very much alone. I was too upset to eat, and I wouldn't drink anything other than soda water with lime, so I sat there looking into the glass of clear liquid, staring at the bubbles and feeling sorry for myself.

"Is this seat taken, Sailor?" The English accent was unmistakable and I looked up into the eyes of my very attractive and long-suffering wife.

"How did you find me?"

"We women have mysterious ways," she said, slipping into the booth next to me. "You look like you lost your best friend."

"I thought you were my best friend," I said, looking at her.

"Well, you haven't lost me, so things can't be that bad," she whispered.

That's when I kissed her. I kissed her for a long, long time, with all of the pent-up emotion and frustration of too-many weeks. That kiss was the only good, real thing in my life at that moment and I wanted it never to end.

"David, you're making a scene," she whispered when she finally pulled away enough to talk.

"Appearances be damned," I reminded her, quoting her words she said to me at the airport. "I'll give it all up, Barb. It doesn't mean anything to me anymore. You're the only thing that matters."

She ran her fingers over the side of my face. "I said 'for better or for worse,' Darling. You should have reminded me of that."

"There won't be any 'worse,' Barbara. Never again. I promise."

We walked back to the courthouse where I continued pacing the hallways, but this time it was different. No matter what the verdict would be, I had won.

Few places in the world are as empty as a courthouse at night. The rooms that serve as stages for all the best and worst human dramas are lifeless and still; their walls echoing with the sounds of conflicts both recent and long ago. This is the arena, and we trial lawyers are the gladiators. Our lives are spent here, in these rooms. Polite society brands us as moral lepers and mocks our profession, but we are the ones they turn to when they want their rights protected or need their transgressors punished. Let them tell their stale jokes about sharks and the lack of lawyers in heaven; sooner or later the Evil, the Oppressed, the Injured and the Careless will all come before the bar of Justice. And each of them will expect a lawyer to pour out part of his or her life in support of a stranger's cause. That's what we do in these rooms, I told my wife. We pour out our lives for people who in the end don't give a damn about us.

Bobby Greenburg was huddled in a corner with some people who might be Melwin Fanchie's family. Even

Melwin had a mother, I supposed, or someone who cared about whether he would spend the rest of his life behind bars. I hadn't noticed those people earlier, and I wondered what they thought of me. Was I the incarnation of everything they ever hated, or did they see me as just another lawyer doing a job?

Off in another corner, Peaches Bailey sat alone doing needlepoint. Her client was in a holding cell down the hall, but no family member sat with Peaches. Joe Stempo was dead, as was his youngest daughter who had escaped being sentenced for her part in his murder. Somewhere far away the two remaining Stempo daughters tried to forget their childhoods, while their mother waited in a steel cage, wondering if the jury had already decided she would die in prison.

It was nine o'clock; still no word. Melwin's jury had been deliberating since three-thirty. Even with an hour off for dinner, that meant they had been at it for four-and-a-half hours. They might be "hung" – unable to reach a verdict. My deal with the General gave me responsibility for a loss. If Grace was acquitted and Melwin's jury was unable to reach a verdict I would probably be told, very politely and professionally, that I might be happier practicing my chosen profession elsewhere. Would some other lawyer prosecute Melwin again? Would things be done differently next time? Would I be remembered as the one who made a crucial error in this case, the one who let two killers slip away?

At nine-fifteen the bailiff called us into the courtroom with the news that the Fanchie jury had reached a verdict. I don't know how my adversaries felt, but my head was pounding and my back ached as I took my place at the counsel table closest to the jury box. Barbara reached across the courtroom bar and squeezed my arm for a moment before she sat down in the first row of the gallery. My hands felt like blocks of ice, and I rubbed them together in an effort to warm them while we waited for the deputies to bring Grace and Melwin from the holding cells. When everyone was assembled, one of the bailiffs told us to rise. The judge came out, took her seat and told two other bailiffs to bring in the juries. Twelve people came in, some of them looking very self-conscious in their unaccustomed roles. The air was heavy in the room as the judge asked the members of the Fanchie jury if they had reached a verdict.

"We have, Your Honor," said the older man who I had picked out as the foreman many hours earlier.

"All right. The other jury has already reached a verdict, and I have that up here. Please give the bailiff your verdict so that I may examine it as to form."

Once again Sarah Ives showed no emotion as she read the verdict form. I could hear the blood pounding in my ears, and I offered a silent prayer that whatever happened, justice would be done.

"The Clerk will publish the verdicts," the judge announced, handing the papers to the woman at her side.

The court clerk took the papers and began reading, "In the Circuit Court of the Twenty-first Judicial Circuit of Florida, in and for Calusa County, Honorable Sarah Wolfe Ives presiding, State of Florida, plaintiff, versus Grace Stempo, defendant. Verdict. We, the jury, find the defendant Grace Stempo guilty of conspiracy to commit murder and guilty of murder in the first degree. So say we all."

Grace gasped. "No," she said as she put her hands to her mouth. Peaches put a hand on her shoulder but said nothing.

The clerk continued on, "In the Circuit Court of the

Twenty-first Judicial Circuit of Florida, in and for Calusa County, Honorable Sarah Wolfe Ives presiding, State of Florida, plaintiff, versus Melwin Fanchie, defendant. Verdict. We, the jury, find the defendant Melwin Fanchie guilty of conspiracy to commit murder and guilty of murder in the second degree. So say we all."

Melwin hung his head but made no sound. It was over. Blood began returning to my fingertips as the judge polled the juries. One by one each juror responded and said the verdict as read was correct. Sarah thanked them for their service and discharged them. I was suddenly very hungry.

"Is there any legal reason why sentence cannot be imposed on Grace Stempo?" the judge asked after the last juror left the courtroom.

"I intend to file a motion for a new trial, and we're going to appeal the verdict, Your Honor," Peaches announced.

"I understand that, Ms. Bailey. But since the only possible sentence for first-degree murder when the State has not sought the death penalty is life in prison, I don't see any reason to burden the Probation Department by asking for a pre-sentence investigation."

"I agree, Your Honor," Peaches conceded.

"All right, Grace Stempo, please rise." Grace got to her feet unsteadily with Peaches beside her. Grace looked a lot older than she had during the trial, and older still than the night Jim Harcourt arrested her in her living room. "Do you wish to say anything before I impose sentence?" Grace shook her head and the judge continued, "The jury having found you guilty of murder in the first degree and conspiracy to commit murder, I now adjudicate you guilty of those crimes. On the charge of first-degree murder, I hereby sentence you to the Department of Corrections for life, without the possibility of parole for twenty-five years. On the charge of conspiracy, I'm going to sentence you to fifteen years and order that sentence to run concurrently with the life sentence. And may God have mercy on you, Mrs. Stempo, because you sure didn't have any on your husband." Grace sat down heavily with a blank look in her eyes. People at the D.O.C. once told me that it usually takes several weeks for the enormity of a life sentence to sink in.

"Melwin Fanchie," the judge continued, as Bobby and Melwin both stood up, "the jury having found you guilty of murder in the second degree and conspiracy to commit murder, I now adjudicate you guilty of those crimes and remand you to the custody of the Sheriff. I'm going to order a pre-sentence investigation on you and set sentencing down for four weeks from today. Is that convenient for you, Mr. Greenburg?"

"Yes, Your Honor. And I request that the Court set a supercedeas bond and allow my client to remain at liberty until sentencing."

Judge Sarah Ives made that screwed-up face again. "Mr. Greenburg, may I remind you that your client has been convicted of a crime that carries a maximum penalty of life in prison?"

"I'm aware of that, Judge."

"Your motion is denied."

"My client intends to appeal."

"Of course. But you won't be able to file your notice of appeal until we get sentencing out of the way, so I'd just as soon move things along."

"Very well, Judge."

"All right. There being no further business before this Court, we'll stand in recess until nine o'clock tomorrow morning."

The judge left the bench and the courtroom deputies escorted Melwin and Grace over to a side table where a bailiff placed their fingerprints on the judgments of conviction. Their faces were blank as they quietly submitted to the procedure and the bailiff methodically rolled their inked fingers onto the papers. If there were ever any question about it, those papers would be permanent proof of who had been convicted in our courtroom.

"We love you, Honey," the woman who had been waiting in the courtroom with Bobby Greenburg called out as Melwin turned away from the bailiff, his fingerprinting completed. "Can I just talk to him for a minute?" she asked the deputy who stepped in front of her when she made a move to get closer to him.

"Not here, Ma'am," he replied. "You can talk to him over at the jail in a little while." The man who had waited with the woman left with her and Bobby after Melwin and Grace were taken out of the courtroom. It appeared that someone did care about Melwin after all.

"Come on, Peaches," I said quietly as she stuffed papers into her briefcase, "I'll buy you dinner."

"Thanks, David," she said with a sigh. "I appreciate the offer, but if it's all the same to you, I'm just gonna go home an' have a stiff drink."

"I'll buy you one of those, too," I offered.

"Thanks, but some other time." She smiled to let me know there were no hard feelings as she left the courtroom.

"Well, Sailor, it's just you and me," Barbara said, slipping her arm through mine. "Why don't you make me that same offer?"

"They were guilty, you know," I said, turning to her.

"I haven't a doubt about it. Have you?"

"No. It's just that . . . I never get used to seeing them taken away like that, especially when they have family here. Melwin's going to do time, but those two people, whoever they are, will be the ones suffering. They're going to have a tough bunch of years ahead."

"How about Mrs. Stempo?" Barb asked quietly.

"She'll die in prison, and nobody will care. One of her daughters is dead, and the other two are already trying to forget her."

Barb handed me my briefcase. "Come on," she said, "I'm going to buy you that stiff drink, along with a cold supper. And we're both going to stay home tomorrow. We're going to stay in bed all day and not accept any telephone calls."

EPILOGUE

Barb's ending for this whole sordid mess would have been nice, but it didn't happen that way. The Attorney General came into town the next day with an entourage that included his new press secretary, Sylvia Mendez, and his Executive Assistant, Tom Julian. And me, of course. I met them at the airport and shared the airport press conference with them and with Sharon Matthews, a former Assistant State Attorney whom the Governor had appointed to replace Deke Stoner as the State Attorney for the Twenty-first Judicial Circuit. The General congratulated Sharon and praised the Governor for his outstanding selection while I wondered darkly whether she was the unnamed Assistant who had been so helpful to Sylvia Mendez. As someone once said, 'Politics makes strange bedfellows.'

"You did an excellent job, Dave," the General said when he and Tom visited me in my office after the initial dog-and-pony show was over. "I want you to know we're very grateful for the way you handled things."

"It was my pleasure, General," I lied. I may hate politics, but I was talking to my boss, and I'm not stupid.

"Helene Hizer is leaving us to take a job in Washington," he continued. "The Governor will be looking for a new Statewide Prosecutor. I'd like to recommend you . . . with your permission of course."

"Thank you, General," I said sincerely, "but I promised my wife the Stempo case would be my last trial."

"Tom mentioned that," he replied, "but I hoped he might be wrong. We could use someone like you in the capital."

"It would mean a substantial salary increase," Tom added.

The offer was tempting, but moving into the world of Tallahassee politics was not. "My wife has a growing business here in Bonita," I hedged. "And to be honest, I kind of like my life the way it is . . . the way it was." I wondered what Barb would say if she could hear me at that moment.

The Attorney General extended his hand and I took it. "Then you're a fortunate man, Dave," he said. "But if you ever change your mind, we'll find a place for you in Tally. I really appreciate the discretion you showed in this case. You know, sometimes it's best to wash our dirty linen in private. It preserves the public's faith in our legal system."

I wanted to tell him what I really thought, to remind him of the lives that had been wasted and the anguish this case had caused. Had it been worth it? Was 'due process' so sacred? Was the political destruction of Deke Stoner so important? I'm ashamed to say it, but I kept my mouth shut. At that moment I could only think of Jim Harcourt who once said he liked to keep the checks coming in.

The General had to hurry off to a full-blown press conference where Sheriff Bear Harper would announce the creation of a new "gang suppression unit" under the direction of newly-appointed "Lieutenant" Clive Watkins —

who, unfortunately was hospitalized due to a traffic collision – and Sharon Matthews who pledged the full support of the State Attorney's Office. Dealing with the press one-on-one, Sylvia Mendez would hand out press releases explaining how the Florida Department of Law Enforcement – under the direction of the Attorney General – would be working with Sharon and Bear, providing whatever "help and support" they requested to eliminate the developing scourge of gang violence in Calusa County.

Tom Julian and I missed those festivities, preferring to retire to the quiet confines of Chef's Bistro to renew our friendship and for me to cry in my Scotch.

"So that's it, right, Tom?" I said after ordering the second round. "Deke Stoner is eliminated as political competition, the General gets to wave a big flag saying how his office convicted two murderers and saved the county from gang violence, and everything else gets swept under the rug."

"Whoa, Bubba, that's the bottle talkin'. You're makin' certain assumptions that are not supported by the evidence."

"Deanna Tracey, remember her, Tom?" I shot back. "She was my wife's partner. She was a beautiful, innocent young woman who got killed by the Jolly Boys . . . don't deny it . . . you know it as well as I do. The newspaper said it was a 'tragic accident' caused by faulty wiring. Yeah, right. And Clive Watkins . . . he got bought off with what . . . a promotion and a desk job? The whole thing stinks, Tom, and you know it."

Tom looked at me intently and his blue eyes pierced me through his wire-rimmed glasses. "As a matter of fact, David, the F.D.L.E. opened an investigation into the Deanna Tracey case the day after she died. The General ordered them to report directly to me." Tom stirred his second "Bourbon and Branch" that had just been delivered to our table. "We know beyond any doubt whatsoever who killed Deanna . . . and, by the way, who tried to take you out with a rather amateurish bomb at your condo . . . and who tried to run you down at your yacht club where you so foolishly went without an escort. He was a Jolly Boy, all right . . . a crazy punk who was trying to make his way up in the gang world by killin' people. We're not gonna prosecute him because we can't. He's dead. It seems that night at the yacht club one of Jim Harcourt's bullets saved the State a whole bunch of trouble.

"Well how about the other one . . ." I began to ask.

"The other kid? The one in the passenger seat? Yeah, he was in on it too, but he was just a joiner. The better part of his face is gone. It's no use prosecutin' him 'cause he'll be takin' his meals through a straw for the rest of his life. Frankly the D.O.C. doesn't want him. It's too much trouble to take care of him." Tom slugged down his drink and ordered another round. "You got any other questions . . . Bubba?"

"Justice is always done if you just hang around and wait long enough, right Tom?" I said.

"That's right, Darlin', just like I always said. Now if you got any other questions ask 'em quick, 'cause you're cuttin' into my drinkin' time."

Yeah, I do, as a matter of fact . . . just one more. What's your explanation for Deke Stoner? We both knew him, Tom. Okay, maybe he wasn't the most careful lawyer in town, but damn . . . to get caught helping a drug gang? That doesn't make sense."

"C'mon, David," Tom responded. "Surely you don't subscribe to the Big Conspiracy theory of government. It doesn't work that way. You should know that."

"Oh? So how does it work?"

"Somebody does somebody a favor . . . let's say somebody gives somebody a campaign contribution perhaps. In return the somebody who got the favor done returns the favor. An' then the first somebody . . . well, he goes ahead and does another favor . . . maybe a bigger contribution or maybe rustlin' up vounteers . . . all under a committee name or some other cover. After a while the favors start mountin' up . . . on both sides. An' then some jackass named Fanchie gets himself involved in a murder 'cause he's got hot pants for a high school honey, but . . . guess what? . . . everything's still okay 'cause the cops happen to screw up an' nobody's the wiser. An' then some lawyer who nobody knows and who owes nobody a favor stumbles into the situation and . . . this is you, Bubba . . . in case ya' didn't recognize yourself . . . and all hell starts to break loose, and there's an indictment and a criminal trial . . . all for some crappy, simple little murder. And somebody gets called on to defend the jackass 'cause the jackass has been workin' for the people who have been supplyin' the money in the first place. But the defense guy . . . this is Bobby Greenburg, you got that right? . . . he's not that good of a lawyer . . . even though the stupid people the jackass works for think he is . . . and he needs help, and the somebody who owes him a couple of favors provides that help . . . on the que-tee, of course. But somebody . . . that's our mutual friend Sylvia . . . gets wind of that help. Do I have to go on with this?

"That's it?"

"Oh, hell no, that's not it. Once it starts, there's no tellin' where it ends: the I.R.S. will be lookin' at Deke and Bobby soon enough."

"And that's the kind of bullshit that takes down the people we put in elected office?" I demanded.

"You got it, my friend. There's no big conspiracy. It's

just bullshit piled on bullshit, and every once in a while somebody slips on the bullshit and gets caught. Deke Stoner slipped and got caught. Bobby Greenburg might get nailed by the tax boys 'cause he's low on the totem pole, but don't worry about Deke. He's got plenty of connections. He'll end up bein' somebody's house counsel over in Palm Beach or Washington or someplace. Okay? End of story. Now let's drink up."

We had a couple more, talking about old times and about cases we'd won, or lost and should have won, and about old warriors of happy or unhappy memory, and a few other assorted lawyer tales. Predictably, the Sheriff sent a deputy with an unmarked car to pick us up at Chef's and take us to the airport. I suppose some people might have considered it a "favor," but in reality it was just another way of Bear Harper keeping the peace in his county. There was no need to arrest two Assistant Attorneys General on a D.U.I. charge. As the General himself observed earlier that day, it was best to wash our dirty laundry in private—it preserved the public's faith in our system.

There was one more question I needed to have answered, and I caught up with Sylvia Mendez in the airport lounge while everyone waited for the last flight to Tallahassee. She had changed her outfit during the day and now was wearing a silk jumpsuit that clung to her saucy derriere and showed off the rest of her curves in all the right places. "We're on the same side now, Syl, so tell me: who tipped you off to our investigation?"

She licked the salt off a Margarita glass. "Let's just say my information came from a *very* high source Bradley," she purred.

"The General?"

"Not that high."

"John Stange?"

"The Deputy A.G. spends most of his time worrying about next year's budget."

"Not Tom?" I asked, hoping she would not confirm my third guess.

"Hey, someone had to get you off your ass and force you to get an indictment. If it wasn't for me you'd still be looking around for 'one more witness' . . . Bubba." She looked at me with the old glint in her eye. "No hard feelings, Bradley?"

She extended her hand in response to a departure announcement. "I've got to go," she said. "If you're ever in Tally, my offer stands."

I took her hand and replied, "Take care of yourself, Sylvia. There's bears in them thar woods."

She smiled, dropped my hand and walked away. Damn, she looked good in that silk jumpsuit.

-- The End --

ABOUT THE AUTHOR

Joseph A. Tringali has been admitted to the practice of law in both Florida and New York, and served as an Assistant Attorney General for the State of Florida, where he regularly appeared in all federal and state courts. He is a member of the United States Supreme Court bar, a former Mayor of North Palm Beach, Florida, and was elected to three terms on the Village Counsel. He has served as Assistant Corporation Counsel for the City of Buffalo, Assistant District Attorney of Erie County, New York, and Assistant State Attorney for the Fifteenth Judicial Circuit of Florida.

While living in Florida Mr. Tringali served as president of the Guild of Catholic Lawyers of Palm Beach County, and he and his wife served for three years as president and secretary of the Friends of Fisher House of West Palm Beach, a local group dedicated to providing free lodging for families of Veterans being treated at the regional Veterans Administration Hospital.

Mr. Tringali is an active alumnus of the of the University at Buffalo Law School, and a loyal member of Phi Alpha Delta Law Fraternity where he served both on the International Tribunal and as District Justice for New York, Massachusetts and Connecticut. He is a lifelong boating enthusiast and longtime member of Buffalo Yacht Club (New York). He has served as Commodore of North Palm Beach Yacht Club and Commodore of Palm Beach Sailing Club. He is a Life

Member of United States Power Squadrons and holds the grade of Senior Navigator, having successfully completed all of the advanced grade and elective courses in the Squadron's educational program. He is a Past National Rear Commander of USPS, where he was Chair of the National Flag and Etiquette Committee.

As a Major in the Civil Air Patrol, Mr. Tringali commanded the Western New York TAK Squadron which was recognized as "Squadron of the Year" by the Niagara Frontier Group, CAP. In his spare time, he enjoys the study of magic and has received the Order of Merlin from the International Brotherhood of Magicians.

In addition to Harbor of Refuge, Mr. Tringali has completed a sequel, Harbor of Dreams, which will be published soon. He is also the author of I Was That Baby, his personal story of growing up adopted and finding his birth family at 56 years old; and Yachting Customs and Courtesies, a two-volume set of over 1,000 pages that has become a resource for yacht clubs around the world.

Mr. Tringali insists his novels are "pure fiction" although some members of the Palm Beach County Bar unofficially swear they see certain resemblances to colorful but long-deceased local characters. He has also written articles for numerous periodicals including The Florida Bar Journal, Lakeland Boating and Fate magazine.

Mr. Tringali lives in North Palm Beach, Florida, with his wife, the former Mary Lou Privitera, who is a graduate of D'Youville College, and holds a master's degree in public administration from Florida Atlantic University and a doctorate in management from the University of Phoenix. They have two children: Lt. Col. John A. Tringali USAF (Ret.), a pilot for Delta Air Lines, and Elizabeth A. Tringali, PA-C, the owner of Tringali Vibrant Health, a medical practice specializing in wellness and anti-aging in West Palm Beach, Florida.

www.ingramcontent.com/pod-product-compliance
Lightning Source LLC
Chambersburg PA
CBHW022328280326
41934CB00006B/575